4th Workshop on Clinical Natural Language Processing (ClinicalNLP 2022)

Online
14 July 2022

ISBN: 978-1-7138-5625-2

Printed from e-media with permission by:

Curran Associates, Inc.
57 Morehouse Lane
Red Hook, NY 12571

Some format issues inherent in the e-media version may also appear in this print version.

Association for Computational Linguistics
209 N. Eighth Street
Stroudsburg, Pennsylvania 18360

Phone: 1-570-476-8006
Fax: 1-570-476-0860

acl@aclweb.org

Additional copies of this publication are available from:

Curran Associates, Inc.
57 Morehouse Lane
Red Hook, NY 12571 USA
Phone: 845-758-0400
Fax: 845-758-2633
Email: curran@proceedings.com
Web: www.proceedings.com

ClinicalNLP 2022

The 4th Workshop on Clinical Natural Language Processing (ClinicalNLP)

Proceedings of the Workshop

July 14, 2022

Order copies of this and other ACL proceedings from:

Association for Computational Linguistics (ACL)
209 N. Eighth Street
Stroudsburg, PA 18360
USA
Tel: +1-570-476-8006
Fax: +1-570-476-0860
acl@aclweb.org

Preface

This volume contains papers from the 4th Workshop on Clinical Natural Language Processing (Clinical NLP), held at NAACL 2022.

Clinical text offers unique challenges that differentiate it not only from open-domain data, but from other types of text in the biomedical domain as well. Notably, clinical text contains a significant number of abbreviations, medical terms, and other clinical jargon. Clinical narratives are characterized by non-standard document structures that are often critical to overall understanding. Narrative provider notes are designed to communicate with other experts while at the same time serving as a legal record. Finally, clinical notes contain sensitive patient-specific information that raise privacy and security concerns that present special challenges for natural language systems. This workshop focuses on the work that develops methods to address the above challenges, with the goal of advancing state-of-the-art in clinical NLP.

This year, we received the total of 16 submissions, out of which 12 were accepted for presentation.

Organizing Committee

General Chairs

Tristan Naumann, Microsoft Research
Steven Bethard, University of Arizona
Kirk Roberts, UTHealth Houston
Anna Rumshisky, UMass Lowell

Program Committee

Program Committee

John Aberdeen, The MITRE Corporation
Emily Alsentzer, MIT
Sabine Bergler, Concordia University
Cheryl Clark, The MITRE Corporation
Surabhi Datta, UTHealth
Dmitriy Dligach, Loyola University
Jungwei Fan, Mayo Clinic
Jason Fries, Stanford University
Sadid Hasan, CVS Health
Djoerd Hiemstra, Radboud University
Alistair Johnson, MIT
Yoshinobu Kano, Shizuoka University
Byung-Hak Kim, AKASA
Egoitz Laparra, University of Arizona
Sijia Liu, IBM Research
Matthew McDermott, MIT
Bridget McInnes, VCU
Timothy Miller, Boston Children's Hospital
Yifan Peng, Weill Cornell Medicine
Hoifung Poon, Microsoft Research
Preethi Raghavan, IBM Research
Thomas Searle, King's College London
Chaitanya Shivade, Amazon
Bhanu Pratap Singh, UMass - Amherst
Yuqi Si, UTHealth
Sarvesh Soni, UTHealth
Karin Verspoor, The University of Melbourne
Yanshan Wang, Mayo Clinic
Stephen Wu, UTHealth
Dongfang Xu, University of Arizona
Rui Zhang, University of Minnesota

Invited Speakers

Hongfang Liu, Mayo Clinic
Mark Dredze, Johns Hopkins University

Keynote Talk: It's Time to Rethink the Future of Clinical NLP

Mark Dredze
Johns Hopkins University

Abstract: The past decade has seen tremendous progress in the field of clinical natural language processing. Driven by new algorithms and access to clinical text from electronic medical records, clinical NLP is quickly becoming a standard tool used in patient care, secondary use and medical research. At the same time, the field of NLP as a whole is undergoing a rapid transformation driven by large language models. Given these developments, it's time that we rethink the future of clinical NLP.

Bio: Mark Dredze is the John C Malone Associate Professor of Computer Science at Johns Hopkins University. He is affiliated with the Malone Center for Engineering in Healthcare, the Center for Language and Speech Processing, among others. He holds a secondary appointment in the Biomedical Informatics & Data Science Section (BIDS), under the Department of Medicine (DOM), Division of General Internal Medicine (GIM) in the School of Medicine. He obtained his PhD from the University of Pennsylvania in 2009.

Prof. Dredze's research develops statistical models of language with applications to social media analysis, public health and clinical informatics. Within Natural Language Processing he focuses on statistical methods for information extraction but has considered a wide range of NLP tasks, including syntax, semantics, sentiment and spoke language processing. His work in public health includes tobacco control, vaccination, infectious disease surveillance, mental health, drug use, and gun violence prevention. He also develops new methods for clinical NLP on medical records.

Beyond publications in core areas of computer science, Prof. Dredze has pioneered new applications in public health informatics. He has published widely in health journals including the Journal of the American Medical Association (JAMA), the American Journal of Preventative Medicine (AJPM), Vaccine, and the Journal of the American Medical Informatics Association (JAMIA). His work is regularly covered by major media outlets, including NPR, the New York Times and CNN.

Keynote Talk: The Reproducible, Implementable, Transparent, and Explainable (RITE) framework for Real-world Implementation of Clinical Natural Language Processing

Hongfang Liu
Mayo Clinic

Abstract: Over the past decade, Electronic Health Record (EHR) systems have been widely implemented with large amounts of detailed longitudinal patient information, including lab tests, medications, disease status, and treatment outcomes, have consequently been accumulated and made electronically available. These large clinical databases are valuable data sources for clinical and translational research with several large clinical data initiatives (e.g., OHSDI, PCORnet, and CTSA). One common challenge faced by those initiatives is, however, the prevalence of clinical information embedded in unstructured text where natural language processing (NLP) techniques can be leveraged. Despite a plethora of recent advances in adopting NLP for clinical research, there have been barriers towards adoption of NLP solutions in clinical and translation research, especially in multisite settings. In this talk, I will discuss our strategy towards addressing those barriers through proposing a RITE-FAIR (Reproducible, Implementable, Transparent, and Explainable - Findable, Accessible, Interoperable, and Reusable) framework for clinical NLP.

Bio: Hongfang Liu is Dr. Richard F. Emslander Professor of Biomedical Informatics of Mayo Clinic and served as the founding chair of Division of Digital Health Sciences. She also directs biomedical informatics in Mayo Clinic Center of Clinical and Translational Science and Mayo Clinic Comprehensive Cancer Center and leads the ADVANCE program (Accelerating Discovery to Delivery through Advanced Informatics and Analytics for Clinical Excellence). Dr. Liu received her formal training in Mathematics, Statistics, Information and Computer Sciences with extensive research expertise in biomedical informatics. Her primary research interest is in clinical and biomedical Natural Language Processing and terminology/ontology. Dr Liu's work in clinical informatics has resulted in informatics systems that unlock clinical information stored in clinical narratives. Her work accelerates the pace of knowledge discovery, implementation and delivery for improved health care. Her research has been continuously supported by grants from National Science Foundation and National Institute of Health including NSF CAREER award and NCATS Innovation Award. Dr. Liu currently leads the community-wide effort on open health natural language processing (OHNLP) which aims to promote open source and interoperable NLP for clinical and translational research. Dr. Liu is a member of several professional societies, including the American Medical Informatics Association (AMIA) and the International Society for Computational Biology (ISCB). She is a fellow of American College of Medical Informatics (FACMI) and a fellow of International Academy of Health Sciences Informatics (FIAHSI).

Table of Contents

Program

Thursday, July 14, 2022

08:30 - 08:40	*Opening Remarks*
08:40 - 09:25	*Keynote: Mark Dredze*
09:25 - 09:40	*Keynote Q&A*
09:40 - 10:00	*Session 1*
	CLPT: A Universal Annotation Scheme and Toolkit for Clinical Language Processing Saranya Krishnamoorthy, Yanyi Jiang, William Buchanan, Ayush Singh and John E. Ortega
10:00 - 10:20	*Break*
10:20 - 12:00	*Session 2*
	PLM-ICD: Automatic ICD Coding with Pretrained Language Models Chao-Wei Huang, Shang-Chi Tsai and Yun-Nung Chen
	An exploratory data analysis: the performance differences of a medical code prediction system on different demographic groups Heereen Shim, Dietwig Lowet, Stijn Luca and Bart Vanrumste
	Cross-Language Transfer of High-Quality Annotations: Combining Neural Machine Translation with Cross-Linguistic Span Alignment to Apply NER to Clinical Texts in a Low-Resource Language Henning Schäfer, Ahmad Idrissi-Yaghir, Peter A. Horn and Christoph M. Friedrich
	Fine-tuning BERT Models for Summarizing German Radiology Findings Siting Liang, Klaus Kades, Matthias A. Fink, Peter Maximilian Full, Tim Frederik Weber, Jens Kleesiek, Michael Strube and Klaus Maier-Hein
	Clinical Flair: A Pre-Trained Language Model for Spanish Clinical Natural Language Processing Matías Rojas, Jocelyn Dunstan and Fabián Villena
12:00 - 13:30	*Lunch*

Thursday, July 14, 2022 (continued)

13:30 - 15:10 *Session 3*

Exploring Text Representations for Generative Temporal Relation Extraction
Dmitriy Dligach, Steven Bethard, Timothy A Miller and Guergana K Savova

Ensemble-based Fine-Tuning Strategy for Temporal Relation Extraction from the Clinical Narrative
Lijing Wang, Timothy A Miller, Steven Bethard and Guergana K Savova

Learning to Ask Like a Physician
Eric Lehman, Vladislav Lialin, Katelyn Edelwina Yap Legaspi, Anne Janelle R. Sy, Patricia Therese S. Pile, Nicole Rose Alberto, Richard Raymund Reyes Ragasa, Corinna Victoria M. Puyat, Marianne Katharina Vicera Taliño, Isabelle Rose I Alberto, Pia Gabrielle Isidro Alfonso, Dana Moukheiber, Byron C Wallace, Anna Rumshisky, Jennifer J. Liang, Preethi Raghavan, Leo Anthony Celi and Peter Szolovits

What Do You See in this Patient? Behavioral Testing of Clinical NLP Models
Betty Van Aken, Sebastian Herrmann and Alexander Löser

RRED : A Radiology Report Error Detector based on Deep Learning Framework

Dabin Min, Kaeun Kim, Jong Hyuk Lee, Yisak Kim and Chang Min Park

15:10 - 15:30 *Break*

15:30 - 15:50 *Session 4*

m-Networks: Adapting the Triplet Networks for Acronym Disambiguation
Sandaru Seneviratne, Elena Daskalaki, Artem Lenskiy and Hanna Suominen

15:50 - 15:35 *Keynote: Hongfang Liu*

15:35 - 16:50 *Keynote Q&A*

16:50 - 17:00 *Closing Remarks*

CLPT: A Universal Annotation Scheme and Toolkit for Clinical Language Processing

Saranya Krishnamoorthy **Yanyi Jiang** **William Buchanan**
Ayush Singh **John E. Ortega**
inQbator AI at eviCore Healthcare
Evernorth Health Services
firstname.lastname@evicore.com

Abstract

With the abundance of natural language processing (NLP) frameworks and toolkits being used in the clinical arena, a new challenge has arisen – how do technologists collaborate across several projects in an easy way? Private sector companies are usually not willing to share their work due to intellectual property rights and profit-bearing decisions. Therefore, the annotation schemes and toolkits that they use are rarely shared with the wider community. We present the clinical language pipeline toolkit (CLPT) and its corresponding annotation scheme called the CLAO (Clinical Language Annotation Object) with the aim of creating a way to share research results and other efforts through a software solution. The CLAO is a unified annotation scheme for clinical technology processing (CTP) projects that forms part of the CLPT and is more reliable than previous standards such as UIMA, BioC, and cTakes for annotation searches, insertions, and deletions. Additionally, it offers a standardized object that can be exchanged through an API that the authors release publicly for CTP project inclusion.

1 Introduction

With the resurgence of deep learning and neural networks, the interest in using a clinical language framework for classifying clinical text in a digital manner has been heightened in recent years. Several workshops and shared tasks (Harper et al., 2021; Goeuriot et al., 2020; Rumshisky et al., 2020; Wang et al., 2020) have focused on the state-of-the-art approaches and the amount of private enterprises offering clinical solutions backed by machine learning technologies has increased drastically (Parida et al., 2022). Nonetheless, a recent study (Digan et al., 2021) shows that systems like UIMA (Ferrucci and Lally, 2004), CLAMP (Soysal et al., 2018), and cTakes (Savova et al., 2010), despite their age and typical technology stack (Java), are still a standard for clinical language text classification and there are only a few publicly available clinical language frameworks or standardized annotation schemes that provide easy ways to share results and other pertinent information with organizations, private or public. We propose a modern standardized framework that supports collaboration on clinical language research. Here we present the clinical language pipeline toolkit (CLPT), a framework developed with Python designed with software development principles. The CLPT enables researchers and entities to share their project results easily and supports research to be conducted in a fast and reproducible way. The unified annotation scheme for the CLPT is called the clinical language annotation object (CLAO). The CLAO is more reliable for annotation searches, insertions, and deletions than previous standards (e.g. UIMA(Ferrucci and Lally, 2004), cTakes(Savova et al., 2010) and BioC (Comeau et al., 2013)).[1] Additionally, the CLAO can be easily shared and integrated due to its standardization which makes it accessible through an application programming interface (API).

To illustrate the aforementioned concepts which will improve clinical technology processing (CTP) collaboration, we introduce five novel ideas and contributions in this article:

1. A freely available[2] annotation scheme (Clinical Language Annotation Object, CLAO) for CTP projects that can be interchanged between public and private sector organizations through offline and online resources such as APIs or file exchange.

2. A high-level Python framework (Clinical Language Pipeline Toolkit, CLPT) designed purposely in an ambiguous manner with the ob-

[1] The focus of this paper is to introduce the main concepts of the CLPT and the CLAO. We plan to publish efficiency results in a future iteration.

[2] https://github.com/inQbator-eviCore/clpt

Proceedings of the 4th Clinical Natural Language Processing Workshop, pages 1 - 9
July 14, 2022 ©2022 Association for Computational Linguistics

jective of accepting any input of multiple modal types (i.e., speech, images, text, and more).

3. A novel algorithm for processing the annotation scheme that allows faster annotation inserts, deletes, and searches than previous frameworks.

4. An annotation scheme that can be converted to a linked data format which supports graph analytics on documents.

5. Out-of-the-box support for semantically comparing text in high-dimension spaces for state-of-the-art language models.

In the following sections, we first go through related work on annotation and natural language processing (NLP) tools in Section 2. In Section 3.1, we then describe in detail the CLAO scheme. Next, in Section 3.2, we cover the four CLPT modules for creating a typical CTP pipeline. Lastly, we conclude with the availability and future work.

2 Related Work

Several clinical text processing toolkits and annotations schemes have been introduced in the past but none of them provide the same functionality and efficiency as the CLAO and CLPT. Some widely used NLP tools for clinical text processing include the clinical text analysis and knowledge extraction system (cTAKES) (Savova et al., 2010), BioC (Comeau et al., 2013), Brat Rapid Annotation Tool (BRAT) (Stenetorp et al., 2012), General Architecture for Text Engineering (GATE) (Cunningham et al., 2002), Metamap (Aronson and Lang, 2010), Metamap Lite (Demner-Fushman et al., 2017), clinical language annotation, modeling, and processing (CLAMP) (Soysal et al., 2018) and sciSpaCy (Neumann et al., 2019).

BRAT (Stenetorp et al., 2012) is a web-based annotation tool for defining entities and creating annotations. Annotations created by BRAT are stored in a standoff format. Since BRAT XML output is similar to CLPT output, it can be easily adapted to CLAO by creating an adapted script, unlike outputs from cTakes or UIMA which are CAS files that are serialized using Java-style notation. Though the CLPT implements a similar approach of storing the annotation in a CLAO object, the CLAO's annotation scheme supports faster annotation insertion, deletion, and searching by implementing B-tree for indexing (see 3.1 for details).

cTAKES (Savova et al., 2010) is a clinical information retrieval system that combines rule-based methods and machine learning techniques for clinical narrative processing. It has been shown to work well on clinical notes alone but does not cover a broader set of NLP tasks (Neumann et al., 2019). The CLPT has been designed purposely ambiguous in order to accept multi-modal input and perform several NLP tasks.

GATE (Cunningham et al., 2002), CLAMP (Soysal et al., 2018), and BioC (Comeau et al., 2013) provide multiple tools which can be used for language processing tasks, annotating corpora, and performing evaluation. Yet, all three of them are either based on Java or C++. Additionally, GATE (Cunningham et al., 2002) and CLAMP (Soysal et al., 2018) depend on a framework called the unstructured information management architecture (UIMA) (Ferrucci and Lally, 2004). CLPT makes similar offerings as the three aforementioned frameworks but it uses Python which makes it easier to integrate with other modern deep-learning NLP frameworks such as TensorFlow (Abadi et al., 2016), MedSpacy (Eyre et al., (in press, n.d.) and PyTorch (Paszke et al., 2019).

The National Library of Medicine[3] presented a framework called Metamap (Aronson and Lang, 2010) for mapping biomedical text to unified medical language system (UMLS) concepts. Others (Soysal et al., 2018; Peng et al., 2020a) have found Metamap difficult for building machine learning models and hard to predict long entities due to its dictionary lookup method (Peng et al., 2020a). Previous research (Zhang et al., 2021) argues that neither Metamap nor CLAMP incorporate deep learning models directly. We believe that the CLAO and CLPT address several downfalls by creating an easy-to-use annotation scheme along with the targeted focus on deep learning.

We consider the work on sciSpaCy (Neumann et al., 2019) similar to ours because it was developed in Python and takes into account recent classification techniques in deep learning. However, to our knowledge, sciSpaCy (Neumann et al., 2019) does not support some of the default features found in the CLPT, such as a shareable annotation file that can be serialized to disk and efficient entity lookups as are offered in the CLAO.

[3]https://www.nlm.nih.gov

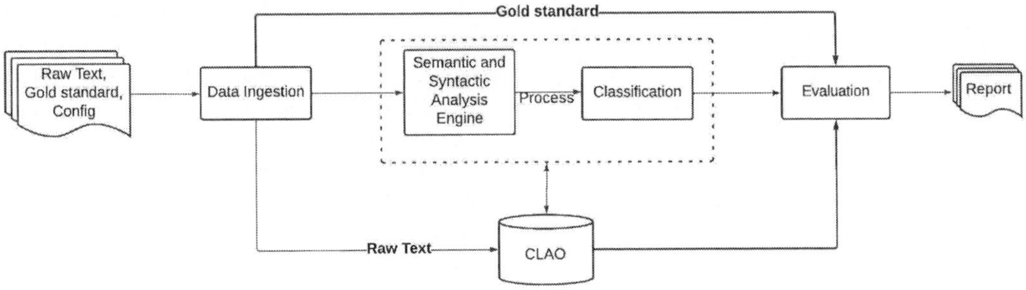

Figure 1: Clinical Language Pipeline Toolkit (CLPT) architecture

3 Methods

3.1 Clinical Language Annotation Object

In this section, we present two core CLAO innovations that provide efficient annotation storage and retrieval. The CLAO receives raw text as input which is cleaned and broken down into minimal units of analysis, expressed in this article as tokens. The CLAO has three main divisions for an annotation: (1) its elements, (2) its attributes and values, and (3) the relations linking the annotation to others (often times for syntactic or semantic representations).

The first step leading to the creation of a CLAO (as seen in Figure 1) is the segmentation of textual data into its minimal elements for annotation. Elements and values for the CLAO are extracted from the segments using sentence (or segment) detection and are stored and finally represented in a common annotation structure represented by a XML-based hybrid standoff format (Ide et al., 2017). We chose to represent the CLAO with a generalized representation in order to provide flexibility so that the annotation scheme was not constrained to the use of specific domains or tools. The version of the CLPT presented here supports exporting the CLAO into a JSON format, future iterations will provide a mechanism to allow users to export the CLAO into a JSON-LD format (Cimiano et al., 2020). JSON-LD is a novel contribution because, unlike other frameworks, it allows queries on the CLAO to be data-driven yet graph-based, similar to previous research (Hellmann et al., 2013; Cimiano et al., 2020) on efficiency. This promotes inter-operability and collaboration through a standard. For convenience, we have provided an example of a serialized CLAO in Appendix A.1.

As another novelty of our annotation implementation, the CLAO supports addition, deletion, and update operations along with the enhancement of annotations through the use of what are known as *B-Trees* for indexing (algorithms for processing stored data that are high performing, Johnson and Sasha (1993)). B-Tree indexing within the CLAO is performed at an asymptotic speed of $O(log\, n)$ for operations on CLAO entities – providing for a small storage footprint, easy scaling (without the need for rehashing as in the case of typical hash maps), and optimum segment loading.

The B-tree based algorithm, called a *blist*, used for indexing a CLAO uses an algorithm written by Daniel Stutzbach[4]. It combines a B-tree with an array for searches. In order to qualify that a blist would be the optimum algorithm for indexing a CLAO, we performed two main experiments illustrated in Figures 2 and 3. Both experiments compare the use of a default Python 3 list[5] data structure and the blist from Daniel Stutzbach. Our first experiment consisted in the creation of one-hundred default Python 3 lists and one-hundred blists both containing one million random floating numbers between 0 and 1. The second experiment consisted of random slicing which was done on both data structures (the Python 3 list and the blist)

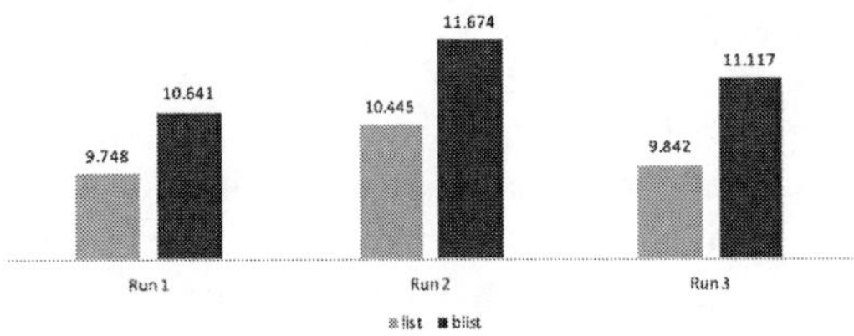

Figure 2: Creation Time Comparison (in Seconds)

[4]https://stutzbachenterprises.com/blist

[5]https://docs.python.org/3/library/stdtypes.html#list

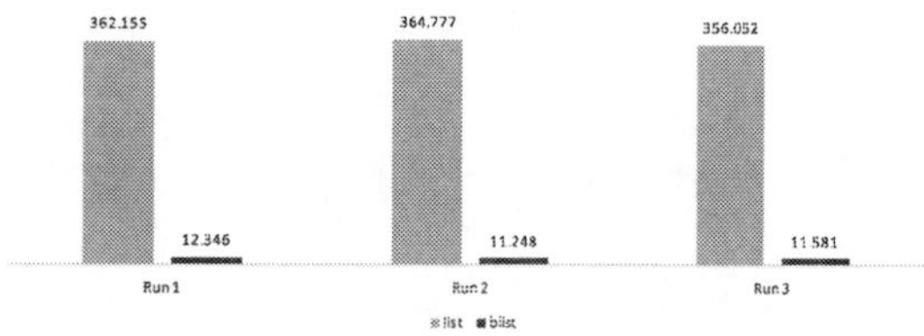

Figure 3: Slicing Time Comparison (in Seconds)

1000 times. The run time for both experiments was recorded and we found that the blist outperformed the Python 3 list as it was approximately 30 times faster thus making it the optimal choice for the CLPT at this time. In future work, we plan on extending the blist algorithm to include an even faster search.

3.2 Clinical Language Pipeline Toolkit

The CLPT is a CTP pipeline meant for exclusive use with the CLAO. We created the CLPT as an easy-to-use first pass for building a CLAO that can then be processed by others. In this short article, we only introduce novel themes along with findings and further plan to extend our work to introduce a larger pipeline backed by a CLAO. The architecture of the CLPT can be considered similar to other architectures like UIMA (Ferrucci and Lally, 2004) and CLAMP (Soysal et al., 2018) in some ways. However, it is our intent to allow further out-of-the-box novel features such as annotations mixed with embeddings. The CLPT, similar to its predecessors, has these four pipelines modules: (1) ingestion, (2) analysis engine, (3) classification, and (4) evaluation as shown in Figure 1. Each module has the option of saving any information to the CLAO as needed, in a repository-like manner. The CLAO is configured via a configuration file that enables any of the four modules, including the analysis and classification components, as explained in the following sections.

3.2.1 Ingestion

The CLPT is designed to be multi-modal, able to accept any form of input such as text, speech, video or images. At this point, we have experimented with text only and left other modalities for future work. The ingestion process is similar to other pipelines in that an object is considered for and serialized to the CLAO format. One main difference between the CLPT and other toolkits is that the CLPT was purposely created with high abstraction and is able to model any type of data. Figure 4 provides an example of the ingestion process which, similar to (Ferrucci and Lally, 2004), uses a document reader (called Document Collector), to read in data. Additionally, users have the option to pass in a configuration file (`.yml` format) designed to allow high-level control as to which modules to use. Nonetheless, there is also a "default" pipeline configuration which requires no intervention. The ingestion module handles the initial creation of the CLAO and passes the CLAO on for further processing to the analysis engine.

3.2.2 Analysis Engine

Our deep learning contribution is based on adding embeddings to the CLAO. Since embeddings are a key difference between the CLPT and other toolkits, we cover them here in further detail. Our embeddings can be used as part of creating a model for processing or loading a pre-trained model. Given that the majority of modern work on clinical NLP uses deep learning and/or embeddings, we felt it necessary to promote their inclusion in the CLPT. Our novel technique of storing embeddings by use of the CLAO has not been performed in the past. Additionally, we provide sub-word embedding combined with hashing trick for efficiency (Bojanowski et al., 2017) which are able to handle out-of-vocabulary (OOV) words. Embeddings are stored in CLAO objects efficiently, allowing comparison between tokens and spans of tokens. This is done by assigning a vector to each token or spans of tokens where the CLAO returns an average of all of the embeddings within it. Furthermore, CLPT offers a configuration mechanism for changing this span embedding method of calculation. Allowing for this flexibility can be considered a novel approach as it allows users to easily test various embedding types for experiments.

3.2.3 Classification

The classification module extracts knowledge from the CLAO by retrieving information from the upstream CLPT component(s). In this module, machine learning and other techniques (e.g., heuristics) are applied to further augment annotations for classification tasks before evaluation. Some of the major components to be released in the CLPT (See Appendix Figure 6), for the classification module are: (1) *acronym expansion* (similar to CARD (Wu et al., 2017)); (2) *mention detection* split into two phases, first a step to identify the mentions and then a step to group them together; (3) *fact extraction* to extract clinical concepts from the mentions which help to better disambiguate clinical notes and provide fact-based evidence for classification; (4) *relationship extraction* further expansion of mention detection to allow linking entities and the creation of a knowledge graph – to be presented as future work.

3.2.4 Evaluation

The CLPT provides an evaluation module (shown in Figure 7) as a separate module rather than the addition of classification or other processing techniques. The aim is to allow several forms of evaluation while, at a minimum, providing the baseline measurements such as precision, recall, F1-score, and accuracy. The baseline evaluation can be extended to cover any other common metrics but at this time we leave that for future work. The evaluation module takes two inputs: a CLAO and a gold standard. The CLAO is what will allow us to compare against the gold standard and both are required.

4 Concluding remarks and future work

We have introduced a novel and efficient toolkit for creating CTP pipelines with several new contributions. The thought has been to make a centralized format for exchanging information amongst entities, albeit academic or private. This will allow entities to compare and contrast results by comparing CLAOs that adhere to a standardized guideline. We contribute this to the public community as a way to use a more updated framework for modern CTP techniques. It is our thought that the CLPT can increase productivity and the exchange of information. The current implementation of the CLPT and the CLAO is in its infancy; the plan is to develop more functionality such as multi-modal inputs, the creation of a knowledge graph, and improved evaluation methods.

Additionally, we plan on extending the current implementation which performs classification using public machine learning models and heuristics by training models with the CLPT. Once those models have been trained, we also plan on adding the capability for fine-tuning those models for several clinical tasks able to handle diverse NLP problems like seminal work (Peng et al., 2020b) has done.

References

Martín Abadi, Ashish Agarwal, Paul Barham, Eugene Brevdo, Zhifeng Chen, Craig Citro, Greg S Corrado, Andy Davis, Jeffrey Dean, Matthieu Devin, et al. 2016. Tensorflow: Large-scale machine learning on heterogeneous distributed systems. *arXiv preprint arXiv:1603.04467*.

Alan R Aronson and François-Michel Lang. 2010. An overview of metamap: historical perspective and recent advances. *Journal of the American Medical Informatics Association*, 17(3):229–236.

Piotr Bojanowski, Edouard Grave, Armand Joulin, and Tomas Mikolov. 2017. Enriching word vectors with subword information. *Transactions of the Association for Computational Linguistics*, 5:135–146.

Philipp Cimiano, Christian Chiarcos, John P McCrae, and Jorge Gracia. 2020. Linguistic linked open data cloud. In *Linguistic Linked Data*, pages 29–41. Springer.

Donald C Comeau, Rezarta Islamaj Doğan, Paolo Ciccarese, Kevin Bretonnel Cohen, Martin Krallinger, Florian Leitner, Zhiyong Lu, Yifan Peng, Fabio Rinaldi, Manabu Torii, et al. 2013. Bioc: a minimalist approach to interoperability for biomedical text processing. *Database*, 2013.

Hamish Cunningham, Diana Maynard, Kalina Bontcheva, and Valentin Tablan. 2002. Gate: an architecture for development of robust hlt applications. In *Proceedings of the 40th Annual Meeting of the Association for Computational Linguistics*, pages 168–175.

Dina Demner-Fushman, Willie J Rogers, and Alan R Aronson. 2017. Metamap lite: an evaluation of a new java implementation of metamap. *Journal of the American Medical Informatics Association*, 24(4):841–844.

William Digan, Aurélie Névéol, Antoine Neuraz, Maxime Wack, David Baudoin, Anita Burgun, and Bastien Rance. 2021. Can reproducibility be improved in clinical natural language processing? a study of 7 clinical nlp suites. *Journal of the American Medical Informatics Association*, 28(3):504–515.

Hannah Eyre, Alec B Chapman, Kelly S Peterson, Jianlin Shi, Patrick R Alba, Makoto M Jones, Tamara L Box, Scott L DuVall, and Olga V Patterson. (in press, n.d.). Launching into clinical space with medspacy: a new clinical text processing toolkit in python. In *AMIA Annual Symposium Proceedings 2021*.

David Ferrucci and Adam Lally. 2004. Uima: an architectural approach to unstructured information processing in the corporate research environment. *Natural Language Engineering*, 10(3-4):327–348.

Lorraine Goeuriot, Hanna Suominen, Liadh Kelly, Antonio Miranda-Escalada, Martin Krallinger, Zhengyang Liu, Gabriella Pasi, Gabriela Gonzalez Saez, Marco

Viviani, and Chenchen Xu. 2020. Overview of the clef ehealth evaluation lab 2020. In *International Conference of the Cross-Language Evaluation Forum for European Languages*, pages 255–271. Springer.

Corey Harper, Jessica Cox, Curt Kohler, Antony Scerri, Ron Daniel Jr, and Paul Groth. 2021. Semeval-2021 task 8: Measeval–extracting counts and measurements and their related contexts. In *Proceedings of the 15th International Workshop on Semantic Evaluation (SemEval-2021)*, pages 306–316.

Sebastian Hellmann, Jens Lehmann, Sören Auer, and Martin Brümmer. 2013. Integrating nlp using linked data. In *International semantic web conference*, pages 98–113. Springer.

Nancy Ide, Christian Chiarcos, Manfred Stede, and Steve Cassidy. 2017. Designing annotation schemes: From model to representation. In *Handbook of linguistic annotation*, pages 73–111. Springer.

Theodore Johnson and Dennis Sasha. 1993. The performance of current b-tree algorithms. *ACM Transactions on Database Systems (TODS)*, 18(1):51–101.

Mark Neumann, Daniel King, Iz Beltagy, and Waleed Ammar. 2019. Scispacy: fast and robust models for biomedical natural language processing. *arXiv preprint arXiv:1902.07669*.

Prasanta Kumar Parida, Lingraj Dora, Monorama Swain, Sanjay Agrawal, and Rutuparna Panda. 2022. Data science methodologies in smart healthcare: a review. *Health and Technology*, pages 1–16.

Adam Paszke, Sam Gross, Francisco Massa, Adam Lerer, James Bradbury, Gregory Chanan, Trevor Killeen, Zeming Lin, Natalia Gimelshein, Luca Antiga, et al. 2019. Pytorch: An imperative style, high-performance deep learning library. *Advances in neural information processing systems*, 32.

Jacqueline Peng, Mengge Zhao, James Havrilla, Cong Liu, Chunhua Weng, Whitney Guthrie, Robert Schultz, Kai Wang, and Yunyun Zhou. 2020a. Natural language processing (nlp) tools in extracting biomedical concepts from research articles: a case study on autism spectrum disorder. *BMC Medical Informatics and Decision Making*, 20(11):1–9.

Yifan Peng, Qingyu Chen, and Zhiyong Lu. 2020b. An empirical study of multi-task learning on bert for biomedical text mining. *arXiv preprint arXiv:2005.02799*.

Anna Rumshisky, Kirk Roberts, Steven Bethard, and Tristan Naumann, editors. 2020. *Proceedings of the 3rd Clinical Natural Language Processing Workshop*. Association for Computational Linguistics, Online.

Guergana K Savova, James J Masanz, Philip V Ogren, Jiaping Zheng, Sunghwan Sohn, Karin C Kipper-Schuler, and Christopher G Chute. 2010. Mayo clinical text analysis and knowledge extraction system (ctakes): architecture, component evaluation and applications. *Journal of the American Medical Informatics Association*, 17(5):507–513.

Ergin Soysal, Jingqi Wang, Min Jiang, Yonghui Wu, Serguei Pakhomov, Hongfang Liu, and Hua Xu. 2018. Clamp–a toolkit for efficiently building customized clinical natural language processing pipelines. *Journal of the American Medical Informatics Association*, 25(3):331–336.

Pontus Stenetorp, Sampo Pyysalo, Goran Topić, Tomoko Ohta, Sophia Ananiadou, and Jun'ichi Tsujii. 2012. Brat: a web-based tool for nlp-assisted text annotation. In *Proceedings of the Demonstrations at the 13th Conference of the European Chapter of the Association for Computational Linguistics*, pages 102–107.

Yanshan Wang, Sunyang Fu, Feichen Shen, Sam Henry, Ozlem Uzuner, and Hongfang Liu. 2020. The 2019 n2c2/ohnlp track on clinical semantic textual similarity: Overview. *JMIR Med Inform*, 8(11):e23375.

Yonghui Wu, Joshua C Denny, S Trent Rosenbloom, Randolph A Miller, Dario A Giuse, Lulu Wang, Carmelo Blanquicett, Ergin Soysal, Jun Xu, and Hua Xu. 2017. A long journey to short abbreviations: developing an open-source framework for clinical abbreviation recognition and disambiguation (card). *Journal of the American Medical Informatics Association*, 24(e1):e79–e86.

Yuhao Zhang, Yuhui Zhang, Peng Qi, Christopher D Manning, and Curtis P Langlotz. 2021. Biomedical and clinical english model packages for the stanza python nlp library. *Journal of the American Medical Informatics Association*, 28(9):1892–1899.

A Appendix

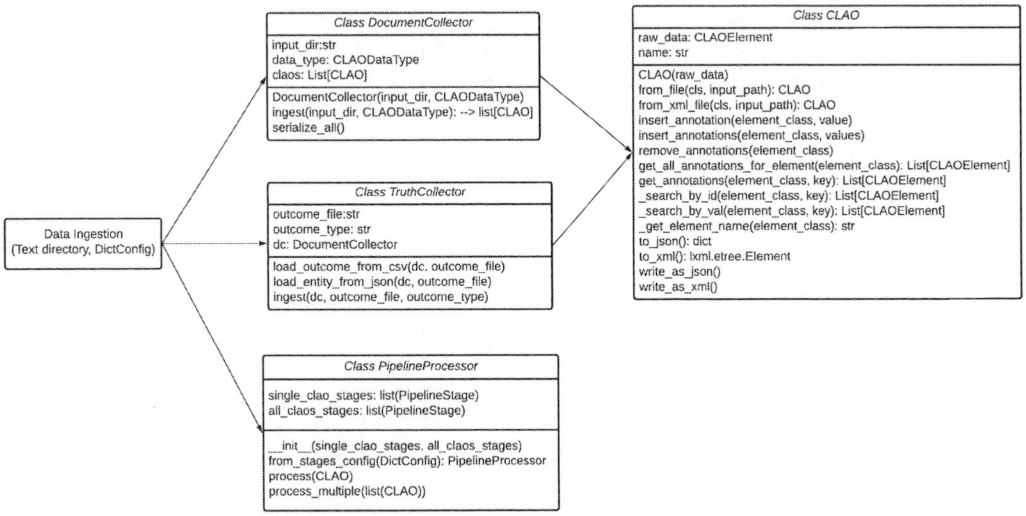

Figure 4: The data ingestion module. It is used to ingest data and create an initial clinical language annotation object (CLAO) which can include text or other types (in future iterations).

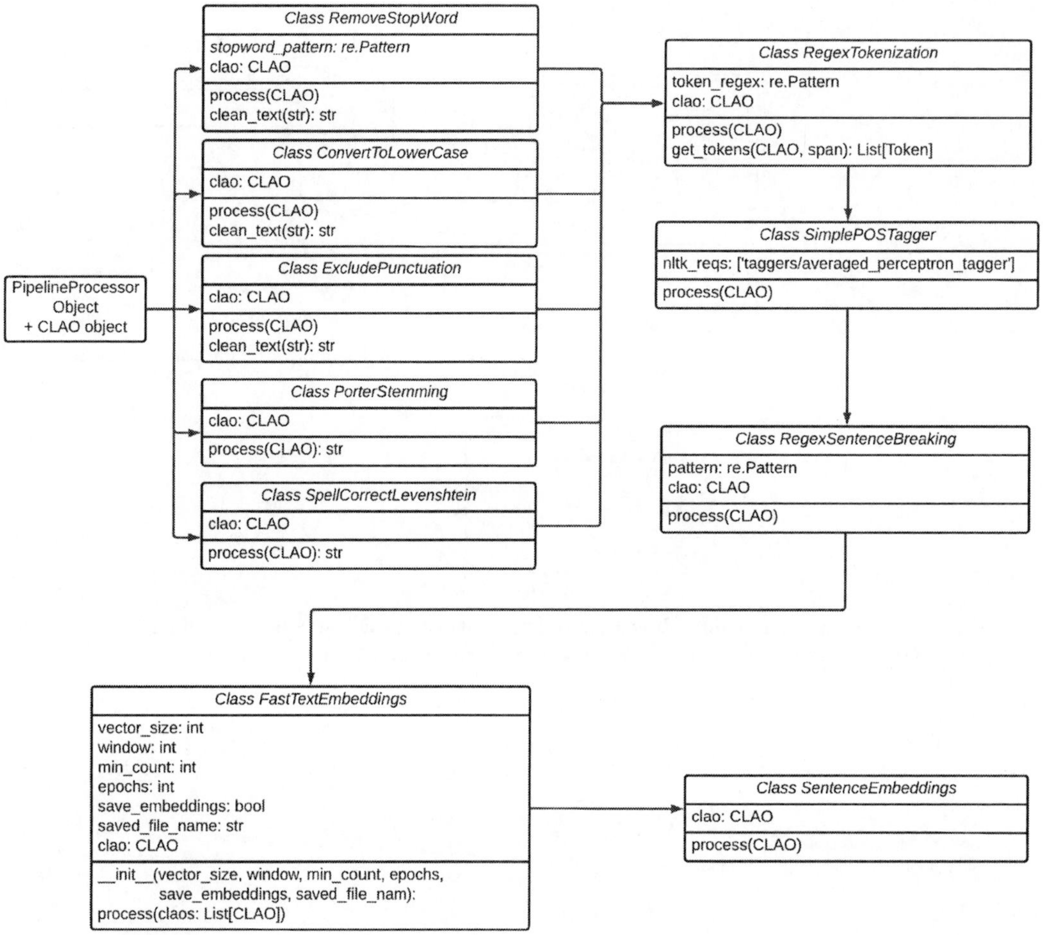

Figure 5: The analysis engine module. Each class has a method named *process()* that pre-processes and stores information from and to a clinical language annotation object (CLAO) during each stage.

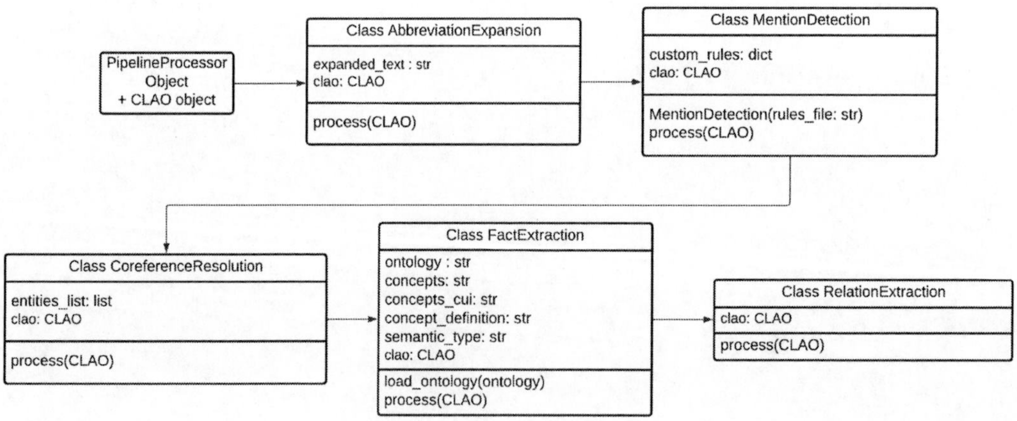

Figure 6: The classification module. This module is used to process and classify input from a clinical language annotation object (CLAO) in turn adding new information to it.

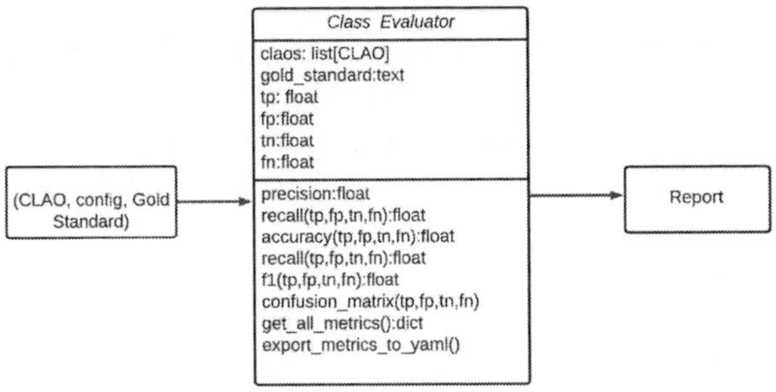

Figure 7: The evaluation module. A module that uses a clinical language annotation object (CLAO) and a gold standard to provide evaluation output in a report format.

A.1 Sample annotation


```
<?xml version='1.0' encoding='UTF-8'?>
<annotation>
    <text start="0" end="41" description="raw_text">Patient has type ii dm. This is not good.</text>
    <sentence id="0" start="0" end="23">
        <entity id="0" start="12" end="22" entity_group="0" token_ids="[2, 5)" type="MENTION" confidence="1"
            label="PROBLEM">Type II Diabetes Mellitus</entity>
        <token id="0" start="0" end="7" pos="NN" stem="patient" embedding_id="0">Patient</token>
        <token id="1" start="8" end="11" pos="VBZ" stem="ha" embedding_id="1">has</token>
        <token id="2" start="12" end="16" pos="VBN" stem="type" embedding_id="2">type</token>
        <token id="3" start="17" end="19" pos="JJ" stem="ii" embedding_id="3">ii</token>
        <token id="4" start="20" end="22" pos="NN" stem="dm" embedding_id="4">dm</token>
        <token id="5" start="22" end="23" pos="." stem="." embedding_id="5">.</token>
    </sentence>
    <sentence id="1" start="24" end="41">
        <token id="6" start="24" end="28" pos="DT" stem="thi" embedding_id="6">This</token>
        <token id="7" start="29" end="31" pos="VBZ" stem="is" embedding_id="7">is</token>
        <token id="8" start="32" end="35" pos="RB" stem="not" embedding_id="8">not</token>
        <token id="9" start="36" end="40" pos="JJ" stem="good" embedding_id="9">good</token>
        <token id="10" start="40" end="41" pos="." stem="." embedding_id="5">.</token>
    </sentence>
    <embedding id="0">[-0.0021704417, -0.010320467, -4.0913405e-06, -0.026113503, 0.003324223]</
        embedding>
    <embedding id="1">[0.03536414, -0.066816024, 0.018991465, 0.03511271, -0.02413405]</embedding>
    <embedding id="2">[-0.04219764, 0.051192448, 0.053828064, 0.013828199, -0.024849724]</embedding>
    <embedding id="3">[-0.011548042, -0.056690447, 0.0042386726, 0.013731264, -0.042996213]</
        embedding>
    <embedding id="4">[-0.015310202, -0.06731376, -0.023788698, -0.070030175, 0.0918083]</embedding>
    <embedding id="5">[-0.07549597, -0.034822427, -0.048076335, 0.05481594, -0.04260452]</embedding>
    <embedding id="6">[-0.08328381, 0.042492405, 0.026664842, 0.000608474, -0.023121541]</embedding>
    <embedding id="7">[-0.095420435, -0.043184925, 0.05082492, -0.015773036, -0.037915066]</embedding
        >
    <embedding id="8">[0.01620562, 0.030467993, -0.0037846065, 0.009880951, 0.0008572937]</embedding>
    <embedding id="9">[0.10948994, 0.040386822, 0.030505553, -0.03049627, 0.04858529]</embedding>
    <entity_group id="0" entity_type="MENTION">Type II Diabetes Mellitus</entity_group>
    <actual_label>0</actual_label>
    <probability>0.67</probability>
    <predicted_label>0</predicted_label>
</annotation>
```


Figure 8: A sample CLAO file comprising of two sentences in a single paragraph.

PLM-ICD: Automatic ICD Coding with Pretrained Language Models

Chao-Wei Huang[⋆†] **Shang-Chi Tsai**[⋆] **Yun-Nung Chen**[⋆]
[⋆]National Taiwan University, Taipei, Taiwan
[†]Taiwan AI Labs, Taipei, Taiwan
f07922069@csie.ntu.edu.tw y.v.chen@ieee.org

Abstract

Automatically classifying electronic health records (EHRs) into diagnostic codes has been challenging to the NLP community. State-of-the-art methods treated this problem as a multi-label classification problem and proposed various architectures to model this problem. However, these systems did not leverage the superb performance of pretrained language models, which achieved superb performance on natural language understanding tasks. Prior work has shown that pretrained language models underperformed on this task with the regular fine-tuning scheme. Therefore, this paper aims at analyzing the causes of the underperformance and developing a framework for automatic ICD coding with pretrained language models. We spotted three main issues through the experiments: 1) large label space, 2) long input sequences, and 3) domain mismatch between pretraining and fine-tuning. We propose **PLM-ICD**, a framework that tackles the challenges with various strategies. The experimental results show that our proposed framework can overcome the challenges and achieves state-of-the-art performance in terms of multiple metrics on the benchmark MIMIC data.[1]

1 Introduction

The clinical notes in electronic health records (EHRs) are written as free-form text by clinicians during patient visits. The notes can be associated with diagnostic codes from the International Classification of Diseases (ICD), which represent diagnostic and procedural information of the visit. The ICD codes are a standardized way to encode information systematically and internationally, which could be used for tracking healthcare statistics, quality outcomes, and billing.

While ICD codes provide several useful applications, manually labelling ICD codes has been shown to be very labor-intensive and domain expertise is required (O'malley et al., 2005). Hence, automatically assigning ICD codes to clinical notes has been of broad interest in the medical natural language processing (NLP) community. Prior work has identified several challenges of this task, including the large number of labels to be classified, the long input sequence, and the imbalanced label distribution, i.e., the long-tail problem (Xie et al., 2019). These challenges make the task extremely difficult, demonstrating that advanced modeling techniques are required. With the introduction of deep learning models, we have seen tremendous performance improvement on the task of automatic ICD coding (Shi et al., 2017; Xie and Xing, 2018; Mullenbach et al., 2018; Li and Yu, 2020; Vu et al., 2020; Cao et al., 2020; Liu et al., 2021; Kim and Ganapathi, 2021; Zhou et al., 2021). These methods utilized convolutional neural networks (CNNs) (Mullenbach et al., 2018; Li and Yu, 2020; Liu et al., 2021) or recurrent neural networks (RNNs) (Vu et al., 2020) to transform the long text in clinical notes into hidden representations. State-of-the-art methods employed a label attention mechanism, i.e., performing attention to hidden representations independently for each label, to combat the extremely large label set (Mullenbach et al., 2018; Vu et al., 2020).

Recently, pretrained language models (PLMs) with the Transformer (Vaswani et al., 2017) architecture have become the dominant forces for NLP research, achieving superior performance on numerous natural language understanding tasks (Devlin et al., 2019; Liu et al., 2019). These models are pretrained on large amount of text with various language modeling objectives, and then fine-tuned on the desired downstream tasks to perform different functionalities such as classification (Devlin et al., 2019) or text generation (Radford et al., 2019; Raffel et al., 2020).

While PLMs demonstrate impressive capabili-

[1]The source code is available at https://github.com/MiuLab/PLM-ICD.

Proceedings of the 4th Clinical Natural Language Processing Workshop, pages 10 - 20
July 14, 2022 ©2022 Association for Computational Linguistics

ties across classification tasks, applying PLMs to automatic ICD coding is still not well-studied. Previous work has shown that applying PLMs to this task is not straightforward (Zhang et al., 2020; Pascual et al., 2021), and the main challenges being:

- The length of clinical notes exceeds the maximum length of PLMs.
- The regular fine-tuning scheme where we add a linear layer on top of the PLMs does not perform well for multi-label classification problems with a large label set.
- PLMs are usually pretrained on general-domain corpora, while clinical notes are very medical-specific and the language usage is different.

As a result, the performance of PLMs reported in the prior work is inferior to the state-of-the-art models that did not use pre-trained models by a large margin (Pascual et al., 2021). Their best model achieved 88.65% in terms of micro-AUC, compared with the state-of-the-art 94.9% from the ISD model (Zhou et al., 2021). This result highlighted that the performance of PLMs on this task was still far from the conventional models.

In this paper, we aim at identifying the challenges met during applying PLMs to automatic ICD coding and developing a framework that could overcome these challenges. We first conduct preliminary experiments to verify and investigate the challenges mentioned above, and then we propose proper mechanisms to tackle each challenge. The proposed mechanisms are: 1) domain-specific pretraining for the domain mismatch problem, 2) segment pooling for the long input sequence problem, and 3) label attention for the large label set problem. By integrating these techniques together, we propose **PLM-ICD**, a framework specifically designed for automatic ICD coding with PLMs. The effectiveness of PLM-ICD is verified through experiments on the benchmark MIMIC-3 and MIMIC-2 datasets (Saeed et al., 2011; Johnson et al., 2016). To the best of our knowledge, PLM-ICD is the first Transformer-based pretrained language model that achieves competitive performance on the MIMIC datasets. We further analyze several factors that affect the performance of PLMs, including pretraining method, pretraining corpora, vocabulary construction, and optimization schedules.

The contributions of this paper are 3-fold:

- We perform experiments to verify and analyze the challenges of utilizing PLMs on the task of automatic ICD coding.
- We develop **PLM-ICD**, a framework to fine-tune PLMs for ICD coding, that achieves competitive performance on the benchmark MIMIC-3 dataset.
- We analyze the factors that affect PLMs' performance on this task.

2 Related Work

2.1 Automatic ICD Coding

ICD code prediction is a challenging task in the medical domain. Several recent work attempted to approach this task with neural models. Choi et al. (2016) and Baumel et al. (2018) used recurrent neural networks (RNN) to encode the EHR data for predicting diagnostic results. Li and Yu (2020) recently utilized a multi-filter convolutional layer and a residual layer to improve the performance of ICD prediction. On the other hand, several work tried to integrate external medical knowledge into this task. In order to leverage the information of definition of each ICD code, RNN and CNN were adopted to encode the diagnostic descriptions of ICD codes for better prediction via attention mechanism (Shi et al., 2017; Mullenbach et al., 2018). Moreover, the prior work tried to consider the hierarchical structure of ICD codes (Xie and Xing, 2018), which proposed a tree-of-sequences LSTM to simultaneously capture the hierarchical relationship among codes and the semantics of each code. Also, Tsai et al. (2019) introduced various ways of leveraging the hierarchical knowledge of ICD by adding refined loss functions. Recently, Cao et al. (2020) proposed to train ICD code embeddings in hyperbolic space to model the hierarchical structure. Additionally, they used graph neural network to capture the code co-occurrences. LAAT (Vu et al., 2020) integrated a bidirectional LSTM with an improved label-aware attention mechanism. EffectiveCAN (Liu et al., 2021) integrated a squeeze-and-excitation network and residual connections along with extracting representations from all encoder layers for label attention. The authors also introduced focal loss to tackle the long-tail prediction problem. ISD (Zhou et al., 2021) employed extraction of shared representations among high-frequency and low-frequency codes and a self-distillation learning mechanism to alleviate the long-tail code distribution. Kim and Ganapathi (2021) proposed a framework called Read, Attend, and Code (RAC) to effectively predict ICD codes, which is the current state-of-the-art model on this task. Most recent models focused on developing an effective interaction between note representations and code representations (Cao et al., 2020; Zhou et al., 2021; Kim and Ganapathi, 2021). Our work, instead, is focusing on the choice of the note encoder, where we apply PLMs for their superior encoding capabilities.

2.2 Pretrained Language Models

Using pretrained language models to extract contextualuzed representations has led to consistent improvements across most NLP tasks. Notably, ELMo (Peters et al., 2018) and BERT (Devlin et al., 2019) showed that pretraining is effective for both LSTM and transformer (Vaswani et al., 2017) models. Variants have been proposed such as XL-Net (Yang et al., 2019), RoBERTa (Liu et al., 2019). These models are pretrained on large amount of general domain text to grasp the capability to model textual data, and fine-tuned on common classification tasks.

To tackle domain-specific problems, prior work adapted such models to scientific and biomedical domains, including BioBERT (Lee et al., 2019), ClinicalBERT (Alsentzer et al., 2019), PubMed-BERT (Gu et al., 2020) and RoBERTa-PM (Lewis et al., 2020). These models are pretrained on domain-specific text carefully crawled and processed for improving the downstream performance. The biomedical-specific PLMs reported improved performance on a variety of biomedical tasks, including text mining, named entity recognition, relation extraction, and question answering (Lee et al., 2019).

While PLMs achieved state-of-the-art performance on various tasks, applying PLMs to large-scale multi-label classification is still a challenging research direction. Chang et al. (2019) proposed X-BERT, a framework that is scalable to an extremely large label set of a million labels. Lehečka et al. (2020) showed that the modeling capacity of BERT's pooling layers might be limited for automatic ICD coding. Pascual et al. (2021) also demonstrated inferior performance when applying BERT to this task and pointed out several challenges to be addressed. Specifically, the authors proposed 5 truncation and splitting strategies to tackle the long input sequence problem. Their proposed *All* splitting strategies is similar to our segment pooling mechanism. However, without the label attention mechanism, the model failed to learn.

Model	Length	Macro-F	Micro-F
LAAT	4000	9.9	57.5
	512*	6.8	47.3
BERT	512*	2.8	38.9

Table 1: Results of LAAT and BERT on MIMIC-3 with different maximum input lengths (%). *The length is number of words for LAAT and number of tokens for BERT, so their performance cannot directly comparable.

Zhang et al. (2020) proposed BERT-XML, an extension of BERT for ICD coding. The model was pretrained on a large cohort of EHR clinical notes with an EHR-specific vocabulary. BERT-XML handles long input text by splitting it into chunks and performs prediction for each chunk independently with a label attention mechanism from AttentionXML (You et al., 2019). The predictions are finally combined with max-pooling. Our proposed framework, PLM-ICD, shares a similar idea with BERT-XML that we also split clinical notes into segments to compute segment representations. The main difference is that we leverage an improved label attention mechanism and we use document-level label-specific representations rather than chunk level representations as in BERT-XML. In Section 5, we demonstrate that PLM-ICD can achieve superior results on the commonly used MIMIC-3 dataset compared with BERT-XML.

3 Challenges for PLMs

In this section, we discuss 3 main challenges for PLMs to work on automatic ICD coding and conduct experiments to verify the severity of the challenges.

3.1 Long Input Text

Pretrained language models usually set a maximum sequence length as the size of their positional encodings. A typical value is set to 512 tokens after subword tokenization (Devlin et al., 2019). However, clinical notes are long documents which often exceed the maximum length of PLMs. For instance, the average number of words in the MIMIC-3 dataset is 1,500 words, or 2000 tokens after sub-

Model	Codes	Macro-F	Micro-F
LAAT	50	66.6	71.5
	Full	9.9	57.5
BERT	50	61.5	65.4
	Full	3.2	40.9

Table 2: Results of LAAT and BERT on MIMIC-3 with full codes and top-50 codes (%).

word tokenization.

To demonstrate that this is a detrimental problem for PLMs, we conduct experiments on MIMIC-3 where the input text is truncated to 512 words for the strong model LAAT (Vu et al., 2020), and 512 tokens for BERT. The results are shown in Table 1. Both models perform worse when the input text is truncated, showing that simple truncation does not work for the long input text problem. Note that the same trend can be found for other models for ICD coding. The results reported by Pascual et al. (2021) also show similar problem where the truncation methods such as *Front-512* and *Back-512* performed much worse than models with longer input context.

3.2 Large Label Set

Automatic ICD coding is a large-scale multi-label text classification (LMTC) problem, i.e., finding the relevant labels of a document from a large set of labels. There are about 17,000 codes in ICD-9-CM and 140,000 codes in ICD-10-CM/PCS, while there are 8921 codes presented in the MIMIC-3 dataset. PLMs utilize a special token and extract the hidden representation of this token to perform classification tasks. For example, BERT uses a `[CLS]` token and adds a pooling layer to transform its hidden representation into a distribution of labels (Devlin et al., 2019). However, while this approach achieves impressive performance on typical multi-class classification tasks, it is not very suitable for LMTC tasks. Lehečka et al. (2020) showed that making predictions based on only the representation of `[CLS]` token results in inferior performance compared with pooling representations of all tokens, and hypothesized that this is due to the lack of modeling capacity of using the `[CLS]` token alone.

To examine the PLMs' capability of performing LMTC, we conduct experiments on MIMIC-3 in two settings, `Full` and `Top-50`. The `Full` setting uses the full set of 8,921 labels, while the `Top-50` uses the top-50 most frequent labels. We report the numbers for LAAT directly from Vu et al. (2020). For the BERT model, we use the segment pooling mechanism to handle the long input, which is detailed in Section 4.2. We aggregate the hidden representations of the `[CLS]` token for each segment with mean-pooling as the document representation. The final prediction is obtained by transforming the document representation with a linear layer.

The results are shown in Table 2. BERT achieves slightly worse performance than LAAT in the `Top-50` setting. However, in the `Full` setting, BERT performs significantly worse compared with LAAT. The results suggest that using BERT's `[CLS]` token for LMTC is not ideal, and advanced techniques for LMTC are required for PLMs to work on this task.

3.3 Domain Mismatch

Normally, PLMs are pretrained on large amount of general-domain corpora which contains billions of tokens. The corpora is typically crawled from Wikipedia, novels (Zhu et al., 2015), webpages, and web forums. Prior work has shown that the domain mismatch between the pretraining corpus and the fine-tuning tasks could degrade the downstream performance (Gururangan et al., 2020).

Specifically for the biomedical domain, several pretrained models have been proposed which are pretrained on biomedical corpora to mitigate the domain mismatch problem (Lee et al., 2019; Alsentzer et al., 2019; Gu et al., 2020; Lewis et al., 2020). These models demonstrate improved performance over BERT on various medical and clinical tasks, showing that domain-specific pretraining is essential to achieve good performance.

4 Proposed Framework

The task of ICD code prediction is formulated as a multi-label classification problem (Kavuluru et al., 2015; Mullenbach et al., 2018). Given a clinical note of $|d|$ tokens $\mathbf{d} = \{t_1, t_2, \cdots, t_{|d|}\}$ in EHR, the goal is to predict a set of ICD codes $\mathbf{y} \subseteq \mathcal{Y}$, where $\mathcal{Y}$ denotes the set of all possible codes. Typically, the labels are represented as a binary vector $\mathbf{y} \in \{0,1\}^{|\mathcal{Y}|}$, where each bit y_i indicates whether the corresponding label is presented in the note.

The proposed framework **PLM-ICD** is illustrated in Figure 1. The details of the components

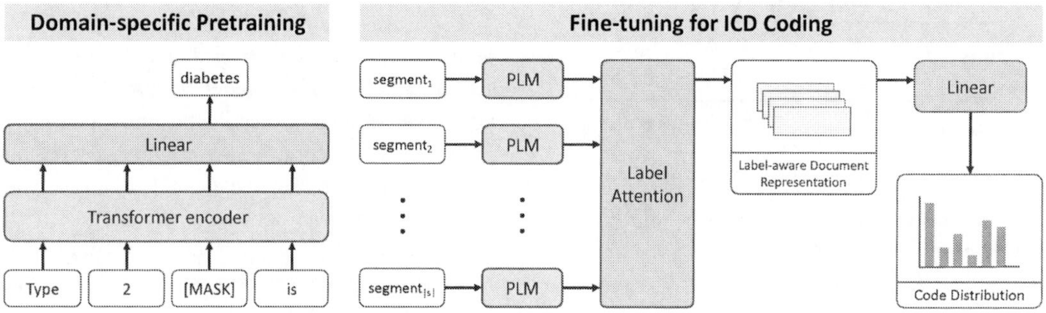

Figure 1: Illustration of our proposed framework. Left: domain-specific pretraining, where a PLM is pretrained on text from specific domains with a language modeling objective. Right: PLM encodes segments of a document separately, and a label-aware attention mechanism is to aggregate the segment representations into label-aware document representations. The document representations are linear-transformed to predict ICD codes.

are described in this section.

4.1 Domain-Specific Pretraining

Automatic ICD coding is a domain-specific task where the input text consists of clinical notes written by clinicians. The clinical notes contain many biomedical terms, and understanding these terms is essential in order to assign ICD codes accurately. While general PLMs are pretrained on large amount of text, the pretraining corpora usually does not contain biomedical text, not to mention clinical records.

In order to mitigate the domain mismatch problem, we propose to utilize the PLMs that are pretrained on biomedical and clinical text, e.g., BioBERT (Lee et al., 2019), PubMedBERT (Gu et al., 2020), and RoBERTa-PM (Lewis et al., 2020). These PLMs are specifically pretrained for biomedical tasks and proven to be effective on various downstream tasks. We take the domain-specific PLMs and fine-tune them on the task of automatic ICD coding. We can plug-and-play the domain-specific PLMs since their architectural design and pretraining objective are identical to their general-domain counterparts. This makes our framework agnostic to the type of PLMs, i.e., we can apply any transformer-based PLMs as the encoder.

4.2 Segment Pooling

In order to tackle the long input text problem described in Section 3.1, we propose **segment pooling** to surpass the maximum length limitation of PLMs. The segment pooling mechanism first splits the whole document into segments that are shorter than the maximum length, and encodes them into segment representations with PLMs. After encoding segments, the segment representations are aggregated as the representations for the full document.

More formally, given a document $d = \{t_1, t_2, ..., t_{|d|}\}$ of $|d|$ tokens, we split it into $|s|$ consecutive segments s_i of c tokens:

$$s_i = \{t_j \mid c \cdot i \leq j < c \cdot (i+1)\}$$

The segments are fed into PLMs separately to compute hidden representations, then concatenated to obtain the hidden representations of all tokens:

$$\mathbf{H} = \text{concat}(PLM(s_1), \cdots, PLM(s_{|s|}))$$

The token-wise hidden representations $\mathbf{H}$ can then be used to make prediction based on the whole document.

4.3 Label-Aware Attention

To combat the problem of a large label set, we propose to augment the PLMs with the label-aware attention mechanism proposed by Vu et al. (2020) to learn label-specific representations that capture the important text fragments relevant to certain labels. After the token-wise hidden representations $\mathbf{H}$ are obtained, the goal is to transform $\mathbf{H}$ into label-specific representations with attention mechanism.

The label-aware attention takes $\mathbf{H}$ as input and compute $|\mathcal{Y}|$ label-specific representations. This mechanism can be formulated into 2 steps. First, a label-wise attention weight matrix $\mathbf{A}$ is computed as:

$$\mathbf{Z} = \tanh(\mathbf{VH})$$
$$\mathbf{A} = \text{softmax}(\mathbf{WZ})$$

where $\mathbf{V}$ and $\mathbf{W}$ are linear transforms. The ith row of $\mathbf{A}$ represents the weights of the ith label, and the softmax function is performed for each label to form a distribution over all tokens. Then, the matrix $\mathbf{A}$ is used to perform a weighted-sum of $\mathbf{H}$ to compute the label-specific document representation:

$$\mathbf{D} = \mathbf{HA}^\top$$

where $\mathbf{D}_i$ represents the document representations for the ith label.

Finally, we use the label-specific document representation $\mathbf{D}$ to make predictions:

$$\mathbf{p}_i = \text{sigmoid}(\langle \mathbf{L}_i, \mathbf{D}_i \rangle)$$

where $\mathbf{L}_i$ is a vector for the ith label, $\langle \cdot \rangle$ represents inner product between two vectors, $\mathbf{p}_i$ is the predicted probability of the ith label. Note that the inner product could also be seen as a linear transform with output size 1. We can then assign labels to a document based on a predefined threshold t.

The training objective is to minimize the binary cross-entropy loss $\mathcal{L}(\mathbf{y}, \mathbf{p})$:

$$-\frac{1}{|\mathbf{y}|} \sum_{i=1}^{|\mathbf{y}|} \Big(\mathbf{y}_i \log \mathbf{p}_i + (1 - \mathbf{y}_i) \log(1 - \mathbf{p}_i) \Big).$$

5 Experiments

In order to evaluate the effectiveness of our proposed framework, we conduct experiments and compare the results with the prior work.

5.1 Setup

We evaluate PLM-ICD on two benchmark datasets for ICD code prediction.

- **MIMIC-2** To be able to directly compare with the prior work (Mullenbach et al., 2018; Li and Yu, 2020; Vu et al., 2020), we evaluate PLM-ICD on the MIMIC-2 dataset (Saeed et al., 2011). We follow the setting from Mullenbach et al. (2018), where 20,533 summaries are used for training, and 2,282 summaries are used for testing. There are 5,031 labels in the dataset.
- **MIMIC-3** The Medical Information Mart for Intensive Care III (MIMIC-3) (Johnson et al., 2016) dataset is a benchmark dataset which contains text and structured records from a hospital ICU. We use the same setting as Mullenbach et al. (2018), where 47,724 discharge summaries are used for training, with 1,632 summaries and 3,372 summaries for validation and testing, respectively. There are 8,922 labels in the dataset.

The preprocessing is done by following the steps described in Mullenbach et al. (2018) with their provided scripts [2]. Detailed training setting is provided in Appendix A.

5.2 Evaluation

We evaluate our methods with commonly used metrics to be directly comparable to previous work. The metrics used are macro F1, micro F1, macro AUC, micro AUC, and precision@K, where $K = \{5, 8, 15\}$.

5.3 Results

We present the evaluation results in this section. All the reported scores are averaged over 3 runs with different random seeds. The results of the compared methods are taken directly from their original paper. We mainly compare our model, PLM-ICD, with the models without special code description modeling. The performance of models with special code description modeling, i.e., HyperCore, ISD, and RAC, are also reported for reference.

5.3.1 MIMIC-3

The results on MIMIC-3 full test set are shown in Table 3. PLM-ICD achieves state-of-the-art performance among all models in terms of micro F1 and all precision@k measures, even though we do not leverage any code description modeling. All the improvements are statistically significant. RAC performs best on AUC scores and macro F1. We note that the techniques proposed by RAC are complementary to our framework, and it is possible to add the techniques to further improve our results. However, this is out of the scope of this paper.

5.3.2 MIMIC-2

The results on MIMIC-2 test set are shown in Table 4. PLM-ICD achieves state-of-the-art performance among all models in terms of micro F1 and

[2] https://github.com/jamesmullenbach/caml-mimic

Model	AUC		F1		P@k		
	Macro	Micro	Macro	Micro	P@5	P@8	P@15
CAML (2018)	89.5	98.6	8.8	53.9	-	70.9	56.1
DR-CAML (2018)	89.7	98.5	8.6	52.9	-	69.0	54.8
MultiResCNN (2020)	91.0	98.6	8.5	55.2	-	73.4	58.4
LAAT (2020)	91.9	98.8	9.9	57.5	81.3	73.8	59.1
JointLAAT (2020)	92.1	98.8	**10.7**	57.5	80.6	73.5	59.0
EffectiveCAN (2021)	91.5	98.8	10.6	58.9	-	75.8	60.6
PLM-ICD (Ours)	**92.6** (.2)	**98.9** (.1)	10.4 (.1)	***59.8***† (.3)	***84.4***† (.2)	***77.1***† (.2)	***61.3***† (.1)
Models with Special Code Description Modeling							
HyperCore (2020)	93.0	98.9	9.0	55.1	-	72.2	57.9
ISD (2021)	93.8	99.0	11.9	55.9	-	74.5	-
RAC (2021)	*94.8*	*99.2*	*12.7*	58.6	82.9	75.4	60.1

Table 3: Results on the MIMIC-3 full test set (%). The best scores among models without special code description modeling are marked in **bold**. The best scores among all models are *italic*. The values in the parentheses are the standard variation of runs. † indicates the significant improvement with $p < 0.05$.

Model	AUC		F1		P@k		
	Macro	Micro	Macro	Micro	P@5	P@8	P@15
CAML (2018)	82.0	96.6	4.8	44.2	-	52.3	-
DR-CAML (2018)	82.6	96.6	4.9	45.7	-	51.5	-
MultiResCNN (2020)	85.0	96.8	5.2	46.4	-	54.4	-
LAAT (2020)	86.8	**97.3**	5.9	48.6	64.9	55.0	39.7
JointLAAT (2020)	**87.1**	97.2	**6.8**	49.1	65.2	55.1	39.6
PLM-ICD (Ours)	86.8 (.2)	**97.3** (.1)	6.1 (.1)	***50.4***† (.2)	***67.3***† (.2)	**56.1**† (.2)	***39.9*** (.2)
Models with Special Code Description Modeling							
HyperCore (2020)	88.5	97.1	7.0	47.7	-	53.7	-
ISD (2021)	*90.1*	*97.7*	*10.1*	49.8	-	*56.4*	-

Table 4: Results on the MIMIC-2 test set (%). EffectiveCAN (2021) and RAC (2021) did not report results on MIMIC-2. The best scores among models without special code description modeling are marked in bold. The best scores among all models are italicized. The values in the parentheses are the standard variation of the runs. † indicates that the improvement is statistically significant with $p < 0.05$.

all precision@k measures, similar to the results on MIMIC-3. All the improvements are statistically significant except for P@15.

In sum, these results show that PLM-ICD is generalizable to multiple datasets, achieving state-of-the-art performance on multiple metrics on both MIMIC-3 and MIMIC-2.

6 Analysis

This section provides analysis on factors that affect PLM's performance on automatic ICD coding.

	Model	Macro-F	Micro-F
	PLM-ICD	10.4	59.8
(a)	- domain pretraining	8.9	54.2
(b)	- segment pooling	7.2	54.6
(c)	- label attention	4.6	48.0

Table 5: Ablation results on the MIMIC-3 full test set (%).

6.1 Ablation Study

To verify the effectiveness of the proposed techniques, we conduct an ablation study on MIMIC-3 full test set. The results are presented in Table 5.

The first ablation we perform is discarding

Model	Macro-F	Micro-F	$\hat{F}$
RoBERTa-PM	10.4	59.8	1.35
BioBERT	9.1	57.9	1.60
ClinicalBERT	8.8	57.8	1.60
PubMedBERT	9.2	59.5	1.41

Table 6: Results with different PLMs on the MIMIC-3 full test set (%). $\hat{F}$ is the fragmentation ratio.

domain-specific pretraining. In this setting, we use the pretrained `RoBERTa-base` model as the PLM, and fine-tune it for ICD coding. As shown in row (a), the performance slightly degrades after discarding domain-specific pretraining. This result demonstrates that domain-specific pretraining contributes to the performance improvement.

The second ablation we perform is discarding segment pooling. In this setting, we replace our segment pooling with the one proposed by Zhang et al. (2020) They applied label attention and made code predictions for each segment separately, and aggregated the predictions with max-pooling. As shown in row (b), replacing our segment pooling results in worse performance. This result indicates that our proposed segment pooling is more effective for aggregating segment representations.

The third ablation is removing the label attention mechanism. We fall back to the normal PLM paradigm, i.e., extracting representations of the `[CLS]` token for classification. This setting is identical to the one described in Section 3.2, where we aggregate the representation of the `[CLS]` token for each segment with mean-pooling, and obtain the final prediction by transforming the aggregated representation with a linear layer. As shown in row (c), removing label attention mechanism results in huge performance degradation. The micro F1 score degrades by 11.8% absolute, while the macro F1 score degrades more than half. This result demonstrates that the label attention mechanism is crucial to ICD coding, which is an observation aligned with the prior work (Mullenbach et al., 2018).

6.2 Effect of Pretrained Models

While we have shown that domain-specific pretraining is beneficial to ICD coding, we would like to explore which domain-specific PLM performs the best on this task. We conduct experiments with different PLMs, including BioBERT (Lee et al., 2019), ClinicalBERT (Alsentzer et al., 2019), PubMedBERT (Gu et al., 2020), and RoBERTa-PM (Lewis et al., 2020).

Model	Macro-F	Micro-F
LAAT	10.4	59.8
CAML	8.7	58.1
BERT-XML	8.2	56.9

Table 7: Results with different attention mechanisms on the MIMIC-3 full test set (%).

Model	Macro-F	Micro-F
Ours	10.4	59.8
HIER-BERT	2.8	42.7
Longformer	5.1	51.6

Table 8: Results with different strategies for tackling the long input problem on the MIMIC-3 full test set (%).

The results are presented in Table 6. RoBERTa-PM achieves the best performance among the 4 examined PLMs This result is in line with the reported results on the BLURB leaderboard (Gu et al., 2020), which is a collection of biomedical tasks.

We also report the fragmentation ratio, i.e., the number of tokens per word after subword tokenization as (Chalkidis et al., 2020). We observe that the PLMs with vocabulary trained on biomedical texts (RoBERTa-PM and PubMedBERT) perform better than the ones inherited vocabulary from BERT-base (BioBERT and ClinicalBERT). The framentation ratio also shows that models with custom vocabulary suffer less on the over-fragmentation problem.

6.3 Effect of Label Attention Mechanisms

We conduct experiments with different label attention mechanisms and report the results in Table 7. We compare the label attention mechanisms from LAAT (Vu et al., 2020), CAML (Mullenbach et al., 2018) and BERT-XML (Zhang et al., 2020). The results show that the label attention used in LAAT is best-suited to our framework.

6.4 Effect of Long Input Strategies

We also conduct experiments to verify the effect of different strategies for tackling the long input problem. As shown in Table 8, our proposed segment pooling outperforms HIER-BERT (Chalkidis et al., 2019) and Longformer (Beltagy et al., 2020), demonstrating the effectiveness of our proposed method.

Max Length	Segment Length	Macro-F	Micro-F
6144	128	9.2	60.0
3072	256	9.4	59.2
3072	128	9.2	59.6
3072	64	8.2	59.3
3072	32	6.9	57.8

Table 9: Results with different maximum lengths on the MIMIC-3 full dev set (%).

6.5 Effect of Maximum Length

We conduct experiments where we alter the maximum length of the documents and segments to explore the different choices of maximum lengths. The results are shown in Table 9.

When fixing the maximum length of the documents to 3,072, we observe that longer segments results in better performance until the segment length reaches 128. Using a longer maximum document length such as 6144 results in slightly better performance. However, longer sequences require more computation. Considering the trade-off between computation and accuracy, we set maximum document length to 3,072 and segment length to 128 as our defaults.

6.6 Effect of Optimization Process

Similar to the prior work (Sun et al., 2019), we also notice that the fine-tuning process is sensitive to the hyperparameters of the optimization process, e.g., batch size, learning rate, and warmup schedule.

With several preliminary experiments conducted on these factors, we observe that the learning rate and the warmup schedule greatly affects the performance. When we reduce learning rate to 2e-5, the model performs 3% worse than using the default parameters in terms of micro F1. The warmup schedule is crucial in our framework. When we use constant learning rate throughout training, the model performs about 4% worse. We do not observe clear difference between different scheduling strategies.

6.7 Best Practices

With the above analyses, we provide a guideline and possible future directions for applying PLMs to ICD coding or tasks with similar properties:

- With the input length exceeding the maximum length of PLMs, segment pooling can be used to extract representations of all tokens. PLMs with longer input length or recurrence could be explored in the future.
- The representation of the `[CLS]` token might be insufficient when dealing with LMTC problems. A label attention mechanism could be beneficial in such scenarios.
- The pretraining corpora plays an important role for domain-specific tasks.
- The hyperparameters of the optimization process greatly affect the final performance, so trying different parameters is preferred when the performance is not ideal.

7 Conclusion

In this paper, we identify the main challenges of applying PLMs on automatic ICD coding, including the long text input, the large label set and the mismatched domain. We propose **PLM-ICD**, a framework with PLMs that tackles the challenges with various techniques. The proposed framework achieves state-of-the-art or competitive performance on the MIMIC-3 and MIMIC-2 datasets. We then further analyze factors that affect PLMs' performance. We hope this work could open up the research direction of leveraging the great potential of PLMs on ICD coding.

Acknowledgements

We thank reviewers for their insightful comments. This work was financially supported from the Young Scholar Fellowship Program by Ministry of Science and Technology (MOST) in Taiwan, under Grants 111-2628-E-002-016 and 111-2634-F-002-014.

References

Emily Alsentzer, John Murphy, William Boag, Wei-Hung Weng, Di Jin, Tristan Naumann, and Matthew McDermott. 2019. Publicly available clinical BERT embeddings. In *Proceedings of the 2nd Clinical Natural Language Processing Workshop*, pages 72–78, Minneapolis, Minnesota, USA. Association for Computational Linguistics.

Tal Baumel, Jumana Nassour-Kassis, Raphael Cohen, Michael Elhadad, and Noemie Elhadad. 2018. Multi-label classification of patient notes: case study on icd code assignment. In *Workshops at the Thirty-Second AAAI Conference on Artificial Intelligence*.

Iz Beltagy, Matthew E. Peters, and Arman Cohan. 2020. Longformer: The long-document transformer. *arXiv:2004.05150*.

Pengfei Cao, Yubo Chen, Kang Liu, Jun Zhao, Shengping Liu, and Weifeng Chong. 2020. HyperCore: Hyperbolic and co-graph representation for automatic ICD coding. In *Proceedings of the 58th Annual Meeting of the Association for Computational Linguistics*, pages 3105–3114, Online. Association for Computational Linguistics.

Ilias Chalkidis, Ion Androutsopoulos, and Nikolaos Aletras. 2019. Neural legal judgment prediction in English. In *Proceedings of the 57th Annual Meeting of the Association for Computational Linguistics*, pages 4317–4323, Florence, Italy. Association for Computational Linguistics.

Ilias Chalkidis, Manos Fergadiotis, Sotiris Kotitsas, Prodromos Malakasiotis, Nikolaos Aletras, and Ion Androutsopoulos. 2020. An empirical study on large-scale multi-label text classification including few and zero-shot labels. In *Proceedings of the 2020 Conference on Empirical Methods in Natural Language Processing (EMNLP)*, pages 7503–7515, Online. Association for Computational Linguistics.

Wei-Cheng Chang, Hsiang-Fu Yu, Kai Zhong, Yiming Yang, and Inderjit Dhillon. 2019. Taming pretrained transformers for extreme multi-label text classification. *arXiv preprint arXiv:1905.02331*.

Edward Choi, Mohammad Taha Bahadori, Andy Schuetz, Walter F Stewart, and Jimeng Sun. 2016. Doctor AI: Predicting clinical events via recurrent neural networks. In *Machine learning for healthcare conference*, pages 301–318. PMLR.

Jacob Devlin, Ming-Wei Chang, Kenton Lee, and Kristina Toutanova. 2019. BERT: Pre-training of deep bidirectional transformers for language understanding. In *NAACL*, pages 4171–4186, Minneapolis, Minnesota. Association for Computational Linguistics.

Yu Gu, Robert Tinn, Hao Cheng, Michael Lucas, Naoto Usuyama, Xiaodong Liu, Tristan Naumann, Jianfeng Gao, and Hoifung Poon. 2020. Domain-specific language model pretraining for biomedical natural language processing. *arXiv preprint arXiv:2007.15779*.

Suchin Gururangan, Ana Marasović, Swabha Swayamdipta, Kyle Lo, Iz Beltagy, Doug Downey, and Noah A. Smith. 2020. Don't stop pretraining: Adapt language models to domains and tasks. In *Proceedings of the 58th Annual Meeting of the Association for Computational Linguistics*, pages 8342–8360, Online. Association for Computational Linguistics.

Alistair EW Johnson, Tom J Pollard, Lu Shen, H Lehman Li-wei, Mengling Feng, Mohammad Ghassemi, Benjamin Moody, Peter Szolovits, Leo Anthony Celi, and Roger G Mark. 2016. Mimic-iii, a freely accessible critical care database. *Scientific data*, 3:160035.

Ramakanth Kavuluru, Anthony Rios, and Yuan Lu. 2015. An empirical evaluation of supervised learning approaches in assigning diagnosis codes to electronic medical records. *Artificial intelligence in medicine*, 65(2):155–166.

Byung-Hak Kim and Varun Ganapathi. 2021. Read, attend, and code: Pushing the limits of medical codes prediction from clinical notes by machines. In *Machine Learning for Healthcare Conference*, pages 196–208. PMLR.

Jinhyuk Lee, Wonjin Yoon, Sungdong Kim, Donghyeon Kim, Sunkyu Kim, Chan Ho So, and Jaewoo Kang. 2019. BioBERT: a pre-trained biomedical language representation model for biomedical text mining. *Bioinformatics*.

Jan Lehečka, Jan Švec, Pavel Ircing, and Luboš Šmídl. 2020. Adjusting bert's pooling layer for large-scale multi-label text classification. In *International Conference on Text, Speech, and Dialogue*, pages 214–221. Springer.

Patrick Lewis, Myle Ott, Jingfei Du, and Veselin Stoyanov. 2020. Pretrained language models for biomedical and clinical tasks: Understanding and extending the state-of-the-art. In *Proceedings of the 3rd Clinical Natural Language Processing Workshop*, pages 146–157, Online. Association for Computational Linguistics.

Fei Li and Hong Yu. 2020. Icd coding from clinical text using multi-filter residual convolutional neural network. In *AAAI*.

Yang Liu, Hua Cheng, Russell Klopfer, Matthew R Gormley, and Thomas Schaaf. 2021. Effective convolutional attention network for multi-label clinical document classification. In *Proceedings of the 2021 Conference on Empirical Methods in Natural Language Processing*, pages 5941–5953.

Yinhan Liu, Myle Ott, Naman Goyal, Jingfei Du, Mandar Joshi, Danqi Chen, Omer Levy, Mike Lewis, Luke Zettlemoyer, and Veselin Stoyanov. 2019. Roberta: A robustly optimized bert pretraining approach. *arXiv preprint arXiv:1907.11692*.

James Mullenbach, Sarah Wiegreffe, Jon Duke, Jimeng Sun, and Jacob Eisenstein. 2018. Explainable prediction of medical codes from clinical text. In *NAACL*, pages 1101–1111, New Orleans, Louisiana. Association for Computational Linguistics.

Kimberly J O'malley, Karon F Cook, Matt D Price, Kimberly Raiford Wildes, John F Hurdle, and Carol M Ashton. 2005. Measuring diagnoses: ICD code accuracy. *Health services research*, 40(5p2):1620–1639.

Damian Pascual, Sandro Luck, and Roger Wattenhofer. 2021. Towards bert-based automatic icd coding: Limitations and opportunities. *arXiv preprint arXiv:2104.06709*.

Matthew Peters, Mark Neumann, Mohit Iyyer, Matt Gardner, Christopher Clark, Kenton Lee, and Luke Zettlemoyer. 2018. Deep contextualized word representations. In *Proceedings of the 2018 Conference of the North American Chapter of the Association for Computational Linguistics: Human Language Technologies, Volume 1 (Long Papers)*, pages 2227–2237, New Orleans, Louisiana. Association for Computational Linguistics.

Alec Radford, Jeffrey Wu, Rewon Child, David Luan, Dario Amodei, and Ilya Sutskever. 2019. Language models are unsupervised multitask learners. *OpenAI blog*, 1(8):9.

Colin Raffel, Noam Shazeer, Adam Roberts, Katherine Lee, Sharan Narang, Michael Matena, Yanqi Zhou, Wei Li, and Peter J. Liu. 2020. Exploring the limits of transfer learning with a unified text-to-text transformer. *Journal of Machine Learning Research*, 21(140):1–67.

Mohammed Saeed, Mauricio Villarroel, Andrew T Reisner, Gari Clifford, Li-Wei Lehman, George Moody, Thomas Heldt, Tin H Kyaw, Benjamin Moody, and Roger G Mark. 2011. Multiparameter intelligent monitoring in intensive care ii (mimic-ii): a public-access intensive care unit database. *Critical care medicine*, 39(5):952.

Haoran Shi, Pengtao Xie, Zhiting Hu, Ming Zhang, and Eric P Xing. 2017. Towards automated icd coding using deep learning. *arXiv preprint arXiv:1711.04075*.

Chi Sun, Xipeng Qiu, Yige Xu, and Xuanjing Huang. 2019. How to fine-tune bert for text classification? In *China National Conference on Chinese Computational Linguistics*, pages 194–206. Springer.

Shang-Chi Tsai, Ting-Yun Chang, and Yun-Nung Chen. 2019. Leveraging hierarchical category knowledge for data-imbalanced multi-label diagnostic text understanding. In *LOUHI*, pages 39–43, Hong Kong. Association for Computational Linguistics.

Ashish Vaswani, Noam Shazeer, Niki Parmar, Jakob Uszkoreit, Llion Jones, Aidan N Gomez, Łukasz Kaiser, and Illia Polosukhin. 2017. Attention is all you need. In *NIPS*, pages 5998–6008.

Thanh Vu, Dat Quoc Nguyen, and Anthony Nguyen. 2020. A label attention model for icd coding from clinical text. In *Proceedings of the Twenty-Ninth International Joint Conference on Artificial Intelligence, IJCAI-20*, pages 3335–3341. International Joint Conferences on Artificial Intelligence Organization.

Pengtao Xie and Eric Xing. 2018. A neural architecture for automated ICD coding. In *ACL*, pages 1066–1076, Melbourne, Australia. Association for Computational Linguistics.

Xiancheng Xie, Yun Xiong, Philip S Yu, and Yangyong Zhu. 2019. Ehr coding with multi-scale feature attention and structured knowledge graph propagation. In *Proceedings of the 28th ACM International Conference on Information and Knowledge Management*, pages 649–658.

Zhilin Yang, Zihang Dai, Yiming Yang, Jaime Carbonell, Ruslan Salakhutdinov, and Quoc V Le. 2019. Xlnet: Generalized autoregressive pretraining for language understanding. *arXiv preprint arXiv:1906.08237*.

Ronghui You, Zihan Zhang, Ziye Wang, Suyang Dai, Hiroshi Mamitsuka, and Shanfeng Zhu. 2019. Attentionxml: Label tree-based attention-aware deep model for high-performance extreme multi-label text classification. *Advances in Neural Information Processing Systems*, 32:5820–5830.

Zachariah Zhang, Jingshu Liu, and Narges Razavian. 2020. BERT-XML: Large scale automated ICD coding using BERT pretraining. In *Proceedings of the 3rd Clinical Natural Language Processing Workshop*, pages 24–34, Online. Association for Computational Linguistics.

Tong Zhou, Pengfei Cao, Yubo Chen, Kang Liu, Jun Zhao, Kun Niu, Weifeng Chong, and Shengping Liu. 2021. Automatic icd coding via interactive shared representation networks with self-distillation mechanism. In *Proceedings of the 59th Annual Meeting of the Association for Computational Linguistics and the 11th International Joint Conference on Natural Language Processing (Volume 1: Long Papers)*, pages 5948–5957.

Yukun Zhu, Ryan Kiros, Rich Zemel, Ruslan Salakhutdinov, Raquel Urtasun, Antonio Torralba, and Sanja Fidler. 2015. Aligning books and movies: Towards story-like visual explanations by watching movies and reading books. In *Proceedings of the IEEE international conference on computer vision*, pages 19–27.

A Training Details

We take the pretrained weights released by original authors without any modification. For the best PLM-ICD model, we use RoBERTa-base-PM-M3-Voc released by Lewis et al. (2020). During fine-tuning, we train our models for 20 epochs. `AdamW` is chosen as the optimizer with a learning rate of $5e-5$. We employ a linear warmup schedule with 2000 warmup steps, and after that the learning rate decays linearly to 0 throughout training. The batch size is set to 8. All models are trained on a GTX 3070 GPU. We truncate discharge summaries to 3072 tokens due to memory consideration, and the length of each segment c is set to 128. The validation set is used to find the best-performing threshold t, and we use it to perform evaluation on the test set.

m-Networks: Adapting the Triplet Networks for Acronym Disambiguation

Sandaru Seneviratne[1], **Elena Daskalaki**[1], **Artem Lenskiy**[1], **Hanna Suominen**[1,2]
[1]The Australian National University (ANU) / Canberra, ACT, Australia
[2]University of Turku / Turku, Finland
{sandaru.seneviratne, eleni.daskalaki,
artem.lenskiy, hanna.suominen}@anu.edu.au

Abstract

Acronym disambiguation (AD) is the process of identifying the correct expansion of the acronyms in text. AD is crucial in natural language understanding of scientific and medical documents due to the high prevalence of technical acronyms and the possible expansions. Given that natural language is often ambiguous with more than one meaning for words, identifying the correct expansion for acronyms requires learning of effective representations for words, phrases, acronyms, and abbreviations based on their context. In this paper, we proposed an approach to leverage the triplet networks and triplet loss which learns better representations of text through distance comparisons of embeddings. We tested both the triplet network-based method and the modified triplet network-based method with m networks on the AD dataset from the SDU@AAAI-21 AD task, CASI dataset, and MeDAL dataset. F scores of 87.31%, 70.67%, and 75.75% were achieved by the m network-based approach for SDU, CASI, and MeDAL datasets respectively indicating that triplet network-based methods have comparable performance but with only 12% of the number of parameters in the baseline method. This effective implementation is available at https://github.com/sandaruSen/m_networks under the MIT license.

1 Introduction

Natural language is often ambiguous and contains phrases, words, acronyms, and abbreviations which have more than one meaning (Charbonnier and Wartena, 2018). The complexity of natural language is further augmented based on which context these words are being used (Navigli, 2009). Scientific and medical communities use domain specific technical terms, which are often shorthanded for ease of use. This has resulted in the prevalence of acronyms in scientific and medical documents (Charbonnier and Wartena, 2018). To understand these expert texts, it is important to disambiguate the meaning of their acronyms. For example, given a sentence with the acronym *RNN*, the possible expansion for the acronym can be *Recurrent Neural Network*, *Random Neural Network*, *Recursive Neural Network*, *Reverse Nearest Neighbour*, etc. Out of these expansions, the one corresponding to the meaning of the sentence should be identified in order to correctly understand the sentence. The task of identifying the correct expansion of acronyms from possible expansions is called *Acronym Disambiguation* (AD).

Methods of pattern matching, language modeling, and machine/deep learning have shown promising results in AD. Early systems for AD used pattern matching (Schwartz and Hearst, 2002) together with approaches based on word embeddings and machine learning (Jaber and Martínez, 2021) where the AD task is considered as a classification problem. Recent efforts in AD mainly include the use of deep learning-based models (Pan et al., 2021; Zhong et al., 2021) and pre-trained language models (Beltagy et al., 2019; Devlin et al., 2019). However, identifying the correct expansion of an acronym calls for better representation of text.

In this study, we approached the problem of AD with the aim of learning effective text representations towards better disambiguation of acronyms. We derived our approach from *Siamese Networks* (Koch et al., 2015) and *Triplet Networks* (TNs) (Hoffer and Ailon, 2015). TNs, inspired by Siamese Networks, aim to learn the information of inputs based on one or a few samples of training data using a triplet loss to provide better representations for data.

The main contributions of this paper were as follows: We leveraged the triplet loss and TNs (Schroff et al., 2015) for AD with the aim of learning sentence embeddings, which can capture the semantic differences of the different expansions of the same acronym. We extended the TN architecture further to include m networks and mapped the

Proceedings of the 4th Clinical Natural Language Processing Workshop, pages 21 - 29
July 14, 2022 ©2022 Association for Computational Linguistics

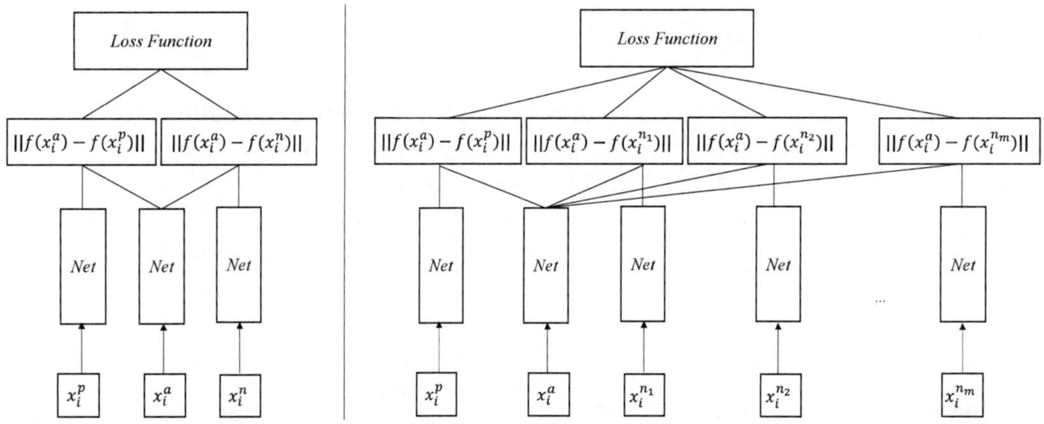

Figure 1: **Triplet Network Architecture and Modified Triplet Network Architecture**. The triplet network architecture (left, Formula (1)) considers the anchor sentence x_i^a, positive sentence x_i^p, and negative sentence x_i^n for a sample when computing the triplet loss. Modified architecture (right, Formula (2)) considers the anchor sentence, positive sentence, and all the possible negative sentences for a sample. This includes m number of similar architectures.

AD task as a binary classification problem, which predicts if the suggested expansion for an acronym is correct or not. To the best of our knowledge this is the first attempt of adapting the TN-based methods and triplet loss for disambiguating the acronyms. We evaluated and verified the proposed approach on the AAAI-21 Scientific Document Understanding AD task dataset (SDU dataset) (Veyseh et al., 2020), sense inventory for clinical abbreviations and acronym dataset (CASI dataset) (Moon et al., 2014), and on a sample of the Medical Abbreviation Disambiguation Dataset (MeDAL) (Wen et al., 2020). We made our implementation available at https://github.com/sandaruSen/m_networks under the MIT license.

2 Related Work

Extensive body of prior research for AD in scientific and medical domains exists because understanding scientific and medical text requires both AD and domain knowledge. Earliest approaches for AD included the use of a number of rules and patterns (Schwartz and Hearst, 2002), training of classifiers based on a set of features which represent the context of the input like, part-of-speech tags, case representation of the words, or word stems (Finley et al., 2016; Wu et al., 2017), and computation of the cosine similarity between the text with the acronym and the possible expansions based on word embeddings (Tulkens et al., 2016). Recent efforts in AD include the use of deep learning-based methods and pre-trained language models (Pan et al., 2021; Singh and Kumar, 2021; Zhong et al., 2021).

With the introduction of transformers, the transformer–based pre-trained language models have been extensively used for the AD task. BERT (Bidirectional Encoder Representations from Transformers) models such as (Devlin et al., 2019), SciBERT (BERT-based language model for performing scientific tasks) (Beltagy et al., 2019), and RoBERTa (Robustly Optimized BERT Pretraining Approach) (Liu et al., 2019) are the language models that are exploited to formulate the problem of AD as a classification task for AD. The SDU@AAAI-21 AD task consisted of systems with transformer-based language models, which differed based on how the inputs and the outputs to the systems were defined (Veyseh et al., 2021). In our work, we explored triplet loss and TNs for AD using pre-trained language models. TNs and triplet loss have been effectively used for representation learning by distance comparisons among pairs of examples. They were initially introduced for computer vision related tasks (Schroff et al., 2015) and are now used in many natural language processing (NLP) tasks (Santos et al., 2016; Ein-Dor et al., 2018; Lauriola and Moschitti, 2020; Wei et al., 2021). We believe that through the triplet loss, the models will be able to learn subtle yet complex differences among the different expansions of the same acronym.

3 Methods

The goal of AD was to identify the correct expansion for a given acronym in text. Considering a dictionary of acronyms D with acronyms as keys $[A_1, A_2, ..., A_j]$ where j is the number of acronyms. For each acronym A_i, the m possible expansions were represented as $[e_1, e_2, ..., e_m]$. Given a sentence x_i with an acronym A_i, the correct expansion should be obtained from D out of the expansion list of the corresponding A_i.

We modeled the AD task based on a TN as well as a modified version of the TN architecture with the triplet loss. The TN allowed the AD task to be expressed as a binary classification problem to predict which expansion is the most relevant to the given acronym based on the context it appears (Appendix A). For the modified version of the TN, we included m number of architectures considering the possible negatives for a sample at once. This resulted in an anchor sentence, a positive sentence, and a list of negative sentences as inputs to the architectures (Figure 1).

Denoting anchor, positive, and negative embeddings as x_i^a, x_i^p, and x_i^n, respectively, where $i = 1, 2, \ldots, k$, and considering a d-dimensional embedding in the vector space $f(x) \in \mathbb{R}^d$ and α a margin that is enforced between positive and negative pairs, the loss for the TN was defined as follows using the L_2 distances for the TN:

$$||f(x_i^a) - f(x_i^p)||_2^2 + \alpha < ||f(x_i^a) - f(x_i^n)||_2^2. \quad (1)$$

For the modified version of the TN with m networks, the loss was computed considering all the possible negatives. Adapting the triplet loss to the modified architecture, the distance between the anchor and the positive sentence should be less than the minimum of the distances between the anchor and the negative sentences. We could denote the loss considering all the m number of negatives $x_i^{n_1}$, $x_i^{n_2}$, $\ldots$, $x_i^{n_m}$ as follows:

$$||f(x_i^a) - f(x_i^p)||_2^2 + \alpha < \min(||f(x_i^a) - f(x_i^{n_1})||_2^2, ||f(x_i^a) - f(x_i^{n_2})||_2^2, \ldots, ||f(x_i^a) - f(x_i^{n_m})||_2^2). \quad (2)$$

Sentence triplet creation, which includes identifying an anchor sample x_i^a, a positive sample x_i^p, and a negative sample x_i^n (Table 1), was considered crucial when using TNs. For each possible expansion of an acronym, we randomly extracted one sentence matching the expansion from the training dataset. These sentences were considered as anchor sentences. We then used all sentences in the training dataset to create positive samples. Acronyms in sentences were replaced by their respective correct expansion to obtain positive sentences. We then applied the following guidelines to create the negative samples: i) For each positive sentence with an acronym, we obtained all the possible expansions except for the correct expansion. ii) We replaced the acronym in the sentence with these expansions to obtain a list of sentences with other expansions. iii) Each of these negative sentences was used to create the final list of triplets.

The triplet selection ensured effective training of the models. Hence, it is advised to consider triplets, which violate the triplet constraint (Formula (1)). In our approach, we considered the same positive sentence with the respective acronym replaced by other expansions of the acronym as negatives. Even though the text in the sentences was very much similar to each other, replacing the acronym with possible expansions resulted in a change in the semantic meaning of the overall sentences. Hence, we believe considering sentences with other possible expansions as negative sentences satisfied the necessity of having *hard negatives*, which were difficult to discriminate from the correct expansion.

Anchor Sentence	The purpose of *RL* is for the agent to learn an optimal, or nearly-optimal, policy that maximizes the reward function.
Positive Sentence	All agents can then operate in parallel, allowing one to exploit a number of already available *reinforcement learning* techniques for parallel learning.
Negative Sentences	[All agents can then operate in parallel, allowing one to exploit a number of already available *robust locomotion* techniques for parallel learning., All agents can then operate in parallel, allowing one to exploit a number of already available *representation learning* techniques for parallel learning., ...]

Table 1: An example of anchor, positive, and negative sentences for the acronym *RL* and the expansion *reinforcement learning*.

Architecture or Model	Number of Parameters	F score on SDU	F score on CASI	F score on MeDAL
Baseline method by Singh and Kumar (2021)	$109,920,002$	84.24%	**78.16%**	74.91%
Triplet Network-based method	$\mathbf{13,576,768}$	85.70%	56.49%	75.19%
m Network-based method	$\mathbf{13,576,768}$	**87.31%**	70.67%	**75.75%**

Table 2: Results of the validation data of SDU dataset and test data of CASI and MeDAL datasets.

In the training stage, we used the anchor sentence, positive sentence, and negative sentence as the input to the TN-based system and anchor sentence, positive sentence, and possible negative sentences as the input to the m-network-based system. For each of the sentences, we obtained an embedding, which was then used to calculate the triplet loss. In the inference stage, we used the given sentence with the acronym as the anchor sentence and we created a list of sentences by replacing the acronym in the sample sentence with possible expansions. We computed the distances between each of the possible sentences and the anchor sentence to obtain the sentence closest to the anchor sentence.

4 Experiments

We used the SDU dataset (Veyseh et al., 2020), CASI dataset (Moon et al., 2014), and MeDAL dataset (Wen et al., 2020) (see Appendix B for further information). The SDU dataset contained data from $6,786$ English scientific papers published at arXiv and consisted of $62,441$ sentences. The dataset also consisted of a dictionary of acronyms and their possible expansions. We used the publicly available training and development data of the SDU dataset for our experiments. CASI dataset was created using admission notes, consultation notes, and discharge summaries from hospitals affiliated with the University of Minnesota. $37,500$ samples from CASI dataset was split into train, validation, and test subsets and a dictionary with the acronyms was created for the experiments. The MeDAL dataset was created from $14,393,619$ articles in PubMed. We created a sample dataset and a dictionary of acronyms from MeDAL dataset for experiments (Table 3 of Appendix B).

We performed a basic preprocessing on the sentences, which were quite long, by sampling tokens in the sentences as proposed by Singh and Kumar (2021). We used $N/2$ tokens to the left and right of the acronym for sentences with length of more than 120, considering $N = 120$.

As a *baseline model*, we experimented with the system proposed by Singh and Kumar, 2021 which modeled the AD task as a span prediction task. The proposed system fine-tuned the complete SciBERT model with 12 layers to predict the start and end indices of the correct expansion of an acronym given all the possible expansions, leveraging the SciBERT's ability to encode pair of sequences together.

We used the pre-trained SciBERT model architecture as the base model for experiments on SDU dataset and the pre-trained BioBERT (BERT-based language model for performing biomedical tasks) (Lee et al., 2020) model as the base model for experiments on the CASI and the MeDAL datasets with their first 11 encoder layers frozen followed by dropout of 0.5 to avoid over-fitting and a dense layer to map the feature embeddings output by the base models with dimensions of 768 to 64 (Appendix C). These 64 dimensional embeddings were used to compute the triplet loss. We trained the models using a learning rate of 5×10^{-4} with the *Adam optimizer* (Kingma and Ba, 2014). The best model over 10 epochs with a batch size of 32 was chosen as the final model.

To evaluate the performance of the proposed architecture in the training set, we computed the macro-averaged F1 score. If the distance between the anchor and the positive sentence is less than the distance between the anchor and negative sentences, the prediction of the model was considered correct. We used F1 also in evaluation. We computed the distances between the anchor and possible sentences from which the sentence with the minimum distance to the anchor was considered the sentence with the correct expansion.

5 Results and Analysis

By comparing the proposed methods with the baseline system on the three datasets, we observed that the methods based on TNs learnt to discriminate among the different expansions of an acronym. Compared to the TN-based method, the m network-based method has comparable performance as the baseline for all the datasets. Both the proposed methods outperformed the baseline on SDU and MeDAL datasets. The m network-based method gave an F1 score of 87.31% on SDU dataset, 70.67% on CASI dataset, and 75.75% on MeDAL dataset (Table 2).

To investigate the semantic similarity and the representation of the output embeddings in the vector space, we visualized output representations obtained by the m network-based architecture for the SDU, CASI, and MeDAL datasets by reducing the dimensions using *principal component analysis* (PCA) (Figure 3 of Appendix D). For the SDU dataset, we used the acronym *RL* with *reinforcement learning* to obtain the positive and respective negative sentences. Similarly, for the CASI dataset the acronym *DM* with *diabetes mellitus* expansion and for the MeDAL dataset the acronym *RSM* with *respiratory muscle strength* expansion were used.

6 Discussion

In this paper, we have suggested a new approach for disambiguating the acronyms to effectively identify the correct expansion through better representation learning using TNs by creating high quality sentence embeddings, which can capture the semantic differences among the different expansions of the same acronym. Namely, we have presented how methods based on TNs and triplet loss can be used for AD. To address the effective learning of context representations for identifying the correct expansion of acronyms, our methods leverage the contextual information of text and semantic similarity among expansions. In particular, our paper has introduced m networks inspired by TNs. Our experiments have demonstrated that methods based on TNs have comparable performance on both scientific and medical domains. However, the applicability of the proposed methods on CASI dataset should be further investigated. Finally, the number of parameters in TN-based methods is only 12% of the number of parameters in the baseline method resulting in smaller size of the models (Table 2). The TN-based methods have used the representations from the last layer of the BERT-based models where as the baseline method fine-tuned the complete model with all 12 layers for the predictions[1]. We have tested the proposed methods on the SDU, CASI, and MeDAL datasets.

The TN-based method for AD can be used for data augmentation when the training data is limited. Given that the original TN architecture only considers one negative sample at a time, considering all the possible expansions of each acronym one at a time can be used to augment the training data size. This addresses the issue of limited training data for deep learning architectures. However, in the modified TN-based architecture with m networks, at the training stage all the possible negatives are considered for a sample at once. Therefore, data augmentation is not possible in this case.

In this paper, our main goal was to approach the AD problem as an effective representation learning problem to discriminate among the possible expansions of an acronym based on the context it appears. Earliest approaches on AD relied on rules and patterns (Schwartz and Hearst, 2002) to identify the correct expansion of an acronym which evolved to use of machine learning-based approaches with different features (Finley et al., 2016; Wu et al., 2017) and computing of semantic similarity between the text with acronym and the possible expansions. Recent efforts involved pre-trained language models for the AD task. Most of these systems were validated on one domain of focus (i.e., scientific text, medical text, or general text). We approached the problem focusing on learning better representations for text through TNs and triplet loss using pre-trained language models. Furthermore, we tested the proposed approaches on both the scientific and medical domains.

As future work, we intend to experiment with different constrastive losses (Sohn, 2016; Chen et al., 2020). Specifically, our aspiration is to compare and contrast the proposed approach with InfoNCE (Van den Oord et al., 2018), a popular contrastive loss which includes multiple negatives and normalises across examples in a mini batch.

7 Ethical Considerations

We have proposed an approach for AD using TN-based methods with the aim of learning effective representations for data. We have used SciBERT trained on scientific publications and BioBERT trained on biomedical domain corpora (PubMed abstracts and PMC full-text articles) for our experiments. Instead of finetuning all the layers in the pre-trained language models, we have finetuned

[1]However, given that m network-based method consists of m architectures, the number of updates on parameters increases.

only the last encoder layer by freezing the first 11 encoder layers thereby bringing the latest deep learning advances to AD in a computationally efficient way. However, the m network architecture despite its smaller number of parameters has m architectures. This has resulted in more updates in the parameters increasing the computational time in the training stage.

The proposed approaches have been tested and validated on three datasets: SDU dataset, CASI dataset, and MeDAL dataset. According to the National Statement on Ethical Conduct in Human Research (2007) — Updated 2018 (National Health and Medical Research Council, 2018), a new ethics approval is not required for our experiments and, to the best of our knowledge, the three original datasets have been created ethically. All the three datasets are publicly available (see Appendix B).

Identifying the correct expansion of acronyms is important in improving the understandability of scientific/medical text due to the prevalence of technical acronyms which are shorthanded for ease of use. For people with limited expertise knowledge, understanding scientific/medical documents can be difficult, stressful and cause misunderstandings. The proposed methods can be used in scientific/medical text simplification tasks to provide lay people with better understanding of text through the disambiguation of acronyms.

Acknowledgement

This research was funded by and has been delivered in partnership with Our Health in Our Hands (OHIOH), a strategic initiative of the ANU, which aims to transform health care by developing new personalized health technologies and solutions in collaboration with patients, clinicians and healthcare providers. We gratefully acknowledge the funding from the ANU School of Computing for the first author's PhD studies.

References

Iz Beltagy, Kyle Lo, and Arman Cohan. 2019. Scibert: A pretrained language model for scientific text. In *Proceedings of the 2019 Conference on Empirical Methods in Natural Language Processing and the 9th International Joint Conference on Natural Language Processing (EMNLP-IJCNLP)*, pages 3615–3620.

Jean Charbonnier and Christian Wartena. 2018. Using word embeddings for unsupervised acronym disambiguation. In *Proceedings of the 27th International Conference on Computational Linguistics*.

Ting Chen, Simon Kornblith, Mohammad Norouzi, and Geoffrey Hinton. 2020. A simple framework for contrastive learning of visual representations. In *International conference on machine learning*, pages 1597–1607. PMLR.

Jacob Devlin, Ming-Wei Chang, Kenton Lee, and Kristina Toutanova. 2019. BERT: Pre-training of deep bidirectional transformers for language understanding. In *Proceedings of the 2019 Conference of the North American Chapter of the Association for Computational Linguistics: Human Language Technologies, Volume 1 (Long and Short Papers)*, pages 4171–4186, Minneapolis, Minnesota. Association for Computational Linguistics.

Liat Ein-Dor, Yosi Mass, Alon Halfon, Elad Venezian, Ilya Shnayderman, Ranit Aharonov, and Noam Slonim. 2018. Learning thematic similarity metric using triplet networks. In *Proceedings of the 56th Annual Meeting of the Association for Computational Linguistics (ACL 2018), Melbourne, Australia*, pages 15–20.

Gregory P Finley, Serguei VS Pakhomov, Reed McEwan, and Genevieve B Melton. 2016. Towards comprehensive clinical abbreviation disambiguation using machine-labeled training data. In *AMIA Annual Symposium Proceedings*, volume 2016, page 560. American Medical Informatics Association.

Elad Hoffer and Nir Ailon. 2015. Deep metric learning using triplet network. In *International workshop on similarity-based pattern recognition*, pages 84–92. Springer.

Areej Jaber and Paloma Martínez. 2021. Participation of uc3m in sdu@ aaai-21: A hybrid approach to disambiguate scientific acronyms. In *SDU@ AAAI*.

Diederik P Kingma and Jimmy Ba. 2014. Adam: A method for stochastic optimization. *arXiv preprint arXiv:1412.6980*.

Gregory Koch, Richard Zemel, Ruslan Salakhutdinov, et al. 2015. Siamese neural networks for one-shot image recognition. In *ICML deep learning workshop*, volume 2. Lille.

Ivano Lauriola and Alessandro Moschitti. 2020. Context-based transformer models for answer sentence selection. *arXiv preprint arXiv:2006.01285*.

Jinhyuk Lee, Wonjin Yoon, Sungdong Kim, Donghyeon Kim, Sunkyu Kim, Chan Ho So, and Jaewoo Kang. 2020. Biobert: a pre-trained biomedical language representation model for biomedical text mining. *Bioinformatics*, 36(4):1234–1240.

Yinhan Liu, Myle Ott, Naman Goyal, Jingfei Du, Mandar Joshi, Danqi Chen, Omer Levy, Mike Lewis, Luke Zettlemoyer, and Veselin Stoyanov. 2019. Roberta: A robustly optimized bert pretraining approach. *arXiv preprint arXiv:1907.11692*.

Sungrim Moon, Serguei Pakhomov, Nathan Liu, James O Ryan, and Genevieve B Melton. 2014. A sense inventory for clinical abbreviations and acronyms created using clinical notes and medical dictionary resources. *Journal of the American Medical Informatics Association*, 21(2):299–307.

National Health and Medical Research Council. 2018. National Statement on Ethical Conduct in Human Research (2007). https://www.nhmrc.gov.au/about-us/publications/national-statement-ethical-conduct-human-research-2007-updated-2018. [Online; accessed 06-January-2022].

Roberto Navigli. 2009. Word sense disambiguation: A survey. *ACM computing surveys (CSUR)*, 41(2):1–69.

Chunguang Pan, Bingyan Song, Shengguang Wang, and Zhipeng Luo. 2021. Bert-based acronym disambiguation with multiple training strategies. *arXiv preprint arXiv:2103.00488*.

Cicero dos Santos, Ming Tan, Bing Xiang, and Bowen Zhou. 2016. Attentive pooling networks. *arXiv preprint arXiv:1602.03609*.

Florian Schroff, Dmitry Kalenichenko, and James Philbin. 2015. Facenet: A unified embedding for face recognition and clustering. In *Proceedings of the IEEE conference on computer vision and pattern recognition*, pages 815–823.

Ariel S Schwartz and Marti A Hearst. 2002. A simple algorithm for identifying abbreviation definitions in biomedical text. In *Biocomputing 2003*, pages 451–462. World Scientific.

Aadarsh Singh and Priyanshu Kumar. 2021. Scidr at sdu-2020: Ideas-identifying and disambiguating everyday acronyms for scientific domain. In *In SDU@AAAI-21*.

Kihyuk Sohn. 2016. Improved deep metric learning with multi-class n-pair loss objective. *Advances in neural information processing systems*, 29.

Stéphan Tulkens, Simon Šuster, and Walter Daelemans. 2016. Using distributed representations to disambiguate biomedical and clinical concepts. In *Proceedings of the 15th Workshop on Biomedical Natural Language Processing*.

Aaron Van den Oord, Yazhe Li, and Oriol Vinyals. 2018. Representation learning with contrastive predictive coding. *arXiv e-prints*, pages arXiv–1807.

Amir Pouran Ben Veyseh, Franck Dernoncourt, Thien Huu Nguyen, Walter Chang, and Leo Anthony Celi. 2021. Acronym identification and disambiguation shared tasks for scientific document understanding. In *In SDU@AAAI-21*.

Amir Pouran Ben Veyseh, Franck Dernoncourt, Quan Hung Tran, and Thien Huu Nguyen. 2020. What does this acronym mean? introducing a new dataset for acronym identification and disambiguation. In *Proceedings of the 28th International Conference on Computational Linguistics*, pages 3285–3301.

Jason Wei, Chengyu Huang, Soroush Vosoughi, Yu Cheng, and Shiqi Xu. 2021. Few-shot text classification with triplet networks, data augmentation, and curriculum learning. In *Proceedings of the 2021 Conference of the North American Chapter of the Association for Computational Linguistics: Human Language Technologies*, pages 5493–5500.

Zhi Wen, Xing Han Lu, and Siva Reddy. 2020. Medal: Medical abbreviation disambiguation dataset for natural language understanding pretraining. In *Proceedings of the 3rd Clinical Natural Language Processing Workshop*, pages 130–135.

Yonghui Wu, Joshua C Denny, S Trent Rosenbloom, Randolph A Miller, Dario A Giuse, Lulu Wang, Carmelo Blanquicett, Ergin Soysal, Jun Xu, and Hua Xu. 2017. A long journey to short abbreviations: developing an open-source framework for clinical abbreviation recognition and disambiguation (card). *Journal of the American Medical Informatics Association*, 24(e1):e79–e86.

Qiwei Zhong, Guanxiong Zeng, Danqing Zhu, Yang Zhang, Wangli Lin, Ben Chen, and Jiayu Tang. 2021. Leveraging domain agnostic and specific knowledge for acronym disambiguation. In *SDU@ AAAI*.

A Triplet Networks and Triplet Loss

Triplet loss uses anchor, positive, and negative samples to learn effective representations. Anchor sample comes from a specific class. Positive samples belong to the same class as the anchor sample and the negative samples belong to a different class than the class of the anchor sample. The triplet loss encourages to minimize the distance between similar embeddings (i.e., anchor and positive embeddings) and maximize the distances between dissimilar embeddings (anchor and negative embeddings) enforcing a margin between the embeddings.

B Data Samples and Their Availability

The datasets used in this study are all publicly available from the following sources: AD dataset from SDU@AAAI21, CASI, and MeDAL. The dataset statistics are shown in Table 3. The distribution of the number of samples based on the number of acronym expansion pairs is shown in Figure 2.

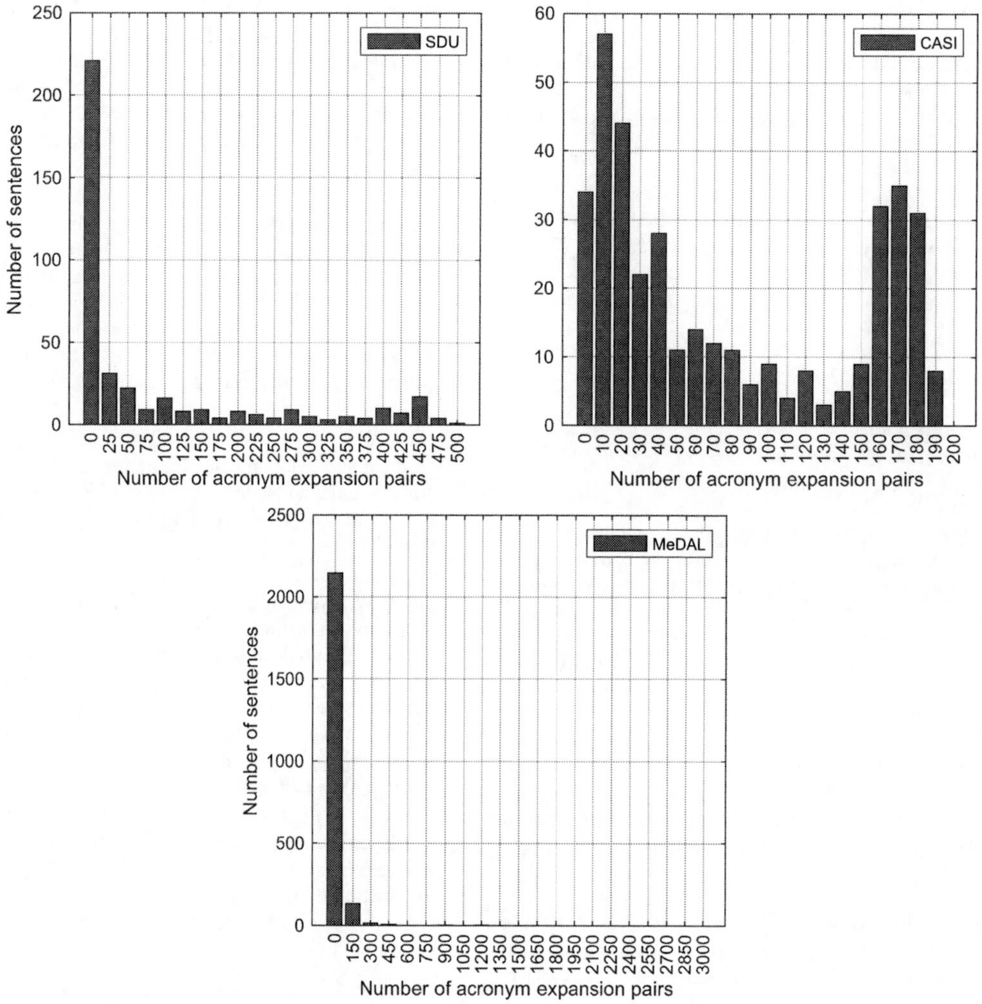

Figure 2: The distribution of samples based on the number of acronym expansion pairs for SDU, CASI, and MeDAL datasets.

C Implementation Details

Our implementation used the pre-trained SciBERT and BioBERT model architectures. We conducted out experiments on 1 RTX 3090 graphics cards with 24 GB memory and CUDA 11.4. Our implementation is based on PyTorch 1.8.2.

D Sample Output Representations

Figure 3 shows sample output representations obtained by the m network-based architecture for the SDU, CASI, and MeDAL datasets by reducing the dimensions using PCA. For the SDU dataset, the acronym *RL* with *reinforcement learning* were used to obtain the positive and respective negative sentences. Similarly, for CASI dataset the acronym *DM* with *diabetes mellitus* expansion and for MeDAL dataset the acronym *RMS* with *respiratory muscle strength* expansion were used.

	Data subset	**No. samples**	**Ratio**
SDU	Training	50,034	80%
	Development	6,189	8%
	Test	6,218	12%
CASI	Training	29,600	80%
	Development	3,700	10%
	Test	3,700	10%
MeDAL	Training	24,000	80%
	Development	3,000	10%
	Test	3,000	10%

Table 3: Dataset Statistics

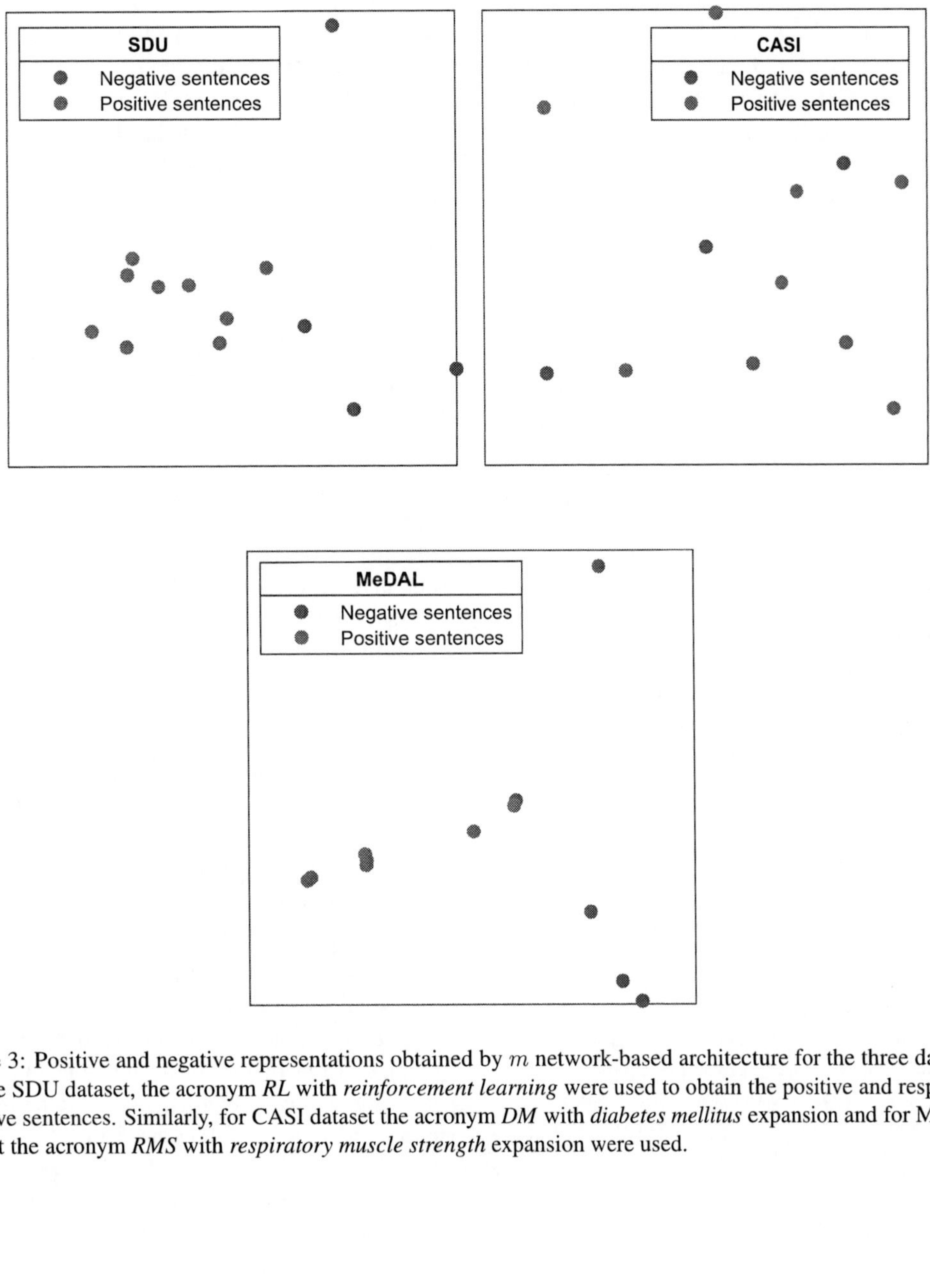

Figure 3: Positive and negative representations obtained by m network-based architecture for the three datasets. For the SDU dataset, the acronym *RL* with *reinforcement learning* were used to obtain the positive and respective negative sentences. Similarly, for CASI dataset the acronym *DM* with *diabetes mellitus* expansion and for MeDAL dataset the acronym *RMS* with *respiratory muscle strength* expansion were used.

Fine-tuning BERT Models for Summarizing German Radiology Findings

Siting Liang[1,*,§], Klaus Kades[2,3,*], Matthias A. Fink[4,5], Peter M. Full[2],
Tim F. Weber[4,5], Jens Kleesiek[6,7], Michael Strube[8], and Klaus Maier-Hein[2,9]

[1]German Research Center for Artificial Intelligence,
[2]Division of Medical Image Computing at German Cancer Research Center (DKFZ),
[3]Faculty of Mathematics and Computer Science, Heidelberg University,
[4]Clinic for Diagnostic and Interventional Radiology, University Hospital Heidelberg,
[5]Translational Lung Research Center (TLRC) Heidelberg,
[6]German Cancer Consortium (DKTK, Partner Sites Essen and Heidelberg),
[7]Institute for Artificial Intelligence in Medicine (IKIM), University Medicine Essen,
[8]Heidelberg Institute for Theoretical Studies gGmbH,
[9]Pattern Analysis and Learning Group, University Hospital Heidelberg,
Germany

siting.liang@dfki.de, k.kades@dkfz.de

Abstract

Writing the conclusion section of radiology reports is essential for communicating the radiology findings and its assessment to physician in a condensed form. In this work, we employ a transformer-based Seq2Seq model for generating the conclusion section of German radiology reports. The model is initialized with the pretrained parameters of a German BERT model and fine-tuned in our downstream task on our domain data. We proposed two strategies to improve the factual correctness of the model. In the first method, next to the abstractive learning objective, we introduce an extraction learning objective to train the decoder in the model to both generate one summary sequence and extract the key findings from the source input. The second approach is to integrate the pointer mechanism into the transformer-based Seq2Seq model. The pointer network helps the Seq2Seq model to choose between generating tokens from the vocabulary or copying parts from the source input during generation. The results of the automatic and human evaluations show that the enhanced Seq2Seq model is capable of generating human-like radiology conclusions and that the improved models effectively reduce the factual errors in the generations despite the small amount of training data.

1 Introduction

For patients with cancer, imaging findings are critical for primary diagnosis and treatment guidance during further disease progression. Depending on the tumor entity and stage, the results of imaging examinations may have a significant impact on the clinician's treatment decisions and strategies. Normally, imaging findings are communicated in clinical routine in the form of written radiology reports. However, it remains difficult to ensure the completeness and comprehensibility of relevant information in traditional written reports. Free-form narrative reports do not have standardized layout and uniform terminology, and key findings may be forgotten, which can lead to serious miscommunication (Weber et al., 2020).

Weber et al., 2020 implemented the application of Structured Oncology Reporting (SOR) to address the problems of traditional radiology reporting. The SOR, which structure is shown in Table 1, demonstrated superiority to the free-text format of radiology reports by providing disease-specific report templates and organizing the content in specific separate sections.

The main goal of this work is to automatically extract information relevant for treatment planning from standardized, real-life radiology reports. Expert validation is on the other hand still essential for this clinical routine application. For this purpose, we build a system that merges the information available in the general information and findings sections of the SOR radiology reports into a conclusion, which can be compared to conclusions generated by human experts.

Our main contributions in this work includes: (i) We tested the effectiveness of applying the generic

*Corresponding authors contributed equally.
§Work completed during master thesis at DKFZ.

Proceedings of the 4th Clinical Natural Language Processing Workshop, pages 30 - 40
July 14, 2022

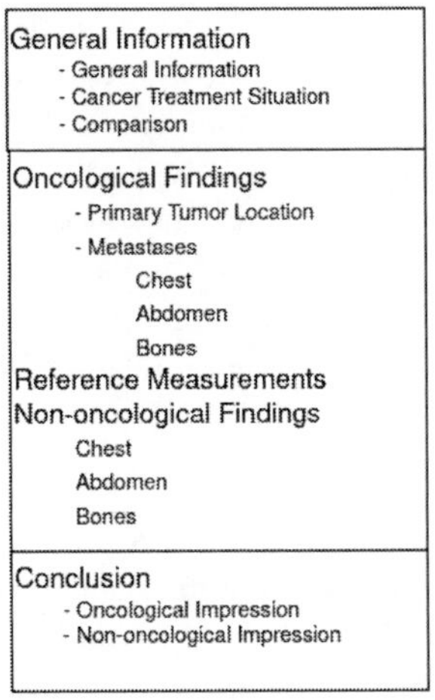

Figure 1: Standardised Layout of SOR (Weber et al., 2020). Each report has a uniform organization: the general section expresses background information on imaging and clinical data, the next section (Findings) describes oncology and non-oncology findings, and the Conclusion section gives oncological and non-oncological impressions.

pretrained German BERT model directly to the target task of generating conclusions of German radiology reports without domain-adaptive pretraining. (ii) Our system improves the factual correctness of the generated conclusions by combining extractive and abstractive learning objectives compared to the Seq2Seq baseline model. (iii) Our expert evaluation shows that the summarizations generated by our system are very close to the human reference. Since our work focuses on the application of NLP with pretrained language models to automated radiology documentation, the above contributions are limited to German SOR data. However, our experiments suggest that good results can also be obtained in low-resource domains by applying lightweight pretrained language models and minor modifications to standard architectures.

2 Related Work

Existing text summarization models can be broadly classified into three categories: extractive, abstractive and hybrid. Early extractive approaches relied on human-designed features extracted from texts to identify key sentences. Deep learning methods show good performance in various of NLP tasks. The data-driven approaches are able to learn features representations automatically. Extractive models have the advantage of producing semantically and syntactically correct summaries. Abstractive models employing an encoder-decoder framework with attentive recurrent neural networks, e.g. on news article corpus, became a standard architecture in abstractive summarization, which translates the original source content to a concise expression about the main content of the source input (Nallapati et al., 2016a; See et al., 2017; Gu et al., 2016; Kryściński et al., 2018; Chopra et al., 2016). In order to improve the faithfulness of the generated summarization given the facts in the source input, abstractive models are usually enhanced to replicate facts from the source combining extractive and abstractive approaches. Nallapati et al., 2016b incorporated a pointer network (Vinyals et al., 2015) that selects a word from a predefined vocabulary to replace an unknown word predicted by a RNN-based encoder-decoder model. Our work aims to combine both benefits of extractive and abstractive summarization with a transformer-based model.

See et al., 2017 used the pointer network Nallapati et al.2016b as a soft switch to either produce a word from the vocabulary distribution or to select a word from a copy distribution provided by a target-source attention distribution. Chen and Bansal; Kryściński et al., 2018; 2018 also applied the copy mechanism to the RNN-based model, but decomposed the decoder into a first-stage extraction model and a second-stage generator. In the first stage, the encoders in both works processed sequential document representation and provided sentence-level representations to the extractor for selection. In the second stage, Kryściński et al., 2018 used the language model to rewrite the selected sentences into the summary. Chen and Bansal, 2018 trained the decoder from scratch by using ROUGE (Lin, 2004) scores as a reward strategy for reinforcement learning to generate summaries based on the selected sentences. In our work, we integrate the pointer network to a transformer-based encoder-decoder model.

Summarizing radiology findings with neural Seq2Seq learning of Zhang et al.; Zhang et al. is very closely related to our work. Zhang et al., 2018 collected a large set of domain-specific training data to train the RNN-based pointer-generator (See et al., 2017). Because there are usually two sections in radiology reports: background and findings, to provide relevant information for the summary, Zhang et al., 2018 incorporated an extra encoder for encoding the background information and findings separately. In contrast, we feed the combination of sequences of the background and findings section as one input and into one encoder. Zhang et al., 2019b improved the radiology summarization model by optimizing the factual correctness of the summaries via policy learning. In order to combine extraction and abstraction in one model, we propose two target sequences paired with an input sequence. One target sequence is the reference summary and the other is a sequence consisting of key sentences extracted from the input. Our goal with the dual target sequences is to encourage the encoder-decoder model to retain some of the input while generating new phrases for the summaries.

Pretrained language models have advanced the state-of-the-art when fine-tuned in various NLP tasks, as well as in automatic text summarization (Miller, 2019; Liu and Lapata, 2019; Zhang et al., 2019a). Rothe et al., 2019 demonstrated the efficacy of warm-starting the encoder and decoder from checkpoints of publicly available large language models, including BERT(Devlin et al., 2018) and GPT-2(Radford et al., 2019), for text generation task such as machine translation and text summarization. Depending on different initialization combinations, they investigated variants of the Seq2Seq model, such as BERT2Random, BERT2BERT, BERT2GPT, etc. Warm-starting the Seq2Seq model leveraging these pretrained language models checkpoints can reduce computational resources and time by orders of magnitude, while improving the sequence generation performance. We adopt the warm-starting idea and initialize both the encoder and decoder with a generic pretrained German BERT model (deepset.ai, 2019). We fine-tune the model with our German radiology report data and enhance the model by combining extractive and abstractive objectives.

3 Models

The main task of summarizing radiology findings is to transform the salient and clinically significant findings from a source of words and phrases $X = \{x_1, x_2, ..., x_T\}$, to a sequence of concise expressions $Y = \{y_1, y_2, ..., y_T'\}$. Background information in the radiology report conveys important information for short-term or long-term examination of each patient in the clinical routine, which is why abstractive models needs to incorporate background information into the summary generation (Zhang et al., 2018). The content of the source sequence X contains the background information and imaging findings. These findings convey the information about the location of the primary tumour, the presence of metastases at different body regions, and other non-oncological findings. Y is the conclusion of the radiology report, which on the one hand assesses the patient's condition according to the detailed findings and on the other hand concisely summarizes the significant findings from the source sequence X. We use a collection of aligned X and Y pairs to train Transformer-based Seq2Seq models to generate Y.

Baseline Model Warm-starting the Seq2Seq model leveraging pretrained checkpoints can reduce computational resources and time by orders of magnitude, while improving the sequence generation performance (Rothe et al., 2019). We utilize the **BERT2BERT** model defined in Rothe et al., 2019, as our abstractive summarization baseline model.

The encoder and decoder of the model are initialized from a public available BERT checkpoint (deepset.ai, 2019), except the encoder-decoder attention layers in the decoder. Taking advantage of the Transformer architecture and pretrained language models, among the 221 millions trainable parameters in the **BERT2BERT** model, only 26 millions parameters in the encoder-decoder attention layers are initialized randomly, and 195 millions are loaded from the pretrained BERT model. The reduction of randomly initialized, trainable parameters, allows for fewer fine-tuning steps, and the model's ability to perform well on small training data sets.

BERT2BERT + Extraction Most abstractive systems suffer from the problem of creating spurious facts due to their ability to paraphrase. Hybrid systems that combine extraction and abstraction are expected to improve the correctness of the generated facts by using more criteria to extract the original facts from the source (Kryscinski et al., 2019; Cao et al., 2017; Zhang et al., 2019b; Chawla et al., 2019; Falke et al., 2019). Different to previous works, which incorporated separate extraction and abstraction stages (Hsu et al., 2018; Li et al., 2018; Chen and Bansal, 2018), we propose a new learning scenario with little modification to the architecture of the **BERT2BERT** model by adding an extraction learning objective (**BERT2BERT+Ext**). Therefore, during training, we optimize the following combined loss:

$$Loss = loss_{abstraction} + loss_{extraction} \quad (1)$$

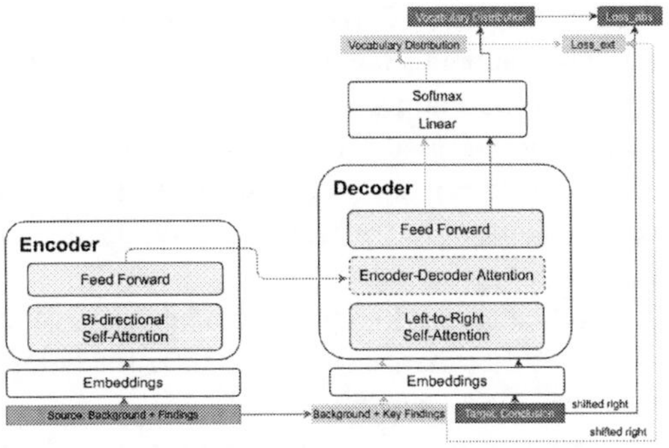

Figure 2: BERT2BERT model adding Extraction Loss. In order to train the decoder to extract the key findings through generation, we supply an additional target sequence ("Background + Key Findings"), which consists of the key findings selected from the source sequence.

The setup is illustrated in Figure 2. Through the extraction objective, the model is trained to reconstruct the key sentences in the generation.

In the original setting of **BERT2BERT**, we only train the model using our source and target sequence pairs (X, Y). As showed in Figure 2, X symbolizes the source input and contains "Background + Findings" and Y is the target input "Conclusion". During training, the decoder of **BERT2BERT+Ext** is fed with additional target sequences ("Background + Key Findings") including the general section and key sentences from the findings sections as input. Section 4.3 explains how to extract these key findings from the finding section from our training data. Extractive loss encourages the model to reconstruct key phrases from the source input. Abstractive loss prompts the model to generate new formulations that are not from the source sequence.

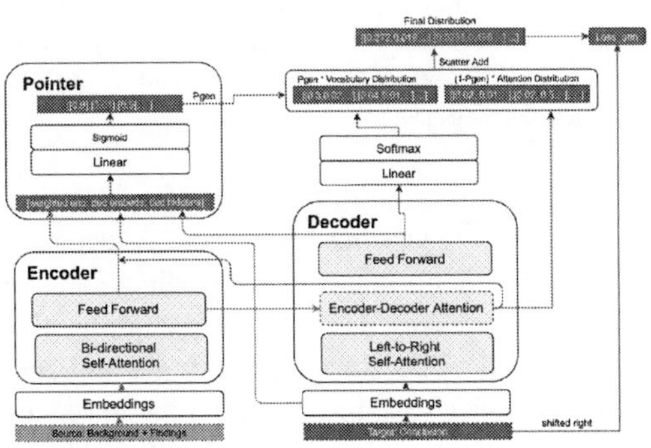

Figure 3: BERT2BERT model incorporating the Pointer Mechanism.

BERT2BERT + Pointer Pointer networks allow the model to copy words from the source sequence through an alignment between the target sequence and the source sequence (See et al., 2017). The benefits of incorporating the pointer to the generation procedure are not only to reduce the number of tokens, which are not known to BERT, but also to ensure factual correctness while generating new phrases. Pointer networks have been used for abstract summaries of Seq2Seq models based on RNNs as a standard architecture. However, to the best of our knowledge, there has been little exploration of incorporating pointer networks into the Transformer encoder-decoder model for summarization tasks. Figure 3 illustrates the combination of **BERT2BERT** and the pointer mechanism (**BERT2BERT+Ptr**). The pointer network consists of one linear layer followed by a sigmoid function which generates a pseudo-probability p_{gen} in the range of $[0, 1]$. In the original function of See et al., 2017, p_{gen} is given by:

$$p_{gen} = sigm(w_{ptr}^T[h_t^x; y_t; s_t] + b_{ptr}) \quad (2)$$

where w_{ptr}^T and b_{ptr} are learnable parameters. p_{gen} is determined by the concatenated representation containing the word embeddings of the input token y_t, the decoder hidden state s_t and the weighted encoder hidden representations h_t^x, at each decoding step t.

See et al., 2017 recycled attention scores directly from the encoder-decoder attention layer. However, in the **BERT2BERT** model, we not only have multiple encoders and decoders, but also multiple heads of the encoder-decoder attention. We can solve the dimension of multiple heads in the attention distribution using the mean of the multi-head attentions (Deaton, 2019). These hidden states from the final encoder are used as context vectors passed to each decoding step. Each decoder state s_t used for predicting the next token is also from the last decoder, as well as the multi-head encoder-decoder attention scores a_t. h_t^x in Equation 3 represents the hidden output from the final encoder weighted by the sum of the heads of the encoder-decoder attention layers at each decoder step from the last decoder, analogous to the RNN-based context vector. h_t^x is given by:

$$h_t^x = \sum_j^{T_x} \sum_i^{N_{heads}} a_t \cdot h_j^x \quad (3)$$

where i is the index of the attention head, j is the position of the source sequence and T_x is the total length of the source sequence. The formula for computing the final distribution $P_{final}(w)$ is as follows:

$$P_{final}(w) = p_{gen} \cdot P_{vocab}(w) + (1 - p_{gen}) \cdot \sum_{i:w_i=w} a_i^t \quad (4)$$

$P_{vocab}(w)$ has the dimension of the size of the vocabulary. a^t contains the values for each token in the source sequence, and each value has a corresponding index i in the vocabulary dimension. The encoder and decoder of **BERT2BERT** share the same vocabulary. Hence, we can sum the values from a^t and P_{vocab} at the same indices.

4 Experiments

4.1 Datasets for Training and Testing

The concept of structured oncology reports (SOR) has been implemented to generate high-quality radiology reports for the general follow-up assessment of cancer patients in the clinical routine at the University Hospital Heidelberg (UKHD) in Germany by Weber et al., 2020. The design and application of SOR can be accessed using the internet link: `http://www.targetedreporting.com/sor/`. For our experiments, we use a collection of 10,514 structured reports from the years 2018 and 2019 from the radiology department of the UKHD. The HIPAA-compliant retrospective study was approved by the Institutional Review Board (S-083/2018), and informed consent was waived. The reports are divided into a training set (80%), a validation set (10%), and a test set (10%).

	training (8410)	valid (1052)	test (1052)
general	2.0	2.0	2.0
findings	21.1 ± 8.2	20.5 ± 7.5	21.7 ± 7.5
conclusion	3.1 ± 2.0	3.4 ± 2.0	3.5 ± 2.0

Table 1: The average number of sentences after segmentation in each section. The general section contains 2 sentences of the background information. The number of sentences in the findings section averages about 22 sentences, with a variation of 7-8 sentences. The conclusion consists of approximately 3-6 sentences.

Sentence Segmentation Each section of the SOR report contains documentation in a tabulated form. Different sections have different table blocks. We need to customize different methods to segment sentences from different sections. In the general section, there are normally two sentences expressing the treatment situation and previous examinations. In the finding sections, we have notes organized in different blocks and free-text content. There are four main blocks: primary tumour location, metastases, reference measurements and non-oncology findings.

The first step is to detect the boundaries of the blocks. After that, we apply a tailor-made regular expression segmenter to split the text in these blocks into sentences. In report texts, periods are usually used to mark the end of sentences and can be used to split text into sentences. However, applying this rule to the findings and conclusion sections requires consideration of several cases, such as abbreviations, dates, and serial numbers, where the period is part of the tokens. We customize the regular expressions to handle the above exceptions. The average number of sentences in each section calculated for each split set can be found in Table 1.

Patient Degree Categories Weber et al., 2020 used a uniform terminology to ensure the formalities of the content in the conclusion section as assessments of patient responses. These terminologies are shown in Table 2.

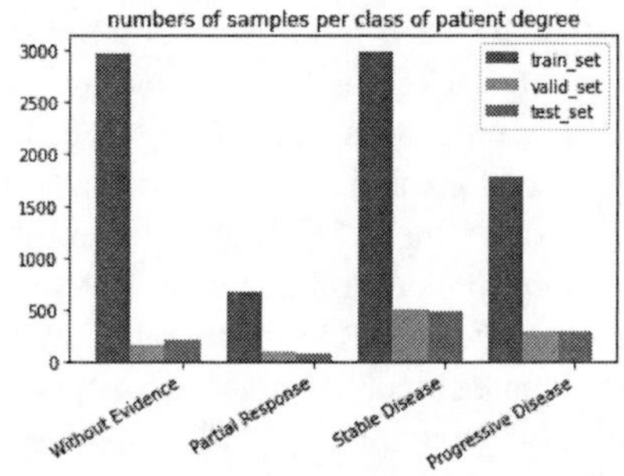

Figure 4: Number of reports for the three data partitions after matching to patient degree categories. We have significantly more reports in the Without Evidence and Stable Disease categories than in the other two categories, and the fewest reports are found in the Partial Response category.

The reports from different patient degree categories challenge our model to varying degrees. For example, a report that contains findings indicating progressive disease is much more complex than a report that does not show findings regarding tumour burden. It would be more appropriate to judge the performance of the model based on the patient degree class of the report. As shown in Figure 4, after dividing the reports into four patient categories, the

Patient Degree	SOR Category	German Template
Without Evidence (WE)	no tumour burden evidence	Oncological regular findings without evidence of recrudesce or metastasis (Onkologisch regelrechter Befund ohne Nachweis von Rezidiv oder Metastasierung)
Partial Response (PR)	significant decrease of tumour burden	Oncological improvement of findings; constancy of findings with a tendency to decrease (Onkologisch Befundverbesserung; Befundkonstanz mit tendenzieller Abnahme)
Stable Disease (SD)	no significant change of tumour burden	Oncological constancy of findings (Onkologisch Befundkonstanz)
Progressive Disease (PD)	significant increase of tumour burden	Oncological worsening of findings; constancy of findings with a tendency to increase (Onkologisch Befundverschlechterung; Befundkonstanz mit tendenzieller Zunahme)

Table 2: Patient degree categories and corresponding uniform terminology in conclusion. The SOR categories are defined by threshold criteria for tumour burden development in the implementation. For example, if there is a significant decrease of tumour burden (more than 30%), the patient degree is defined as Partial Response.

BERT2BERT	baseline
BERT2BERT+Ext	adding extraction learning objective
BERT2BERT+Ptr	integrating pointer network
BERT2BERT+Ext+Ptr	combining extraction and pointer

Table 3: The abstractive models are warm-started with the checkpoints from the **German BERT** (deepset.ai, 2019).

number of reports is imbalance across patient categories, however, is kept similar across the three data splits. The number of training samples is an important factor in the performance of the model. Given uneven quantity and the varying complexity of reports across categories, we expect inconsistent performance of the models across the four patient degree categories.

4.2 Experimental Setup

In our experiments, we evaluate the efficacy of the proposed **BERT2BERT** baseline and its enhancements, shown in Table 3. The implementation of all BERT-based models is based on the open source library **HuggingFace Transformers** by Wolf et al., which is dedicated to supporting state-of-the-art Transformer architectures and to collecting and supplying pretrained models for the community. The models are fine-tuned on 8410 reports and validated on 1052 samples during the training. The maximum number of training epochs is 10 with an early stopping setting according to the validation loss metric: when the validation loss is no longer decreasing within 3 epochs, the training process is terminated. All fine-tuning processes are conducted using one single GPU of 32GB memory and completed in no longer than 6 hours.

Input Sequences We combine the sentences from the background and finding sections in one input sequence and feed them into the encoder of the model. We adopt the idea from Liu and Lapata, 2019 of inserting "[CLS]" tokens between the sentences to construct structured sequences. Since BERT is not a generative model and does not learn an end of text token like GPT-2 does, we use the "[SEP]" token to make the end of the whole sequence, so that the decoder in **BERT2BERT** stops the generation when it sees this special token.

Evaluation Metrics For quantitative evaluation, we firstly apply the ROUGE metric (Lin, 2004) and report the F_1 scores for ROUGE-1 and ROUGE-L about the tokens overlaps between the system-generated summaries against the reference conclusions. Secondly, we propose the patient degree matching metric, evaluating whether the assessments generated by the abstractive models can be categorized to the same patient degree category as their reference. After that, we conduct a human evaluation with two domain experts in which the annotators are asked to score the system-generated conclusions as well as the reference based on three criteria: comprehensibility, oncology and non-oncology correctness.

4.3 Extracting Key Sentences

We propose the **BERT2BERT+Ext** model in Section 3 to improve the extraction ability of the decoder during generation, however, we lack key sentences for training. For finding the most effective way to extract the key sentences, we evaluate several non-neural, automatic extractive methods on the test data:

1. **Longest-k**. This method simply extracts the k longest sentences from the findings. We hypothesize the longer a sentence of findings is, the more information it may communicate in the summary.

2. **Tfidf-Ex**. This approach is built on the scores of TF-IDF (Jones, 1972). TF-IDF produces a vocabulary based on the collection of documents and outputs a TF-IDF vector of vocabulary breadth. We can set a threshold to extract

the top keywords from the TF-IDF vector. The sentences are ranked based on the scores by summing up the TF-IDF of all the keywords found in the sentence of a document. Top k sentences are extracted as the salient sentences.

3. **TextRank** (Mihalcea and Tarau, 2004) algorithm scores sentences based on the graph theory. In the algorithm, a graph is constructed with each sentence in the document as a vertex, and the score of edges between sentences are determined based on the number of overlapping tokens indicating the similarity between sentences.

All the extractive approaches assign an importance score to each sentence from the findings section and rank the sentences according to the scores. We compare the results of the different methods in Table 4. All the three extractive methods return comparable results. The **Longest-k** method is the simplest extractive method for which no computation is required and indicates that phrases from the longest sentences in the finding sections are usually included in the human-written summaries.

	Longest-k	Tfidf-Ex	TextRank
ROUGE-1	**41.9**	40.6	40.4
ROUGE-L	**40.8**	38.7	39.6

Table 4: The recall scores of ROUGE metrics for the different extractive approaches. The scores imply how much of overlaps between the key sentences and the reference is found. The 2 sentences from the general section are always included in the extraction. Because the average number of sentences in the reference summaries does not exceed 6, we evaluate the key sentences given k=4, i.e, 4 key sentences from the findings section.

4.4 Human Evaluation

Since the ROUGE metric only assesses the similarity between the system-generated conclusions and the references, we conduct an expertise evaluation with two domain annotators (one radiologist and one final year medical student) to understand the clinical validity of the conclusions generated by the abstractive models. According to the radiologist, there are two important criteria to judge the clinical validity of the conclusions, namely the degree of correctness of the oncological and non-oncological impressions based on the patient's condition. In addition, we ask the annotators to score the comprehensibility of system-generated and referenced findings with expert judgment to investigate whether the abstractive models could produce medical terms that are as comprehensible as those written by specialists. In the evaluation, we first create a pool of samples, where each sample has scored higher ROUGE-1 scores than the average in the entire test set for all four abstractive models. Next, we randomly select five examples from the pool for each patient degree category, totalling twenty samples. We present the general information, findings secions and the four system-generated conclusions as well as the reference conclusion of each sample to the annotators in a random order. They are asked to score the conclusions on a likert scale from 0 to 5, indicating oncological and non-oncological correctness degrees as well as comprehensibility from very poor to very good. A score of 3 indicates satisfaction. The annotators have no prior knowledge of the models nor the reference. The annotator instructions are given in Appedix A. The annotation was performed with the open source text annotation tool doccano (Nakayama et al., 2018).

5 Results and Discussion

	whole	WE	PR	SD	PD
BERT2BERT	36.15	55.27	30.86	32.09	30.93
BERT2BERT+Ext	42.13	**58.99**	38.19	38.17	36.68
BERT2BERT+Ext(random)	37.27	57.22	31.43	32.71	31.32
BERT2BERT+Ptr	42.25	55.9	38.66	**39.88**	**39.04**
BERT2BERT+Ext+Ptr	**43.32**	57.91	**40.15**	39.39	38.65
BERT2BERT+Ext+Ptr(random)	42.10	57.37	38.71	39.41	37.81

Table 5: ROUGE-1 F_1 scores of BERT2BERT-based Models on the whole test set and different partitions of four Patient Degree Classes. BERT2BERT+Ext(random) has random selected sentences targets. When the target sentences to be extracted are replaced with randomly selected sentences, no significant improvement is found in BERT2BERT+Ext models.

Table 5 shows the F_1 scores of ROUGE-1 metric across the different settings of the abstractive model overall reports and according to the patient degree categories. The hybrid models outperform the **BERT2BERT** model by nearly 6 points. Integrating extraction or pointer mechanism yields comparable results. According to the metrics, the last hybrid model combining the two facilities achieves only a small improvement compared to enhancing the model only with extraction training or pointer network. One SOR report and the generations of the abstractive models are shown in Appendix B.

Both the baseline model and the hybrid model have less difficulty in generating summaries for the *WE* class. We hypothesize that this is because in this category, there are many training samples (almost one-third of the reports), uniform templates, and barely important information can be extracted from the findings. In the templates of SD, there is only one statement about the findings: "oncological constancy". For the PR and PD classes, there are cases in which an oncological constancy is described, however, with a tendency to an improvement or deterioration, which increases the difficulties of the generation task for the models.

In the case of evaluating oncology facts, their correctness requires more expertise to assess. Hence, we need to present examples of system-generated conclusions to domain experts to assess clinical validity. The results of the expertise assessment are presented in Section 5.

Validation of the Extraction Learning Since we do not have human-annotated labels in the radiology reports indicating the important sentences, we apply the **Longest-k** method explained in 4.3 to extract the key sentences used as target for training **BERT2BERT+Ext**. In **BERT2BERT+Ext(random)** we replaced the target sentences with random ones. The results in Table 5 show that, the performance of **BERT2BERT+Ext(random)** drops in comparison to **BERT2BERT+Ext**. This verifies the importance of target sentences for improving the extraction ability of the **BERT2BERT+Ext** model. In **BERT2BERT+Ext+Ptr(random)**, the scores obtained by integrating the pointer mechanism are not significantly affected when the decoder is trained to extract sentences that include irrelevant sentences. From the ROUGE scores, we can conclude that the hybrid models achieve better results than the baseline model.

Results of Expert Evaluation Figure 5 presents the correctness results of oncological and non-oncological impressions as well as the comprehensibility of the impressions. A score of zero indicates unacceptable generation given the facts in the source input, while a score of five means that the facts in the generation are completely correct.

The results shown in the bar charts are the average scores of the two annotators, normalized by number of the examples in each category. In terms of correctness regarding oncological and non-oncological impressions in the WE patient degree, all conclusions generated by the abstractive models are scored close to 5. In SD category, the generated conclusions are almost as good as the human-written conclusions, except for the baseline model. Summarizing the findings for the PR and PD categories is more challenging for the models due to the complexity of the findings and the small number of training examples. The hybrid models perform better than the baseline, but the correctness of their generations are rated very differently in these two categories. The **BERT2BERT+Ext+Ptr** model performs best in ensuring correctness across patient degree categories in general. Figure 5 shows that, the abstractive models are capable of generating good comprehensible radiology conclusions, except for the baseline model in the PD category. Although the PR class has the fewest training instances, the abstractive models also achieve results above 3.

6 Conclusion

In this work, we experiment and demonstrate the efficacy of the **BERT2BERT**-based abstractive models on summarizing German radiology findings in structured reports. We propose two strategies to improve the **BERT2BERT** model with the aim of optimizing the factual correctness in the conclusions generated by the system, **BERT2BERT+Ext** and **BERT2BERT+Ptr**. Both **BERT2BERT+Ext** and **BERT2BERT+Ptr** models have very few modifications to the baseline model and improve the performance of the model. In **BERT2BERT+Ext**, we train the model to generate summaries, encouraging the model to reconstruct key sentences based on the source text in the training process. **BERT2BERT+Ptr** incorporates the pointer mechanism to modify the decoder's prediction by copying the salient segments directly from the source sequence. Despite the limitations of the models and the imbalanced training data, the issue of unfaithful facts in the conclusions generated by the baseline model is greatly improved by these hybrid models. One pressing issue in the future work is to investigate the potential advantages of these models on free-text radiology data or data in other domains.

Acknowledgments

This research was supported by the German Cancer Consortium (DKTK, Strategic Initiative *Joint Imaging Platform*) and carried out during a master thesis at German Cancer Research Center. This work is further supported by the pAItient project (BMG, 2520DAT0P2).

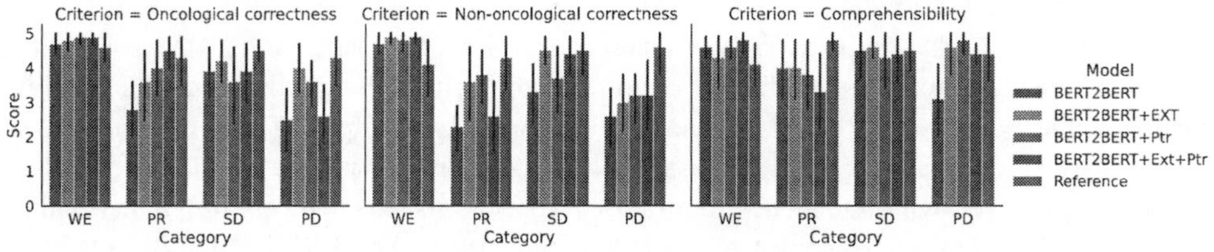

Figure 5: Average scores with standard deviation for the three criteria: Oncological correctness, non-oncological correctness and comprehensibility.

References

Ziqiang Cao, Furu Wei, Wenjie Li, and Sujian Li. 2017. Faithful to the original: Fact aware neural abstractive summarization. *CoRR*, abs/1711.04434.

Kushal Chawla, Kundan Krishna, and Balaji Vasan Srinivasan. 2019. Improving generation quality of pointer networks via guided attention. *CoRR*, abs/1901.11492.

Yen-Chun Chen and Mohit Bansal. 2018. Fast abstractive summarization with reinforce-selected sentence rewriting. In *Proceedings of the 56th Annual Meeting of the Association for Computational Linguistics (Volume 1: Long Papers)*, pages 675–686, Melbourne, Australia. Association for Computational Linguistics.

Sumit Chopra, Michael Auli, and Alexander M. Rush. 2016. Abstractive sentence summarization with attentive recurrent neural networks. In *Proceedings of the 2016 Conference of the North American Chapter of the Association for Computational Linguistics: Human Language Technologies*, pages 93–98, San Diego, California. Association for Computational Linguistics.

John Deaton. 2019. Transformers and pointer-generator networks for abstractive summarization.

deepset.ai. 2019. Open sourcing german bert.

Jacob Devlin, Ming-Wei Chang, Kenton Lee, and Kristina Toutanova. 2018. BERT: pre-training of deep bidirectional transformers for language understanding. *CoRR*, abs/1810.04805.

Tobias Falke, Leonardo F. R. Ribeiro, Prasetya Ajie Utama, Ido Dagan, and Iryna Gurevych. 2019. Ranking generated summaries by correctness: An interesting but challenging application for natural language inference. In *Proceedings of the 57th Annual Meeting of the Association for Computational Linguistics*, pages 2214–2220, Florence, Italy. Association for Computational Linguistics.

Jiatao Gu, Zhengdong Lu, Hang Li, and Victor O. K. Li. 2016. Incorporating copying mechanism in sequence-to-sequence learning. *CoRR*, abs/1603.06393.

Wan Ting Hsu, Chieh-Kai Lin, Ming-Ying Lee, Kerui Min, Jing Tang, and Min Sun. 2018. A unified model for extractive and abstractive summarization using inconsistency loss. *CoRR*, abs/1805.06266.

Karen Spärck Jones. 1972. A statistical interpretation of term specificity and its application in retrieval. *Journal of Documentation*, 28:11–21.

Wojciech Kryscinski, Bryan McCann, Caiming Xiong, and Richard Socher. 2019. Evaluating the factual consistency of abstractive text summarization. *CoRR*, abs/1910.12840.

Wojciech Kryściński, Romain Paulus, Caiming Xiong, and Richard Socher. 2018. Improving abstraction in text summarization. In *Proceedings of the 2018 Conference on Empirical Methods in Natural Language Processing*, pages 1808–1817, Brussels, Belgium. Association for Computational Linguistics.

Wei Li, Xinyan Xiao, Yajuan Lyu, and Yuanzhuo Wang. 2018. Improving neural abstractive document summarization with explicit information selection modeling. In *Proceedings of the 2018 Conference on Empirical Methods in Natural Language Processing*, pages 1787–1796, Brussels, Belgium. Association for Computational Linguistics.

Chin-Yew Lin. 2004. ROUGE: A package for automatic evaluation of summaries. In *Text Summarization Branches Out*, pages 74–81, Barcelona, Spain. Association for Computational Linguistics.

Yang Liu and Mirella Lapata. 2019. Text summarization with pretrained encoders. *CoRR*, abs/1908.08345.

Rada Mihalcea and Paul Tarau. 2004. TextRank: Bringing order into text. In *Proceedings of the 2004 Conference on Empirical Methods in Natural Language Processing*, pages 404–411, Barcelona, Spain. Association for Computational Linguistics.

Derek Miller. 2019. Leveraging BERT for extractive text summarization on lectures. *CoRR*, abs/1906.04165.

Hiroki Nakayama, Takahiro Kubo, Junya Kamura, Yasufumi Taniguchi, and Xu Liang. 2018. doccano: Text annotation tool for human. Software available from https://github.com/doccano/doccano.

Ramesh Nallapati, Bing Xiang, and Bowen Zhou. 2016a. Sequence-to-sequence rnns for text summarization. *CoRR*, abs/1602.06023.

Ramesh Nallapati, Bowen Zhou, and Mingbo Ma. 2016b. Classify or select: Neural architectures for extractive document summarization. *CoRR*, abs/1611.04244.

Alec Radford, Jeff Wu, Rewon Child, David Luan, Dario Amodei, and Ilya Sutskever. 2019. Language models are unsupervised multitask learners.

Sascha Rothe, Shashi Narayan, and Aliaksei Severyn. 2019. Leveraging pre-trained checkpoints for sequence generation tasks. *CoRR*, abs/1907.12461.

Abigail See, Peter J. Liu, and Christopher D. Manning. 2017. Get to the point: Summarization with pointer-generator networks. *CoRR*, abs/1704.04368.

Oriol Vinyals, Meire Fortunato, and Navdeep Jaitly. 2015. Pointer networks.

TF Weber, M Spurny, FC Hasse, O Sedlaczek, GM Haag, C Springfeld, T Mokry, D Jäger, HU Kauczor, and AK Berger. 2020. Improving radiologic communication in oncology: a single-centre experience with structured reporting for cancer patients. *Insights Imaging*, 11(1):106.

Thomas Wolf, Lysandre Debut, Victor Sanh, Julien Chaumond, Clement Delangue, Anthony Moi, Pierric Cistac, Tim Rault, Rémi Louf, Morgan Funtowicz, and Jamie Brew. 2019. Huggingface's transformers: State-of-the-art natural language processing. *CoRR*, abs/1910.03771.

Xingxing Zhang, Furu Wei, and Ming Zhou. 2019a. HIBERT: Document level pre-training of hierarchical bidirectional transformers for document summarization. In *Proceedings of the 57th Annual Meeting of the Association for Computational Linguistics*, pages 5059–5069, Florence, Italy. Association for Computational Linguistics.

Yuhao Zhang, Daisy Yi Ding, Tianpei Qian, Christopher D. Manning, and Curtis P. Langlotz. 2018. Learning to summarize radiology findings. *CoRR*, abs/1809.04698.

Yuhao Zhang, Derek Merck, Emily Bao Tsai, Christopher D. Manning, and Curtis P. Langlotz. 2019b. Optimizing the factual correctness of a summary: A study of summarizing radiology reports. *CoRR*, abs/1911.02541.

A Annotator Instructions

We have discussed the criteria with domain experts for judging the correctness of system-generated conclusions. We define an annotation task for grading generated assessments according to certain criteria. The following instructions are presented to annotators for evaluating the generated summaries. are a senior medical student and a radiologist.

Evaluation Criteria We consider four summary models and the reference conclusion. Each model generates a radiological summary (assessment) under the specification of a source text (general examination information and radiological findings). You will be presented with the source text, the four generations from the models, and the assessment written by the physician. Please rate the generations of each model and the reference according to the following criteria: Oncolgical correctness, nononcolgical correctness, and readability:

- Oncological correctness: is the summary and the details about metastases (none, new, proliferation or regressive) correct? (0) not assessable; (1) not at all correct ; (2) correct to a small extent ; (3) half correct; (4) correct to a large extent; (5) everything correct.
- Nononcological correctness: is the general date, organ, and other information correct? (0) not assessable; (1) not at all correct ; (2) correct to a small extent ; (3) half correct; (4) correct to a large extent; (5) everything correct.
- Readability: is the generation easy to understand, without broken expressions or unknown words? (0) not assessable; (1) many unknown words, difficult to read and comprehend; (2) several unknown words and aborted expressions, not fluent; (3) several unknown words; (4) fluent and coherent, but some unknown words; (5) correct words and expressions, fluent and coherent.

If the generation is not assessable, select 0 - not assessable. Otherwise, the scale are grades from 1 to 5 and must be assigned for each criterion.

B SOR Report Example

We present one SOR example from (Weber et al., 2020) in Table 6 along with the generations of the

General Section	Untersuchungsregion Thorax (CT), Abdomen (CT) Behandlungssituation Ausgangsbefund. Vergleich Letzte Vergleichsuntersuchung: 17.11.2017.
Findings Section	Primärtumor / Lokalrezidiv Soweit messtechnisch erschwert erfassbar progrediente diffus infiltrierende Raumforderung des Pankreaskopfs mit Gangstau im Pankreasschwanz und vollständiger Ummauerung des Truncus coeliacus, mindenstens 180° Ummauerung der A. liniealis . Bekannter kompletter Verschluss der extrahepatischen Pfortader und V. mesenteria superior mit ausgeprägten Kollateralen . Regionäre Lymphknoten Gering prominenterer vermehrter Lymphknotenbesatz mesenterial, exemplarisch mit einem KAD von 7 mm, zuvor 5 mm (8-137) . Metastasen Lunge und Pleura: Keine . Thorakale Lymphknoten und Weichteile: Keine . Leber: Keine . Abdominale Lymphknoten und Weichteile: Keine . Peritoneum: Kein eindeutiger Nachweis einer Peritonealkarzinose, jedoch Infiltration der Mesenterialwurzel durch den Primarius und Nachweis geringer freier Flüssigkeit im kleinen Becken . Skelett: Keine . Referenzmessungen Keine Referenzmessungen . Thorax Portsystem in situ . Kein katheterassoziierter Thrombus . Abdomen Unveränderte Nebenmilze . Konstante geringe Cholestase Skelett Im Übrigen ohne besondere Auffälligkeiten .
Conclusion	Onkologische Beurteilung Onkologisch Befundkonstanz mit tendenzieller Zunahme der Tumorlast gegenüber 17.11.2017. Progredient diffus infiltrierende Raumforderung des Pankreaskopfs. Andere Befunde Keine Angabe.(Progressive diffusely infiltrating mass of the pancreatic head.)
BERT2BERT	Onkologische Beurteilung Onkologisch Befundverschlechterung gegenüber dem Ausgangsbefund vom 11.04.2018 und 12.05.2019. In diesem Zeitraum zunehmende Peritonealkarzinose mit Ummauerung der VMS, sowie Ummauerung des TCs bei bekanntem Magenkarzinom. Andere Befunde Keine Angabe.(During this period, increasing peritoneal carcinomatosis with walling of the VMS, as well as walling of the TC in known gastric carcinoma.)
BERT2BERT +Ext	Onkologische Beurteilung Onkologisch Befundkonstanz gegenüber 17.11.2017. In diesem Zeitraum keine wesentliche Änderung des Pankreasschwanzes mit Infiltration der Pfortader und Ummauerung der Truncus coeliacus, AMS / VMS sowie Arteria hepatica communis durch die AMS - suspekte Lymphknotenmetastasen. Andere Befunde Keine Angabe.(During this period, no significant change in the tail of the pancreas with infiltration of the portal vein and walled truncus coeliacus, AMS / VMS and arteria hepatica communis by the AMS - suspicious lymph node metastases.)
BERT2BERT +Ptr	Onkologische Beurteilung Onkologische Befundverschlechterung zum 17.11.2017. In diesem Zeitraum neu aufgetretene Lymphknotenmetastase im Oberbauch mit ausgeprägter Infiltration der Pfortader und der V. Pankreatitis. Unveränderte Darstellung der bekannten Peritonealkarzinose. Andere Befunde Keine Angabe.(Newly appeared lymph node metastasis in the upper abdomen during this period with marked infiltration of the portal vein and pancreatic vein. Unchanged presentation of known peritoneal carcinomatosis.)
BERT2BERT +Ext+Ptr	Onkologische Beurteilung Onkologisch Befundkonstanz mit tendenzieller Zunahme der Tumorlast gegenüber 17.11.2017. In diesem Zeitraum moderate Zunahme des Primärtumors im Pankreasschwanz. Bekannter Verschluss der extrahepatischen Pfortader und Ummauerung der A. gastrica sinistra und Infiltration der Pfortader. Andere Befunde Keine Angabe.(Moderate increase in primary tumor in the pancreatic tail during this period. Known occlusion of the extrahepatic portal vein and walling of the gastrica sinistra artery and infiltration of the portal vein.)

Table 6: In conclusion is a human-written summary reference. Followings are the generations by the Seq2Seq models given the input text combining general and finding sections. In this example, words in red are unfaithful generations comparing to the input and extracted information (highlighted in green) that appears in the source sequence.

abstractive models given the input from the general and findings sections in the report. The date of the previous radiology examination is very important information for short-term or long-term response assessments. The baseline BERT2BERT model tends to predict more new phrases and always generate a spurious date. While the other hybrid models are able to address this issue and more constraint to the original phrases from the source input.

RRED : A Radiology Report Error Detector based on Deep Learning Framework

Dabin Min[1*], Kaeun Kim[1*], Jong Hyuk Lee[1], Yisak Kim[123], Chang Min Park[123]
[1]Department of Radiology, Seoul National University Hospital
[2]Interdisciplinary Program in Bioengineering, Seoul National University Graduate School
[3]Department of Radiology, Seoul National University College of Medicine
{reonaledo, jonghyuklee, yisakk, morphius}@snu.ac.kr
kaeun.kim@uwaterloo.ca

Abstract

Radiology report is an official record of radiologists' interpretation of patients' radiographs and it's a crucial component in the overall medical diagnostic process. However, it can contain various types of errors that can lead to inadequate treatment or delay in diagnosis. To address this problem, we propose a deep learning framework to detect errors in radiology reports. Specifically, our method detects errors between findings and conclusion of chest X-ray reports based on a supervised learning framework. To compensate for the lack of data availability of radiology reports with errors, we develop an error generator to systematically create artificial errors in existing reports. In addition, we introduce a Medical Knowledge-enhancing Pre-training to further utilize the knowledge of abbreviations and key phrases frequently used in the medical domain. We believe that this is the first work to propose a deep learning framework for detecting errors in radiology reports based on a rich contextual and medical understanding. Validation on our radiologist-synthesized dataset, based on MIMIC-CXR, shows 0.80 and 0.95 of the area under precision-recall curve (AUPRC) and the area under the ROC curve (AUROC) respectively, indicating that our framework can effectively detect errors in the real-world radiology reports.

1 Introduction

Radiology report is a document containing official interpretation of patients' radiographs which is used as an important communication tool between radiologists and referring physicians (Wallis and McCoubrie, 2011). The major components of the report include basic demographic information (e.g. patient's name, identifying number), **findings** which explains the image findings along with pertinent clinical information, and **conclusion** (also called impression) which is a list of summary statements of radiographic study conclusion and recommendations for further evaluation and patient management (Wilcox, 2006). Medical treatment decisions are often based on the findings and conclusions of the radiology report (Sistrom and Langlotz, 2005). This explains how the radiologic contribution to inappropriate or delayed diagnosis overall is likely to be substantial (Bruno et al., 2015).

Radiology report errors can be categorized and defined in different ways, mostly based on their causes. Kim and Mansfield classified the errors in 12 types which include errors caused by underreading, location of the lesion, and faulty reasoning. Pinto et al. claim that radiology report errors can be classified based on 4 main reasons why radiologists are sued which include observer errors, errors in interpretation, and failure to suggest proper recommendations. Sangwaiya et al. has analyzed errors on location and size discrepancy of lesions in radiology reports. Combining these works, we conclude that the errors that contribute most to inappropriate or delayed diagnosis are radiologists failing to identify and interpret abnormalities, and discrepancies in size or location of the lesions reported.

Although there have been sufficient discussions in previous studies on methods to reduce errors in radiology reports, research on algorithms to directly detect such errors has been conducted at a very basic level. Lee et al. proposed a software that detects the laterality error for the side or sites between the radiology report and its examination name. Minn et al. proposed an algorithm to detect gender and laterality mismatch in report and its metadata. Zech et al. proposed a LSTM (Hochreiter and Schmidhuber, 1997) based neural model to detect inappropriate insertions, deletions, and substitutions of words in radiology reports. As such, existing studies on error detection in radiology reports were conducted only on local parts such as gender, laterality, and a single word, and most

*These authors contributed equally.

Proceedings of the 4th Clinical Natural Language Processing Workshop, pages 41 - 52
July 14, 2022 ©2022 Association for Computational Linguistics

of these were done by simple matching without considering deep contextual meanings. Unfortunately, in real life, radiologists' error occur due to more complicated reasons that cannot be covered by these approaches. Considering how radiologists record their interpretation and communicate with referring physicians, capturing and understanding the contextual meaning of each section in the report is an important part for practical error detectors that can be used in real life.

In the field of NLP, many pre-trained language models (PLMs) are showing remarkable achievement in various tasks of natural language understanding since the advent of ELMo (Peters et al., 2018) and BERT (Devlin et al., 2018). Recently, several studies on PLM that utilize world knowledge for language understanding have appeared, showing outstanding results not only in the general domain but also in domain-specific tasks (Zhang et al., 2019; Sun et al., 2019, 2020, 2021; Wang et al., 2020). Specifically, PLMs specialized in the medical domain such as ClinicalBERT (Alsentzer et al., 2019) and BioMegatron (Shin et al., 2020) have shown notable performance in the medical NLP tasks.

Despite the remarkable achievement in the field of NLP, the main barrier to apply these technologies, is the absence of radiology reports with errors to perform PLM supervised learning. Two reasons are identified behind the lack of accessible data. First, identifying errors in radiology reports can only be done by well-trained radiologists which is time-consuming and requires costly manual work. Second, in fact, radiology report errors do not occur as often enough for them to be collected and used to train deep learning models. It is estimated that in a daily practice, the rate of radiology report errors that are substantial to result in inappropriate or delayed diagnosis is less than 4% (Berlin, 2007). Also, when considering the different types of errors, classifying and collecting enough data for each type of error is an unrealistic approach.

Here, we introduce two novel approaches to identify errors in radiology reports based on the understanding of the nature of radiology reports while overcoming the challenge created by inadequate radiology report error data: 1) To compensate for the lack of data availability of radiology reports with errors, we introduce an artificial **error generator**. The error generator synthesizes errors that mimic radiologists behaviors that potentially cause errors in daily practice. It can generate different types of errors by employing appropriate and relevant medical knowledge. 2) In order to incorporate medical knowledge for detecting complex errors, we introduce a **Medical Knowledge-enhancing Pre-training** task, which is inspired by ERNIE1.0(Sun et al., 2019), to our BERT based error detector. This additional pre-training task allows the detector to directly learn medical abbreviations and frequent phrases in radiology report.

To validate our proposed approach, experiments are performed on MIMIC-CXR (Johnson et al., 2019) with part of it including intentionally generated error by a board-certified radiologists. Furthermore, through additional experiments, the proposed model was able to identify errors in original MIMIC-CXR which was verified by human evaluation. The experiment results show that the error detector can detect errors in real-world data while it is trained on artificial errors generated by the error generator. Additionally, external validation, experiments on domain adaptation, and several ablation studies well prove the generalizability of the error detector and the performance of the knowledge-enhancing pre-training task.

In summary, our main contributions are as follows:

1. We propose **RRED** (**R**adiology **R**eport **E**rror **D**etector) which is a deep learning framework that can detect radiology report errors based on rich understanding of context and medical knowledge.
2. We propose an **error generator** that systematically generates realistic errors in the radiology reports by integrating medical knowledge.

2 Method

Figure 1 illustrates the suggested complete framework. The following sections describe the Error Generator and the Error Detector independently.

2.1 Error Generator

While there can be many types of errors in radiology reports, this study aims to detect errors occurring when writing the conclusion section based on the findings section. In order for the error generator to synthesize realistic radiology report errors, we have categorized the errors into two types based on previous works on categorization of errors in radiology reports. For clarity, Appendix C, Table 9 provides examples of each type of error.

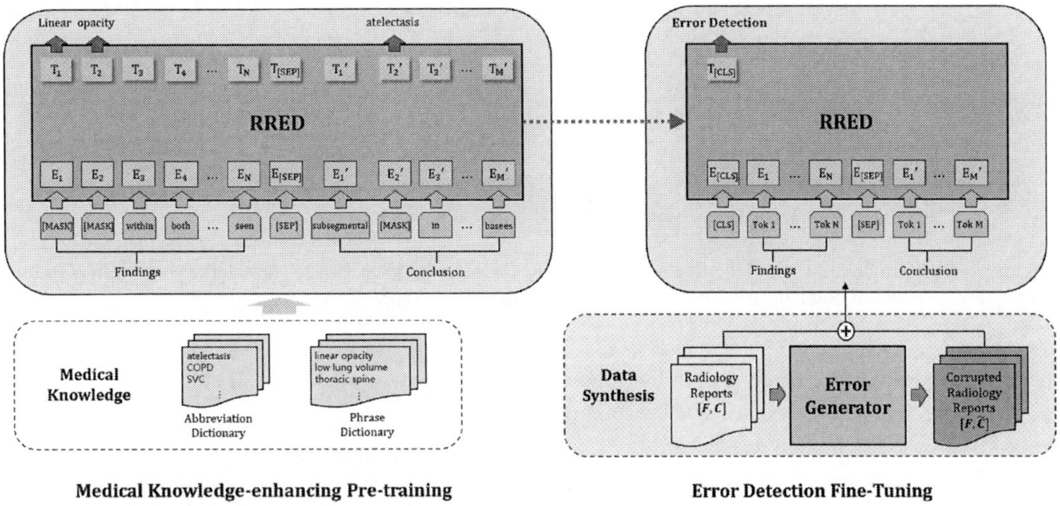

Figure 1: The overall framework of RRED.

2.1.1 Interpretive Error

Interpretive error is any error that changes the interpretation of the findings section in one way or another. This type of error can be subdivided into 3 classes based on their causes.

Faulty reasoning Errors in which findings were identified but attributed to the wrong cause. This occurs due to lack of knowledge or experience of the interpreter or due to lack of information provided in the findings section. For instance, when the conclusion section identifies cardiomegaly while the findings section only identifies pneumothorax, this is clearly an error.

Absence of abnormalities Errors in which abnormalities described in the findings sections are missed in the conclusion section.

Presence of incorrect findings Errors in which abnormalities are described in the conclusion section while the finding section clearly states that there are no findings.

2.1.2 Factual Error

Factual error is any error in which the interpretation and identification of abnormalities are correct while there are discrepancies in the description of the lesion itself. This can be subdivided into 2 classes:

Discrepancy in location of the lesion Errors in which the direction of the lesion location is mistaken (e.g. left $\rightarrow$ right, lower $\rightarrow$ upper).

Discrepancy in numerical measurement of the lesion This type of error includes errors in which the measured unit is incorrectly recorded in the conclusion section (e.g. cm $\rightarrow$ mm, mm $\rightarrow$ m) or when decimal points are misplaced or missed (e.g. $12.20 \rightarrow 1.220$, $8.25 \rightarrow 82.5$).

When factual errors occur, surgeries and biopsies can be operated on the wrong side of the body which can potentially harm the patient physically.

The error generator generates realistic errors from existing radiology reports which can create synthesized datasets that can be used to train the error detector. The synthesized data is required to be realistic enough to train a robust error detector that can detect errors in real life radiology practice. The following sections will describe the details of the error generator.

2.1.3 Error Generator Overview

The error generator consists of two steps: 1) Labeling each report using CheXpert labeler (Irvin et al., 2019) 2) Applying errors based on the tree structure which is based on the CheXpert classes mentioned in the following subsection.

2.1.4 CheXpert Labeler and its tree structure

CheXpert labeler predicts the probability of 14 different classes shown in Figure 2. The error generator first uses this to label each of the radiology reports provided. Two board certified radiologists expanded the labels of CheXpert to group similar labels which creates a tree structure. These similar labels can be interchangeable depending on the interpretation of the radiologist, therefore, cannot be considered incorrect when a different label is used within the similar label group. Figure 2 indicates the similar groups in different colors (other than

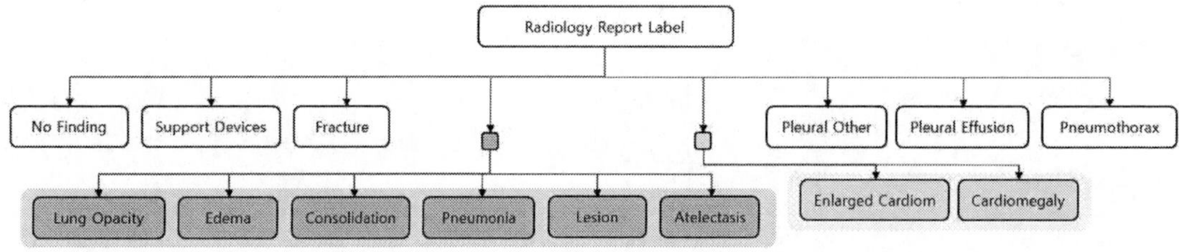

Figure 2: Diagram that illustrates the tree structure of the CheXpert labeler's labels. The labels highlighted in blue and yellow are two different similar label groups, in which the labels can be interchangeable within their own group.

white). In other words, labels within the blue region are interchangeable and the labels within the yellow region are also interchangeable.

2.1.5 Applying errors

Each type of error is applied using the labels labeled by the CheXpert labeler. To avoid any uncertainties, the entire set of labels CheXpert can label is indicated by U. Also, any report that has a label "No Finding" is noted by NF. In order to generate realistic errors, generating faulty reasoning error, absence of abnormalities, or factual error in reports in NF should be avoided. When there are no findings in the provided report, there is no medical significance in misidentifying the cause, removing findings, or creating errors in measurement or location of a lesion.

Faulty reasoning error is applied by randomly swapping the conclusion of the report with other reports' conclusion which has a different label from the original label. Since the CheXpert labeler is a multi-label labeler, the generator precisely and randomly selects a conclusion from the set $\{\mathrm{U} - \mathrm{NF} - \{original\ labels\}\}$. **Absence of abnormalities** is applied by randomly swapping the conclusion of the report with reports in NF. **Presence of incorrect findings** can only be applied when the given radiology report is in NF. It is applied by randomly swapping the conclusion of the reports in $\{\mathrm{U} - \mathrm{NF}\}$.

Discrepancy in location of the lesion is applied by detecting the keywords that indicate the location of the lesion. The keywords are the following: left, right, upper, lower, high, low, big, and small. When the keywords are identified, they are replaced by their counter-keywords which are: right, left, lower, upper, low, high, small, and big, respectively. **Discrepancy in numerical measurement of the lesion** is applied by first detecting any numerical measurement of a lesion (with its unit). Then, by a 50-50 chance, either the unit or the numerical value is changed.

2.2 Error Detector

The Error Detector uses a BERT-base architecture, which showed remarkable achievement in natural language understanding, to detect errors based on syntactic and semantic understanding of the radiology report. The parameters are initialized to the ClinicalBERT parameters which showed better performance in the medical domain.

2.2.1 Medical Knowledge-enhancing Pre-training Task

Radiology reports frequently contain medical abbreviations and phrases with specific meanings and we want the model to be able to capture richer local and global contexts for these. So, we introduce a Medical Knoweldge-enhancing Pre-training task (MKP), inspired by the Knowledge Integrated Masked Language Modeling task of ERNIE1.0, to obtain an integrated representation of such medical knowledge.

Specifically, we selected abbreviations and phrases from a radiology report to directly mask the corresponding tokens and predict the whole masked tokens. Abbreviations were identified using a medical abbreviation dictionary from imantsm and Aristotelis, and phrases were identified using a phrase dictionary created by keyBERT (Grootendorst, 2020) on MIMIC-CXR. For each report, one of the abbreviations or phrases detected in the dictionaries was randomly selected and all corresponding tokens were masked. For other tokens, probabilistic masking strategy was applied in the same way as BERT's masked-language modeling (MLM). To assist the model to capture the meaning of abbreviations and phrases effectively, border tokens of the abbreviation and phrase tokens were not masked.

2.2.2 Training Process

Pre-training MKP is performed on the MIMIC-CXR dataset which includes 91,544 chest X-ray reports. Because ClinicalBERT, which shows a sufficient level of understanding of medical domain text, is used as the initial weight, heavy pre-training for large-scale corpus is not performed. The maximum sequence length, batch size and training epochs were set to 512, 32 and 50 respectively. We performed experiments with models pre-trained for 100 and 150 epochs, but there were no significant differences observed in error detection task performance between these models.

Fine-tuning The training objective of the error detector is to perform a binary classification between original reports and corrupted reports. The training set, namely machine-synthesized dataset, consists of original reports and corrupted reports generated by the error generator. The error detector takes the concatenation of the findings and conclusion sections of the radiology report with a separator token as an input. The input representation is created by adding different segment embedding to distinguish them from each other. Also, positional embedding is added in the same way as BERT. Taking into account the general length of each section in a radiology report, the maximum lengths of findings and conclusion are 338 tokens and 172 tokens, respectively.

3 Experiments

In this section, we describe the datasets, implementation details, and experiment results of the error detection task on several datasets.

3.1 Datasets

3.1.1 MIMIC-CXR

MIMIC-CXR is a publicly available dataset consisting of chest X-rays and corresponding radiology reports, collected from patients between 2011 and 2016 at the Beth Israel Deaconess Medical Center Emergency Department. We used the train-test split disclosed in THE MEDIQA 2021 shared task (Abacha et al., 2021), which consists of 91,544 train sets and 2,000 test sets sampled by simple criterion such as acceptable length. Out of the 91,544 training examples, errors were generated on 88,388 examples (96.55% of the training set) where the percentage of interpretation error and factual error were 85.06% and 14.94%, respectively. For the test set, errors were generated on 1,933 examples (96.65% of the test set) where the percentage of the interpretation error was 79.51% and the percentage of the factual error was 20.49%.

3.1.2 Open-I

Open-I (Demner-Fushman et al., 2016) is another publicly available chest X-ray and radiology report dataset. It is collected from the Indiana Network for Patient Care, consisting of 2,928 reports. We used this dataset as an external dataset to check the generalizability of the model, meaning that both pre-training and fine-tuning is only performed on MIMIC-CXR, and the Open-I is tested in a completely unseen state. Using the error generator, errors were generated on 2,813 examples (96.07% of the dataset) where the percentage of the interpretation error and factual error were 89.69% and 10.31%, respectively.

3.1.3 Radiologist-synthesized dataset

To verify that the error detector trained on the dataset generated by the error generator can work on the real-world error generated by the radiologist, we prepared a dataset in which two board-certified radiologists manually injected errors into the MIMIC-CXR test set of THE MEDIQA 2021 split. Errors were injected into the conclusion section of 111 randomly selected reports out of a total of 2,000 reports, and 7 types of errors were generated to comprehensively verify the various types of errors that could actually occur.

The following types were considered as interpretive errors: Written as a wrong cause that is easy to confuse due to lack of knowledge or experience (Type 1-A, 18%), written as a completely nonsensical disease (Type 1-B, 18%), written in the absence of abnormalities (Type 1-C, 18%), written in the presence of incorrect findings (Type 1-D, 18%). The following types were considered as factual errors: Discrepancy in location of the lesion (Type 2-A, 19%), discrepancy in the numerical measurement of the lesion (Type 2-B, 4%). Additionally, free-form errors that do not fall into any of the six categories (Type 3, 5%).

3.2 Experimental Setups

After generating corrupted MIMIC-CXR using the error generator, we fine-tune the detector model on machine-synthesized data. This machine-synthesized data has 141,420 reports for the training set and 35,356 reports for the validation set. We tune the initial learning rate $\in$ {1e-6, 5e-6, 1e-5,

5e-5, 2e-4, 2e-3}, batch size $\in$ {16, 32}, number of epochs $\in$ {1, 3, 5, 10, 20}. Adam optimizer is used and other hyperparameters are fixed to their default values. The optimal setting is determined by AUPRC on MIMIC-CXR and the decision threshold for binary classification is set to a value representing precision 0.99 on the training set.

3.3 Experimental Results on datasets with Synthesized Error

The performance of our proposed framework for each dataset is shown in Table 1. Test results on MIMIC-CXR and Open-I, which are machine-synthesized datasets using our error generator, showed very high scores in all metrics including the area under precision recall curve (AUPRC) and the area under the ROC curve (AUROC). Showing these results even without training on Open-I, which is collected from a completely different hospital, means that the proposed framework has high generalizability to unseen data. A domain adaptation strategy can be attempted to further improve performance on the external dataset, and the experimental results are provided in Appendix B.

Experimental results on the radiologist-synthesized dataset also showed a significant level of performance. This means that the proposed framework that learns from errors generated by the error generator is highly applicable to real-world data. According to the experimental results, it is expected that the proposed model can detect 63% of all reports with errors with 87% of precision in the actual field. As shown in the precision-recall curve in Appendix A, Figure 3 and Figure 4, precision and recall can be set to an appropriate level by adjusting the decision threshold. Recall by each type of error with different precision criterion is also provided in Appendix A, Table 7.

3.4 Human Evaluation of RRED

To evaluate the practical ability of the proposed framework detecting actual errors in real world dataset, the trained model was inferred to the entire original MIMIC-CXR and the results are evaluated. As a result of inference, it is predicted that errors exist in 408 reports, which is 0.44% of the 93,544 reports. For 100 randomly selected cases, a board-certified radiologist was asked to answer 'Yes'/'No' to the following questions:

1. **Question 1**: There is an error between the findings and the conclusion.

2. **Question 2**: Among those where the answer to Question 1 is 'Yes', factual error that is not appropriate for findings, exists in conclusion. (e.g., discrepancies in laterality, numbers and the existence of unreported facts.)

3. **Question 3**: Among those where the answer to Question 1 is 'Yes', interpretive error that is not appropriate for findings, exists in conclusion. (e.g., faulty reasoning, missing important interpretation.)

The percentages of 'Yes' for the three questions are shown in Table 2. It can be seen that the actual error rate is 81% for the 100 selected cases, which is fairly consistent with the evaluation result on radiology-synthesized data showing about 87% of precision. In addition, it is observed that about 73% of the detected errors are factual errors, about 65% are interpretive errors and 31% are both. The detected examples of report with errors in MIMIC-CXR is shown in Table 3. Through this human evaluation result, we can expect that the proposed framework can be effectively applied in real radiology practice to detect factual errors and interpretive errors.

3.5 Effect of Medical Knowledge-enhancing Pre-training

Three experiments are performed to verify the effectiveness of the proposed Medical Knowledge-enhancing Pre-training (MKP) in various aspects. Table 4 shows the mean performance improvement by MKP for each dataset. The improvement for the machine-synthesized datasets (MIMIC-CXR, Open-I, and Open-I*) seem to be marginal as they are already scoring close to 1.0, but they show a consistent improvement for most metrics. For radiologist-synthesized dataset, the performance gains are more noticeable. Table 5 shows that the level of recall for types 1-A and 1-D, which are interpretive errors, increased. These observations suggest that MKP gives the model a higher level of understanding of medical context and knowledge, allowing the model to detect more complex types of errors.

Table 6 is the ablation result showing the performance change when each component is excluded from MKP. We can see that the masking strategy on medical abbreviations and phases is highly useful. When compared to the result of MLM only, it pushes the AUPRC score from 0.773 to 0.798 on

	AUPRC	AUROC	Precision(ppv)	Recall(sensitivity)	Specificity	Accuracy
MIMIC-CXR	0.998 (0.00)	0.998 (0.00)	0.992 (0.00)	0.964 (0.00)	0.993 (0.00)	0.979 (0.00)
Open-I	0.993 (0.00)	0.994 (0.00)	0.986 (0.00)	0.935 (0.01)	0.988 (0.00)	0.963 (0.00)
Radi-synth*	0.798 (0.03)	0.950 (0.02)	0.870 (0.05)	0.633 (0.03)	0.994 (0.00)	0.974 (0.00)

Table 1: Performance on MIMIC-CXR, Open-I and our Radiologist-synthesized dataset(*). These are the mean performance and its standard deviation from 10 random bootstrap experiments. Since there are no other studies to compare the performance, we only showed the performance of the proposed model without the baseline.

	Percentage of 'Yes'
Question 1	81.00
Question 2	72.84
Question 3	65.43
Question 2 & 3	31.00

Table 2: Quality of RRED assessed by a board-certified radiologist evaluator.

radiology-synthesized dataset. In particular, when the phrase masking is excluded, the performance is significantly reduced(AUPRC 0.798→0.769) showing that knowledge integration for phrases can provide significant understanding ability. Finally, the MLM on radiology report also seems to have an important effect on improving the overall understanding of the report itself.

4 Discussion

Through the evaluation of RRED, we mainly focus on precision rather than recall. This is because this study aims to develop a practical and reliable error detector that can be used in daily practice with a low false alarm rate. We believe that minor errors are worth missing if the alarm can provide a strong guarantee of actual errors to the radiologists.

Despite the fact that the experimental results show notable effectiveness of our approach, there are some limitations. First, the types of errors that have been implemented and experimented with, do not represent the entire scope of radiology report errors. While interpretive and factual errors are critical in the process of diagnosis, expanding the type of errors would be beneficial to reflect real-life errors in radiology practice. Second, the error generator relies on simple random swapping to generate interpretive errors. Although the experimental results show how this method is effective in large dataset like MIMIC-CXR, it is evident that this does not fully reflect the true nature of the real-life interpretive error. If the error generator can improve its' ability to imitate the behavior of radiologists, the error detector is expected to capture complex interpretive errors more precisely.

5 Conclusion

In this paper, we present **RRED**, a **R**adiology **R**eport **E**rror **D**etector based on a rich understanding of context and medical knowledge with supervised deep learning framework. We also propose a error generator for generating synthetic report data with errors to train the detector model. Through various types of evaluations, we showed that our framework can be effectively applied to real world data to detect errors that could cause inappropriate or delayed diagnosis. We also showed the significant effects of the MKP which is a proposed pre-training task to integrate medical knowledge into pre-training language model.

To the best of our knowledge, this is the first work proposing PLM based error detection model for radiology reports. In future works, we plan to develop **RRED2.0** with improved error generator and detector: 1) We will investigate more systematic approaches to generate a broader range of errors in radiology reports, in an effort to expand and improve the usability of the radiology report error detector. 2) We will expand this work to develop a vision-language error detector that can detect errors also in the findings section which is intended to record findings when reading radiographs.

We expect this work to become a practical foolproof system that can reduce critical errors in radiology reports to improve the quality of radiology reporting process and further, the entire diagnosis process.

References

Asma Ben Abacha, Yassine M'rabet, Yuhao Zhang, Chaitanya Shivade, Curtis Langlotz, and Dina Demner-Fushman. 2021. Overview of the mediqa 2021 shared task on summarization in the medical domain. In *Proceedings of the 20th Workshop on Biomedical Language Processing*, pages 74–85.

Emily Alsentzer, John R Murphy, Willie Boag, Wei-Hung Weng, Di Jin, Tristan Naumann, and Matthew

Error Type	Findings	Conclusion
Factual	The cardiomediastinal and hilar contours are stable. There has been interval increase in the **right pleural effusion** with a rounded contour concerning for loculation. There is no left pleural effusion. There is no pneumothorax. There is no focal consolidation concerning for pneumonia. Pulmonary vasculature is within normal limits.	Enlarged **left pleural effusion**, now possibly loculated.
Interpretive	A portable frontal chest radiograph shows the **large left lower lobe mass seen on recent CT chest**. New opacity adjacent to the aortic knob could represent pneumonia or fluid tracking up into the fissure. There is no appreciable pleural effusion or pneumothorax. The visualized upper abdomen is unremarkable.	Possible small left upper lobe pneumonia or pleural effusion extending into the major fissure. Large left lung mass, **less likely malignant**.
Both	Elevation of the **left hemidiaphragm** is new since prior exams, **with minimal adjacent relaxation atelectasis of the left lower lobe**. The cardiomediastinal contours are within normal limits. The bilateral hila are unremarkable. The lungs are clear without focal consolidation. There is no evidence of pulmonary vascular congestion. There is no pneumothorax or pleural effusion.	New **right hemidiaphragmatic** elevation. **Consider evaluation right hemidiaphragm function**. Otherwise, no acute cardiopulmonary process.

Table 3: Examples of actual errors detected in MIMIC-CXR by RRED. We can see that the error actually exists in the highlighted area for each error type. In the example of factual error, the location is described differently. In the example of interpretive error, the mass of the left lung is overestimated as less malignant. In the last example, there is not only a discrepancy of location, but also the important information of the findings is over-summarized.

	AUPRC	AUROC	Precision(ppv)	Recall(sensitivity)	Specificity	Accuracy
MIMIC-CXR	0.001 (<.001)	0.001 (<.001)	0.003 (<.001)	0.018 (<.001)	0.003 (<.001)	0.010 (<.001)
Open-I	0.001 (.065)	0.002 (<.001)	-0.001 (.410)	0.011 (<.001)	-0.001 (.300)	0.005 (<.001)
Open-I*	0.001 (.016)	0.000 (.071)	0.003 (<.001)	-0.007 (<.001)	0.002 (<.001)	-0.002 (<.001)
Radi-synth	0.057 (<.001)	0.006 (<.001)	0.061 (<.001)	0.047 (.005)	0.003 (<.001)	0.005 (<.001)

Table 4: Mean performance improvement by Medical Knowledge-enhancing Pre-training for each dataset and p-values of paired t-test. Open-I* indicates the performance of RRED tested after domain adaptation on the Open-I.

	1-A	1-B	1-C	1-D	2-A	2-B	3	Total
w/o MKP	0.20	**0.55**	0.65	0.50	**0.81**	0.20	0.00	0.50
w/ MKP	**0.50**	**0.55**	**0.70**	**0.75**	**0.81**	**0.60**	**0.2**	**0.64**

Table 5: Comparison of recall for each type of error between models with and without MKP.

	AUPRC	AUROC	Precision(ppv)	Recall(sensitivity)	Specificity	Accuracy
Full MKP	**0.798 (0.03)**	0.950 (0.01)	0.870 (0.05)	**0.633 (0.03)**	0.994 (0.00)	**0.974 (0.00)**
– Abbreviation	0.792 (0.03)	**0.951 (0.01)**	**0.873 (0.04)**	0.609 (0.03)	**0.995 (0.00)**	0.972 (0.00)
– Phrase	0.769 (0.04)	**0.951 (0.01)**	0.863 (0.05)	0.632 (0.03)	0.994 (0.00)	0.973 (0.00)
– Abbreviation & Phrase *	0.773 (0.04)	0.945 (0.02)	0.841 (0.05)	0.618 (0.03)	0.993 (0.00)	0.971 (0.00)
No Pre-training	0.741 (0.03)	0.944 (0.01)	0.810 (0.06)	0.586 (0.03)	0.992 (0.00)	0.968 (0.00)

Table 6: Ablation results of Medical Knowledge-enhancing Pre-training (MKP). These are the mean performance and its standard deviation from 10 random bootstrap experiments on Radiologist-synthesized Dataset. – Abbreviation & Phrase * indicates the case where only MLM is considered.

McDermott. 2019. Publicly available clinical bert embeddings. *arXiv preprint arXiv:1904.03323*.

Aristotelis. 2018. wordlist-medicalterms-en.

Leonard Berlin. 2007. Radiologic errors and malpractice: a blurry distinction. *American Journal of Roentgenology*, 189(3):517–522.

Michael A Bruno, Eric A Walker, and Hani H Abujudeh. 2015. Understanding and confronting our mistakes: the epidemiology of error in radiology and strategies for error reduction. *Radiographics*, 35(6):1668–1676.

Dina Demner-Fushman, Marc D Kohli, Marc B Rosenman, Sonya E Shooshan, Laritza Rodriguez, Sameer Antani, George R Thoma, and Clement J McDonald. 2016. Preparing a collection of radiology examinations for distribution and retrieval. *Journal of the American Medical Informatics Association*, 23(2):304–310.

Jacob Devlin, Ming-Wei Chang, Kenton Lee, and Kristina Toutanova. 2018. Bert: Pre-training of deep bidirectional transformers for language understanding. *arXiv preprint arXiv:1810.04805*.

Maarten Grootendorst. 2020. Keybert: Minimal keyword extraction with bert.

Sepp Hochreiter and Jürgen Schmidhuber. 1997. Long short-term memory. *Neural computation*, 9(8):1735–1780.

imantsm. 2022. medical_abbreviations.

Jeremy Irvin, Pranav Rajpurkar, Michael Ko, Yifan Yu, Silviana Ciurea-Ilcus, Chris Chute, Henrik Marklund, Behzad Haghgoo, Robyn Ball, Katie Shpanskaya, et al. 2019. Chexpert: A large chest radiograph dataset with uncertainty labels and expert comparison. In *Proceedings of the AAAI conference on artificial intelligence*, volume 33, pages 590–597.

Alistair EW Johnson, Tom J Pollard, Seth J Berkowitz, Nathaniel R Greenbaum, Matthew P Lungren, Chih-ying Deng, Roger G Mark, and Steven Horng. 2019. Mimic-cxr, a de-identified publicly available database of chest radiographs with free-text reports. *Scientific data*, 6(1):1–8.

Young W Kim and Liem T Mansfield. 2014. Fool me twice: delayed diagnoses in radiology with emphasis on perpetuated errors. *AJR Am J Roentgenol*, 202(3):465–470.

Young Han Lee, Jaemoon Yang, and Jin-Suck Suh. 2015. Detection and correction of laterality errors in radiology reports. *Journal of digital imaging*, 28(4):412–416.

Matthew J Minn, Arash R Zandieh, and Ross W Filice. 2015. Improving radiology report quality by rapidly notifying radiologist of report errors. *Journal of digital imaging*, 28(4):492–498.

Matthew E. Peters, Mark Neumann, Mohit Iyyer, Matt Gardner, Christopher Clark, Kenton Lee, and Luke Zettlemoyer. 2018. Deep contextualized word representations. In *Proceedings of the 2018 Conference of the North American Chapter of the Association for Computational Linguistics: Human Language Technologies, Volume 1 (Long Papers)*, pages 2227–2237, New Orleans, Louisiana. Association for Computational Linguistics.

Antonio Pinto, Luca Brunese, Fabio Pinto, Riccardo Reali, Stefania Daniele, and Luigia Romano. 2012. The concept of error and malpractice in radiology. In *Seminars in Ultrasound, CT and MRI*, volume 33, pages 275–279. Elsevier.

Minal Jagtiani Sangwaiya, Shyla Saini, Michael A Blake, Keith J Dreyer, and Mannudeep K Kalra. 2009. Errare humanum est: frequency of laterality errors in radiology reports. *American Journal of Roentgenology*, 192(5):W239–W244.

Hoo-Chang Shin, Yang Zhang, Evelina Bakhturina, Raul Puri, Mostofa Patwary, Mohammad Shoeybi, and Raghav Mani. 2020. BioMegatron: Larger biomedical domain language model. In *Proceedings of the 2020 Conference on Empirical Methods in Natural Language Processing (EMNLP)*, pages 4700–4706, Online. Association for Computational Linguistics.

Chris L Sistrom and Curtis P Langlotz. 2005. A framework for improving radiology reporting. *Journal of the American College of Radiology*, 2(2):159–167.

Yu Sun, Shuohuan Wang, Shikun Feng, Siyu Ding, Chao Pang, Junyuan Shang, Jiaxiang Liu, Xuyi Chen, Yanbin Zhao, Yuxiang Lu, et al. 2021. Ernie 3.0: Large-scale knowledge enhanced pre-training for language understanding and generation. *arXiv preprint arXiv:2107.02137*.

Yu Sun, Shuohuan Wang, Yukun Li, Shikun Feng, Xuyi Chen, Han Zhang, Xin Tian, Danxiang Zhu, Hao Tian, and Hua Wu. 2019. Ernie: Enhanced representation through knowledge integration. *arXiv preprint arXiv:1904.09223*.

Yu Sun, Shuohuan Wang, Yukun Li, Shikun Feng, Hao Tian, Hua Wu, and Haifeng Wang. 2020. Ernie 2.0: A continual pre-training framework for language understanding. In *Proceedings of the AAAI Conference on Artificial Intelligence*, volume 34, pages 8968–8975.

A Wallis and P McCoubrie. 2011. The radiology report—are we getting the message across? *Clinical radiology*, 66(11):1015–1022.

Ruize Wang, Duyu Tang, Nan Duan, Zhongyu Wei, Xuanjing Huang, Guihong Cao, Daxin Jiang, Ming Zhou, et al. 2020. K-adapter: Infusing knowledge into pre-trained models with adapters. *arXiv preprint arXiv:2002.01808*.

John R Wilcox. 2006. The written radiology report. *Applied Radiology*, 35(7):33.

John Zech, Jessica Forde, Joseph J Titano, Deepak Kaji, Anthony Costa, and Eric Karl Oermann. 2019. Detecting insertion, substitution, and deletion errors in radiology reports using neural sequence-to-sequence models. *Annals of translational medicine*, 7(11).

Zhengyan Zhang, Xu Han, Zhiyuan Liu, Xin Jiang, Maosong Sun, and Qun Liu. 2019. Ernie: Enhanced language representation with informative entities. *arXiv preprint arXiv:1905.07129*.

A Appendix

Figure 3 and Figure 4 shows the Precision-Recall curve and ROC curve on Radiologist-synthesized dataset, respectively.

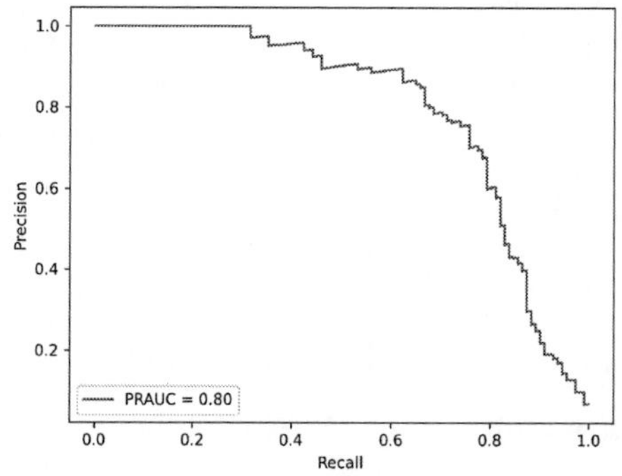

Figure 3: Precision-Recall curve on Radiologist-synthesized dataset

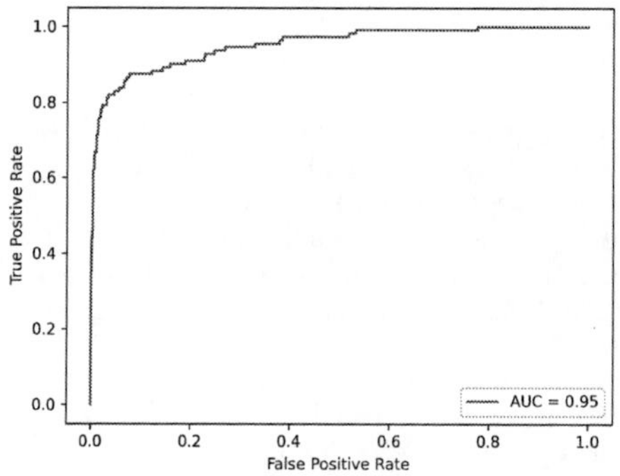

Figure 4: ROC curve on Radiologist-synthesized dataset

Table 7 shows that, even with an precision of 1.0, about 31% of errors can be detected, which means that a certain amount of errors can be detected even with a false-alarm rate close to zero in the real world. When precision is set to 0.96, the recall for factual error (type 2) rises remarkably. Also, the recall of interpretive error (type 1) is increased when it is set to 0.8 to 0.9. The recommended precision settings for a false alarm rate is around 0.96, and for a better detection of interpretive errors is around 0.8 to 0.9.

B Appendix

Table 8 shows the experimental results regarding the effectiveness of the domain adaptation strategy that can ideally improve the performance on

Precision(ppv)	1-A	1-B	1-C	1-D	2-A	2-B	3	Total
1	0.1	0.35	0.5	0.35	0.38	0.2	0	0.31
0.96	0.1	0.35	0.55	0.4	0.71	0.6	0	0.41
0.9	0.35	0.5	0.65	0.6	0.81	0.6	0	0.56
0.8	0.55	0.6	0.7	0.8	0.86	0.6	0.2	0.68

Table 7: Recall by error type with different precision criterion

	AUPRC	AUROC	Precision(ppv)	Recall(sensitivity)	Specificity	Accuracy
Domain Adaptation X	0.993 (0.00)	0.994 (0.00)	0.986 (0.00)	0.935 (0.01)	0.988 (0.00)	0.963 (0.00)
Domain Adaptation O	**0.997 (0.00)**	**0.998 (0.00)**	**0.994 (0.00)**	**0.944 (0.00)**	**0.995 (0.00)**	**0.970 (0.00)**
Difference (P Value of paired t-test)	0.004 (<.001)	0.004 (<.001)	0.008 (<.001)	0.009 (<.001)	0.007 (<.001)	0.008 (<.001)

Table 8: Performance increase by domain adaptation on Open-I dataset

external dataset. For domain adaptation, 1 epoch training is performed on 500 reports of Open-I after fine-tuning on MIMIC-CXR. Even with this light training, a statistically significant level of consistent performance improvement is observed for all metrics. Therefore, when applying the proposed framework to the real life scenarios, performance improvement can be expected if domain adaptation is performed with synthetic data generated by the error generator.

C Appendix

Table 9 provides some examples of errors generated by the error generator using MIMIC-CXR.

Error Class	Sub-class	Examples		
		Findings	**Error-free Conclusion**	**Conclusion with synthesized error**
Inter-pret-ation Error	**Faulty Reasoning**	Heart size is mildly enlarged. The mediastinal and hilar contours are normal. The pulmonary vasculature is normal. Lungs are clear. There is minimal blunting of the left costophrenic sulcus suggestive of a trace left pleural effusion. No right-sided pleural effusion is present. There is no pneumothorax. No acute osseous abnormalities detected.	Small left pleural effusion. Otherwise, no acute cardiopulmonary abnormality.	Improved left lower lobe atelectasis but are persistent consolidation is concerning for aspiration pneumonia. The same is true for the smaller region can of consolidation in the left lung base medially. NG tube in appropriate position.
	Absence of abnormalities	AP portable chest radiograph demonstrates interval placement of a nasogastric tube, which appears to descend the thorax in an uncomplicated course. The terminal tip appears at the anticipated location of the gastroesophageal junction. For standard placement within the stomach advance approximately 8 cm. Streaky opacity in the left lung base is reflective of atelectasis. Bibasilar atelectasis is persistent on the right and slightly improved on the left. Lung volumes are overall low. There is no pneumothorax or pleural effusion. Note is made of chronic deformity of the right humeral neck.	Interval placement of an enteric tube. Recommend advancement approximately 8 cm for more appropriate positioning within the gastric lumen. Bibasilar atelectasis.	No acute cardiopulmonary abnormality.
	Presence of incorrect findings	PA and lateral views of the chest were provided demonstrating clear lungs without focal consolidation, effusion or pneumothorax. The cardiomediastinal silhouette is normal. Bony structures are intact. No free air below the right hemidiaphragm.	No acute intrathoracic process.	In comparison to ___, there is increased opacity of the left mid lung, which may represent fluid trapped in an accessory minor fissure. This could be confirmed with a additional lateral view of the chest or CT. Increased left pleural effusion
Factual Error	**Discrepancy in location of the lesion**	A right PICC ends in the mid SVC. There has been a significant decrease in size of the right pleural effusion but no change in marked right lower lobe atelectasis. There is no pneumothorax. Apical bullous disease is stable. Left basilar atelectasis has improved. There is no new consolidation. The cardiomediastinal silhouette is normal.	Decrease in size of right pleural effusion after thoracentesis. No pneumothorax. Persistent marked right lower lobe atelectasis. Near resolution of left basilar atelectasis. Resolved results were discussed with ___ at 4:30 p.m. on ___ via telephone by Dr ___.	Decrease in size of right pleural effusion after thoracentesis. No pneumothorax. Persistent marked right upper lobe atelectasis. Near resolution of left basilar atelectasis. Resolved results were discussed with ___ at 4:30 p.m. on ___ via telephone by Dr ___.
	Discrepancy in numerical measurement of the lesion	Bilateral atelectasis is mild. An approximately 2.6 x 2.1-cm lobulated opacity projecting over the left apex is new since ___ and has a mass-like appearance. No pleural effusion, pneumothorax, or edema. The heart is top-normal in size, unchanged. No acute osseous abnormality. Biapical pleural thickening is worse on the left.	New 2.6-cm lobulated opacity projecting over the left apex since ___ could be an underlying mass. Chest CT nonemergent is recommended to further evaluate left apex lobulated mass in setting of reported history of a right breast mass.	New 26.0 cm lobulated opacity projecting over the left apex since could be an underlying mass Chest CT non emergent is recommended to further evaluate left apex lobulated mass in setting of reported history of a right breast mass

Table 9: Examples of different types of errors in radiology reports. The column, **Conclusion with synthesized error**, shows the synthesized error from the error generator for each type.

Cross-Language Transfer of High-Quality Annotations: Combining Neural Machine Translation with Cross-Linguistic Span Alignment to Apply NER to Clinical Texts in a Low-Resource Language

Henning Schäfer[1,2] **Ahmad Idrissi-Yaghir**[2,3] **Peter A. Horn**[1] **Christoph M. Friedrich**[2,3]
[1]Institute for Transfusion Medicine, University Hospital Essen,
Hufelandstraße 55, 45147 Essen, Germany
[2]Department of Computer Science, University of Applied Sciences and Arts Dortmund
(FH Dortmund), Emil-Figge-Straße 42, 44227 Dortmund, Germany
[3] Institute for Medical Informatics, Biometry and Epidemiology (IMIBE),
University Hospital Essen, Hufelandstraße 55, 45147 Essen, Germany
{henning.schaefer,peter.horn}@uk-essen.de
{ahmad.idrissi-yaghir,christoph.friedrich}@fh-dortmund.de

Abstract

In this work, cross-linguistic span prediction based on contextualized word embedding models is used together with neural machine translation (NMT) to transfer and apply the state-of-the-art models in natural language processing (NLP) to a low-resource language clinical corpus. Two directions are evaluated: (a) English models can be applied to translated texts to subsequently transfer the predicted annotations to the source language and (b) existing high-quality annotations can be transferred beyond translation and then used to train NLP models in the target language. Effectiveness and loss of transmission is evaluated using the German Berlin-Tübingen-Oncology Corpus (BRONCO) dataset with transferred external data from NCBI disease, SemEval-2013 drug-drug interaction (DDI) and i2b2/VA 2010 data. The use of English models for translated clinical texts has always involved attempts to take full advantage of the benefits associated with them (large pre-trained biomedical word embeddings). To improve advances in this area, we provide a general-purpose pipeline to transfer any annotated BRAT or CoNLL format to various target languages. For the entity class medication, good results were obtained with 0.806 $F1$-score after re-alignment. Limited success occurred in the diagnosis and treatment class with results just below 0.5 $F1$-score due to differences in annotation guidelines.

1 Introduction

Clinical texts contain many important buried information that can be accessed through natural language processing (NLP). Systematic analysis of this vast amount of data can improve clinical care and aid in decision making. There are many other applications already in use, such as cohort selection, pharmacovigilance, and quality reporting (Spasić et al., 2020). Clinical text is often available as unstructured texts: Retrospective analysis therefore involves an enormous amount of work (Wu et al., 2019). By using NLP, biomedical concepts can be extracted and processed using named entity recognition (NER), allowing large amounts of text on specific topics of interest to be retrospectively analyzed. While biomedical text is intended for publications, clinical text is written by and aimed at health care professionals. They are written under time pressure and are heterogeneous in terms of abbreviations, omission of words, and medical jargon to keep information density high (Leaman et al., 2015).

Compared to English texts, the processing of non-English clinical texts by NLP is far from what is actually possible by the current state-of-the-art (Névéol et al., 2018; Schneider et al., 2020). This is due to the fact that in the U.S., Health Insurance Portability and Accountability (HIPAA) clearly regulates which 18 different identifiers of protected health information (PHI) must be removed in order for a document to be considered anonymized, creating many facilitators for de-identification of clinical texts (Yogarajan et al., 2020; Ahmed et al., 2020). Based on these rules, large clinical datasets such as Medical Information Mart for Intensive Care III (MIMIC-III) (Johnson et al., 2016) and shared tasks with high-quality annotations have been published, resulting in research and tools for processing English clinical texts being widely developed.

Proceedings of the 4th Clinical Natural Language Processing Workshop, pages 53 - 62
July 14, 2022 ©2022 Association for Computational Linguistics

With regard to the availability of NLP tools for other languages, there are major differences, for example in the processing of German clinical texts: Anonymization is left to individual institutions, data protection officers, and ethics committees, which means that there are no uniform regulations. The state-of-the-art for German texts lags behind and, despite great efforts (Hahn et al., 2018), continues to be limited to rule-based systems (Roller et al., 2020) or is often based on in-house data (Richter-Pechanski et al., 2021), which means that neither the data nor the trained models can be shared (Carlini et al., 2021). Freely available large anonymized datasets with high-quality annotated German clinical texts are therefore non-existent.

In order to bridge this gap, this work provides a general-purpose pipeline to transfer annotated datasets in BRAT or CoNLL format to various target languages[1]. Approaches based on neural machine translation (NMT) have recently been applied to NER tasks (Xie et al., 2018; Mayhew et al., 2017; Yan et al., 2021). Improved translation quality through advances in neural machine translation (Ng et al., 2019; Tran et al., 2021) have reached a level that allows the transfer of predictions or annotated data in combination with word alignments (Jalili Sabet et al., 2020; Dou and Neubig, 2021) to other languages.

In this work, the Berlin-Tübingen-Oncology Corpus (BRONCO) (Kittner et al., 2021) is used and treated as a zero-resource dataset, for which English models and external biomedical and clinical datasets are used instead. The aim is to evaluate whether low-resource languages can benefit from the available English resources. The methodology of this work can be applied to other clinical datasets and languages, as word alignment with contextualized embeddings through multilingual BERT (Devlin et al., 2019) covers 104 languages. Accordingly, multilingual models are available for translation, e.g., the mBART (Tang et al., 2021) many-to-many model covers 50 languages.

2 Data

The BRONCO corpus (Kittner et al., 2021) is the first small, fully anonymized dataset for German clinical texts, that can be accessed via a data usage agreement form request. The dataset contains 200 discharge reports of hepatocellular carcinoma and melanoma, with 50 reports retained by the authors as independent test data. Due to strict data protection regulations and to make de-anonymization more difficult, the discharge summaries were shuffled into sentences so that the clinical context is only preserved at sentence level. It includes three annotated entity classes: diagnosis, medication and treatment (see Table 1). According to Kittner et al. (2021) the annotation process was performed by 2 groups of annotators, group A (2 medical experts) and group B (3 medical experts and 3 medical students). Conflicting annotations were resolved in the final version of BRONCO.

Table 1: Berlin-Tübingen-Oncology Corpus (BRONCO) descriptive statistics.

Entity	BRONCO 150	BRONCO 50	Total
Diagnosis	4,080	1,165	5,245
Treatment	3,050	816	3,866
Medication	1,630	383	2,013
Total	8,760	2,364	11,124
No. of Documents	150	50	200
No. of Sentences	8,976	2,458	11,434
No. of Tokens	70,572	19,370	89,942

For the 3 entity classes in BRONCO, 3 existing English external datasets are used. In order to use external data, the underlying documents and annotation guidelines should match if possible.

2.1 Medication

To fine-tune models for recognizing medication entities in BRONCO, the SemEval-2013 drug-drug interaction (DDI) (Segura-Bedmar et al., 2011) corpus will serve as an external English resource. The corpus is semantically annotated and contains documents describing drug-drug interactions from the DrugBank database and MEDLINE, and includes annotated medication text-spans. It is the only corpus that covers both generic names and brand names.

2.2 Diagnosis

The BRONCO entity class diagnosis is defined by the annotation guidelines as a disease, symptom or medical observation that can be matched with the German modification of the International Classification of Diseases (ICD-10). The NCBI disease corpus (Doğan et al., 2014) is used for this purpose, although it differs in terms of document style and annotation guidelines.

[1] https://github.com/0xhesch/CLAT-cross-lingual-annotation-transfer

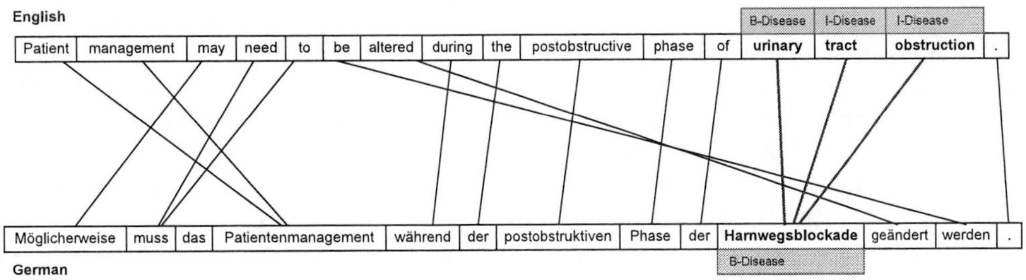

Figure 1: Behaviour of words in relation to the translated target language (here German). There are considerable differences in sentence structure, number of words and required word count for the description of a single medical term. The source to target token positions are to be resolved by word alignment systems to transfer annotations across languages.

Table 2: The table shows a sentence in BIO format from the NCBI dataset, translated into German along with the aligned annotation of the tokens.

Identification	O	Identifizierung	O
of	O	von	O
APC2	O	APC2	O
,	O	,	O
a	O	einem	O
homologue	O	Homologen	O
of	O	des	O
the	O	Tumorsuppressors	B-Disease
adenomatous	B-Disease	der	O
polyposis	I-Disease	adenomatösen	B-Disease
coli	I-Disease	Polyposis	I-Disease
tumour	I-Disease	coli	I-Disease
suppressor	O	.	O
.	O		

2.3 Treatment

Analogous to diagnosis, the BRONCO treatment class is a diagnostic procedure, e.g., surgery or systemic cancer treatment, found in the German Operationen and Prozedurenschlüssel (OPS) coding system. There is no exact match for this, although the treatment class of the i2b2/VA 2010 challenge data (Uzuner et al., 2011) shows overlapping annotation guidelines. Here, the treatment class also comprises medications which has to be taken into account in the methodology.

3 Methods

The experiments are divided into two parts. First, the German clinical dataset is treated as a zero-resource problem. This means that none of the annotated data is used to develop recognition models for the three entity classes diagnosis, medication and treatment. Instead, three existing English high-quality annotated datasets as described in Section 2 are used to train on the entity classes. Inferences are either made based on the translation and are then retroactively aligned to the German text, or models are fine-tuned on the translated form of the English datasets and are directly applied to the German clinical texts.

The second part focuses on the extent to which English pre-trained biomedical language models can be adapted for use in another language. For this purpose, the German dataset is translated and aligned in order to fine-tune large English pre-trained biomedical transformer-based models. The inference is then re-aligned to the German language. This is compared to non-biomedical German and cross-lingual transformer-based language models. In this way, the loss due to translation and subsequent alignment can be determined and weighed against the benefits of large biomedical language models that would not otherwise be available.

Based on current benchmarks (Ng et al., 2019; Tran et al., 2021), the selection for translation models fell on the directional WMT 19 en $\leftrightarrow$ de model from Facebook AI Research (FAIR) as well as the multilingual WMT 21 model that covers 7 different languages. Since careful review of the translation quality of some clinical texts did not reveal any relevant deficiencies, the more resource-friendly WMT 19 model was chosen. For the span alignment of the annotations, Simalign (Jalili Sabet et al., 2020) is used without fine-tuning a parallel corpus. The work of Jalili Sabet et al. (2020) has shown that word alignments via contextualized embeddings from multilingual language models achieve good results. Here, the Itermax algorithm is used with contextualized word embeddings from multilingual BERT (Devlin et al., 2019). Itermax aligns two parallel sentences at token level with cosine-similarity, where for each token the parallel vectors co-represent the context of the token within its sentence. Since for many sentences no mutual argmaxes are available, the suggestion mentioned by the authors to perform this process iteratively is followed. This also allows for token of the source language to be mapped to multiple token in the target language. This seems reasonable for clinical entities. For example, *urinary tract obstruction* is merged to only one token *Harnwegsblockade* in the German language (see Figure 1).

For fine-tuning language models, all experiments use the hyperparameters as described in Table 6. All experiments were conducted on an NVIDIA V100 SXM2 GPU.

3.1 Zero-Resource

Here, two variants seem reasonable. First, datasets with annotations can be translated from en $\rightarrow$ de (forward-passed), thereby training models directly in the target language. On the other hand, low-resource language texts can be translated into English (de $\rightarrow$ en) and the prediction subsequently re-aligned (en $\rightarrow$ de) to the originating language (backward-pass). Both variants are visualized as detailed workflows in Figure 2 (forward-pass) and Figure 3 (backward-pass).

3.1.1 Forward-Pass

For medication, the DDI corpus will be forward-passed to predict medication mentions in German text. The DrugBank, as well as the MEDLINE portion of the dataset, are merged. Except for drugs and brand names, all other entities are omitted. The two entity classes drug and brand name are then merged into a single medication entity class.

For diagnosis, the NCBI data is forward-passed. The general process of translation and word alignment for this class is shown as an example in Figure 1. A sample sentence of the resulting translated German NCBI corpus is shown in Table 2.

For treatment, the i2b2/VA 2010 challenge data is forward-passed. The i2b2 annotation guidelines state, that treatment also covers medication. Prior to training the model on the treatment entity class, drug predictions based on the DDI model that overlap with i2b2 treatment entities are therefore removed.

3.1.2 Backward-Pass

For the backward-pass, the three external resources are used untranslated to directly fine-tune Bio_Discharge_Summary_BERT (Alsentzer et al., 2019), a state-of-the-art biomedical language model that was initialized with BioBERT (Lee et al., 2019) and then further trained on discharge summaries from MIMIC-III.

For prediction, the German BRONCO 150 dataset is then translated into English using FAIR's WMT 19 model de $\rightarrow$ en, without word alignments. The inference on translated BRONCO 150 sentences are then re-aligned with the original German sentences.

3.2 Fine-Tuning

This experiment aims to determine the loss incurred by translation and re-alignment for named entity recognition within the clinical domain and uses a large pre-trained biomedical language model. Note that this does require available annotations. Since the initial baseline of the authors of the BRONCO dataset does not include transformer-based results, this experiment also covers cross-lingual and German-specific pre-trained experiments. At the same time, these experiments will test whether non-biomedical models are suitable for German clinical texts. For this purpose mBERT (Devlin et al., 2019), GBERT (Chan et al., 2020), GELECTRA (Chan et al., 2020) and XLM-R (Conneau et al., 2020) are used in the base, as well as in the large versions if available.

To take advantage of English biomedical pre-trained language models, Bio_Discharge_Summary_BERT is used as described in Figure 3 which means that the inference takes place on the translation and the annotations are retroactively aligned. BRONCO 150 results are reported through 5-fold cross-validation. For BRONCO 50 evaluation, the models are trained on the full BRONCO 150 data. Results on BRONCO 50 are reported independently by the dataset authors. The evaluation is done by providing the models, as well as the pipeline for translation and retroactive alignments. Since the evaluation on BRONCO 50 must be performed by the curators, the range of models is limited here.

4 Results

4.1 Zero-Resource

The results based on the external data are reported for all 3 entity classes to see if there are differences between translating external datasets into the target language or aligning the inference of the English

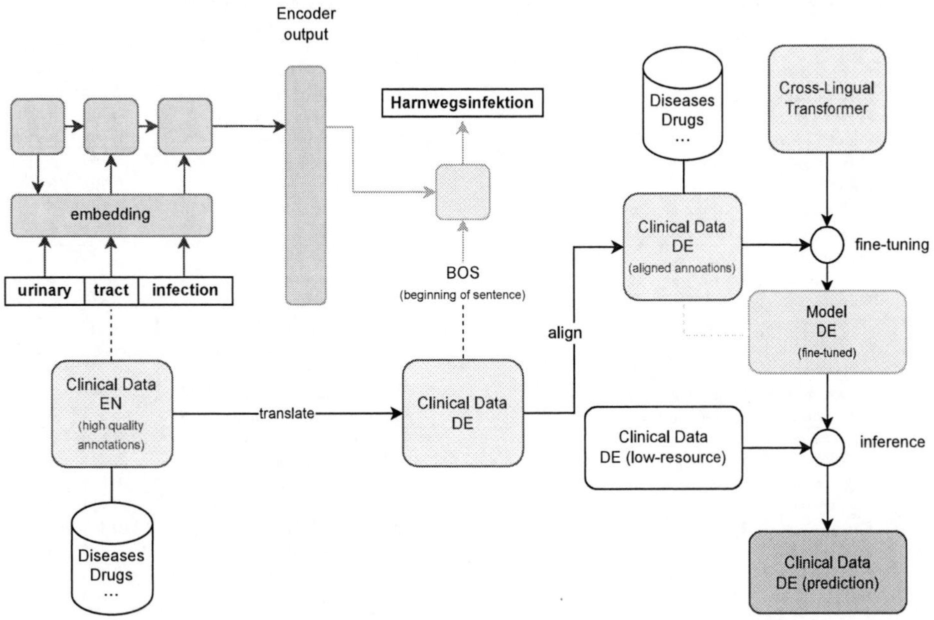

Figure 2: Schematic workflow (forward-pass) to perform prediction for clinical data with few resources. Here, the external English data is translated with annotations and then used to fine-tune cross-lingual language models for the target language. Prediction is then directly applied to the target language.

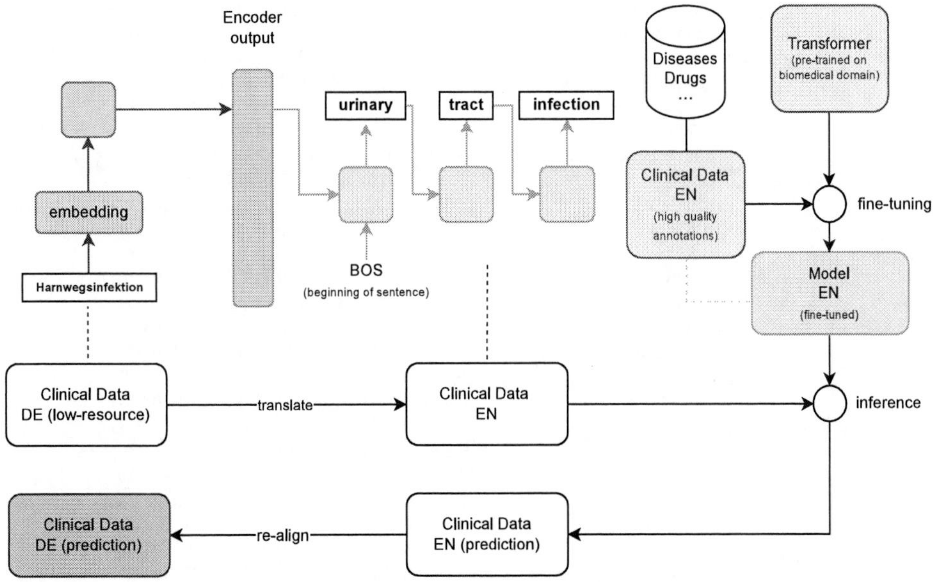

Figure 3: Schematic workflow (backward-pass) to perform prediction for clinical data with few resources. Models trained on external English data are applied to the translation and the prediction is aligned retrospectively.

Table 3: Forward- and backward-pass results on 3 entity classes for BRONCO 150 corpus through external data sources. State denotes if the results were obtained before- or after re-alignment in backward-pass runs.

Target Entity	Method	State	External Data Source	Model	Precision	Recall	F1
Medication	Forward-pass	-	DDI Corpus	deepset/gbert-base	0.637	0.809	0.712
	Forward-pass	-		deepset/gelectra-base	0.605	0.824	0.698
	Forward-pass	-		deepset/gelectra-large	**0.803**	0.769	0.785
	Forward-pass	-		bert-base-multilingual-cased	0.525	0.793	0.631
	Forward-pass	-		xlm-roberta-base	0.600	0.816	0.692
	Forward-pass	-		xlm-roberta-large	0.782	0.798	0.790
	Backward-pass	before re-alignment		Bio_Discharge_Summary_BERT	0.745	0.729	0.737
	Backward-pass	after re-alignment		Bio_Discharge_Summary_BERT	0.788	**0.826**	**0.806**
Diagnosis	Forward-pass	-	NCBI-Disease Corpus	deepset/gbert-base	0.433	0.445	0.439
	Forward-pass	-		deepset/gelectra-base	0.410	0.374	0.391
	Forward-pass	-		deepset/gelectra-large	**0.537**	0.419	0.471
	Forward-pass	-		bert-base-multilingual-cased	0.469	0.370	0.414
	Forward-pass	-		xlm-roberta-base	0.482	0.354	0.408
	Forward-pass	-		xlm-roberta-large	0.476	0.387	0.427
	Backward-pass	before re-alignment		Bio_Discharge_Summary_BERT	0.502	0.378	0.431
	Backward-pass	after re-alignment		Bio_Discharge_Summary_BERT	0.524	**0.474**	**0.498**
Treatment	Forward-pass	-	i2b2/VA 2010	deepset/gbert-base	0.510	0.429	0.466
	Forward-pass	-		deepset/gelectra-base	0.521	0.456	0.486
	Forward-pass	-		deepset/gelectra-large	0.523	0.454	0.486
	Forward-pass	-		bert-base-multilingual-cased	0.473	0.402	0.434
	Forward-pass	-		xlm-roberta-base	0.504	0.411	0.453
	Forward-pass	-		xlm-roberta-large	0.526	0.434	0.475
	Backward-pass	before re-alignment		Bio_Discharge_Summary_BERT	0.476	0.387	0.427
	Backward-pass	after re-alignment		Bio_Discharge_Summary_BERT	**0.536**	**0.463**	**0.497**

Table 4: Average results of 5-fold cross-validation for BRONCO 150 with reported standard deviation. † denotes initial baseline results by Kittner et al. (2021).

Target Entity	Model	Precision	Recall	F1
Medication	CRF†	0.960 (0.008)	0.850 (0.020)	0.900 (0.009)
	CRF+WE†	**0.960 (0.004)**	0.840 (0.009)	0.900 (0.006)
	LSTM†	0.910 (0.050)	0.860 (0.030)	0.880 (0.020)
	LSTM+WE†	0.960 (0.020)	0.870 (0.060)	0.910 (0.040)
	deepset/gbert-base	0.923 (0.019)	0.935 (0.016)	0.929 (0.012)
	deepset/gbert-large	0.929 (0.027)	0.941 (0.018)	0.935 (0.011)
	deepset/gelectra-base	0.850 (0.011)	0.912 (0.013)	0.880 (0.012)
	deepset/gelectra-large	0.951 (0.006)	**0.956 (0.018)**	**0.954 (0.008)**
	bert-base-multilingual-cased	0.926 (0.024)	0.937 (0.009)	0.931 (0.013)
	xlm-roberta-base	0.923 (0.005)	0.932 (0.014)	0.927 (0.006)
	xlm-roberta-large	0.929 (0.011)	0.941 (0.018)	0.935 (0.011)
Diagnosis	CRF†	0.800 (0.010)	0.710 (0.020)	0.750 (0.020)
	CRF+WE†	0.782 (0.006)	0.700 (0.020)	0.740 (0.010)
	LSTM†	0.750 (0.030)	0.690 (0.030)	0.720 (0.010)
	LSTM+WE†	**0.810 (0.080)**	0.740 (0.080)	0.770 (0.080)
	deepset/gbert-base	0.744 (0.012)	0.802 (0.020)	0.772 (0.016)
	deepset/gbert-large	0.769 (0.009)	0.814 (0.015)	0.791 (0.008)
	deepset/gelectra-base	0.692 (0.023)	0.773 (0.026)	0.730 (0.022)
	deepset/gelectra-large	0.789 (0.008)	**0.826 (0.013)**	**0.807 (0.008)**
	bert-base-multilingual-cased	0.740 (0.017)	0.797 (0.022)	0.768 (0.019)
	xlm-roberta-base	0.728 (0.012)	0.792 (0.018)	0.759 (0.013)
	xlm-roberta-large	0.767 (0.012)	0.815 (0.014)	0.790 (0.007)
Treatment	CRF†	**0.860 (0.020)**	0.780 (0.010)	0.820 (0.010)
	CRF+WE†	0.850 (0.020)	0.780 (0.010)	0.810 (0.010)
	LSTM†	0.830 (0.040)	0.790 (0.030)	0.810 (0.020)
	LSTM+WE†	0.850 (0.060)	0.820 (0.070)	0.840 (0.060)
	deepset/gbert-base	0.783 (0.009)	0.830 (0.012)	0.806 (0.009)
	deepset/gbert-large	0.796 (0.023)	0.846 (0.019)	0.820 (0.020)
	deepset/gelectra-base	0.678 (0.015)	0.791 (0.023)	0.730 (0.017)
	deepset/gelectra-large	0.821 (0.009)	0.856 (0.011)	**0.839 (0.010)**
	bert-base-multilingual-cased	0.783 (0.026)	0.839 (0.016)	0.810 (0.022)
	xlm-roberta-base	0.753 (0.005)	0.825 (0.008)	0.788 (0.005)
	xlm-roberta-large	0.821 (0.013)	**0.857 (0.017)**	0.839 (0.014)

Table 5: Results for BRONCO 50. † denotes initial baseline results by Kittner et al. (2021). * denotes that the results are based on the translation and have been re-aligned.

Target Entity	Model	Precision	Recall	F1
Medication	CRF†	0.940	0.870	0.900
	CRF+WE†	**0.950**	0.850	0.900
	LSTM†	**0.950**	0.850	0.890
	LSTM+WE†	0.910	0.890	0.900
	deepset/gbert-base	0.929	**0.958**	**0.943**
	Bio_Discharge_Summary_BERT*	0.921	0.944	0.932
Diagnosis	CRF†	0.790	0.670	0.720
	CRF+WE†	0.770	0.660	0.710
	LSTM†	0.780	0.650	0.710
	LSTM+WE†	0.790	0.650	0.720
	deepset/gbert-base	**0.792**	**0.772**	**0.782**
	Bio_Discharge_Summary_BERT*	0.661	0.689	0.675
Treatment	CRF†	0.830	0.730	0.780
	CRF+WE†	0.810	0.730	0.760
	LSTM†	**0.850**	0.690	0.760
	LSTM+WE†	0.760	0.740	0.750
	deepset/gbert-base	0.782	**0.824**	**0.803**
	Bio_Discharge_Summary_BERT*	0.661	0.742	0.699

models. The results for the forward- and backward-pass are shown in Table 3. For all classes, the backward-pass resulted in better scores, although the difference compared to the forward-pass is not substantial. The results of the German and multilingual models are comparable to the results before the re-alignment step, i.e. on the BRONCO 150 translation. To estimate any loss that may occur due to the translation quality of the WMT 19 en $\leftrightarrow$ de model, the case-sensitive SacreBLEU score (Post, 2018) on the re-translation of BRONCO150 is reported, which resulted in a score of 40.41. The medication class achieved the best results after re-alignment with 0.806 $F1$-score. The classes diagnosis and treatment both remained just below 0.5 $F1$-score, also after re-alignment. Aligning the annotations back to German, increases recall in particular, as e.g. in the case of medication by almost 0.1 $F1$-score. The forward-pass results show that large models are superior. A general outperformance of German-specific language models over multilingual language models is not present.

4.2 Fine-Tuning

Table 4 shows the 5-fold cross-validation results. Here, the BRONCO 150 dataset was fine-tuned using multiple German transformer-based language models and multilingual language models. In addition, the results are also compared to those reported in (Kittner et al., 2021). For all target entities, all transformer-based models except GELECTRA$_{base}$ outperformed the models used by Kittner et al. (2021) and achieved a better $F1$-score. Although, the Conditional Random Field (CRF) and Long Short-Term Memory (LSTM) models reported better precision for all classes, their recall scores were outperformed with the transformer-based models. Overall, the large transformer-based models achieved the highest scores, with GELECTRA$_{large}$ performing the best and reaching an $F1$-score of 0.954 ± 0.008 for medication, 0.807 ± 0.008 for diagnosis and 0.839 ± 0.010 for treatment. The model was followed by XLM-R$_{large}$, which was on par with GBERT$_{large}$ for all the target entities. Altogether, the results show that large German-specific language models perform the best, with XLM-R$_{large}$ being a strong multilingual language model that can even compete with task language-specific models.

The results achieved on the BRONCO 50 dataset show similar findings, where the German-specific language model GBERT$_{base}$ reached the best $F1$-score for all classes. Furthermore, the result achieved through translation and alignment was superior to the models reported in (Kittner et al., 2021) for medication, but these models were not as successful for the classes diagnosis and treatment.

5 Discussion

In the zero-resource setting, there is an advantage in the backward-pass approach over the forward-pass models. Good results could only be achieved for the medication class, but this is not necessarily due to translation and word alignment, but to the nature of the data. For the diagnosis and treatment class, there is no equivalent English dataset that fully matches the annotation guidelines of the German clinical text. The medication class seems unproblematic in that medication terms are more easily aligned, one-to-many token constellations due to translation are rare, and medications are often represented similarly in both languages. Nevertheless, the underlying sentence structure is fundamentally different between English and German, which means that the transfer of the results can be considered successful. Further limitations are discussed in Section 6.

These assumptions are also supported by the fine-tuning results, which show that although translation and alignment result in a loss, it is still competitive compared to the initial baseline. Only in the comparison with multilingual and German transformer architectures the disadvantage becomes clear. Provided that annotations are available, a general advantage of English biomedical models over non-

Table 6: Hyperparameters used for fine-tuning transformer-based models on external data and BRONCO 150.

Hyperparameter	Value
Batch size	64 (16 for large models)
Epochs	4
Manual seed	42
Learning rate	4e-5
Max sequence length	512
Optimizer	AdamW (Loshchilov and Hutter, 2019)
Adam epsilon	1e-8

domain language models on German clinical texts can therefore not be confirmed.

6 Conclusion and Future Work

The results of this work show that English language models can in principle be applied to other languages in clinical contexts. Translated training data can serve as a good basis and approach for languages where there are otherwise no resources. In a zero-resource scenario, the approach is limited to the extent that it works for data where the documents and annotation guidelines match across languages. Cross-linguistic differences in the available standards that annotators work with also play a limiting role here. BRONCO corpus is based on German ICD-10 and German OPS standards, which is also reflected in the annotation guidelines, making it difficult to apply external data.

Transfer in the clinical setting was evaluated with only one language pair (en $\leftrightarrow$ de). Success with other language pairs depends not only on the annotation standard, but also on the similarity of the languages (grammar and morphology). Transfer can only succeed if the quality of translation and word alignment is sufficient, which can be expected between Indo-European languages, but can be much more difficult when transferring between language families.

Practical applications on other low-resource languages is left for future work. It would be interesting to see the effect of adding a few annotated samples to the external data. In this context, zero-shot and few-shot approaches would be a useful addition as a comparator. For comparison, it would also be helpful to have a non-alignment baseline that is fine-tuned to English data and directly infers German test data.

Acknowledgements

We thank Robert Martin of the Faculty of Mathematics and Natural Sciences at the Humboldt University of Berlin for the independent evaluation of the results on the BRONCO 50 test data.

This work was funded by a PhD grant from the DFG Research Training Group 2535 Knowledge- and data-based personalization of medicine at the point of care (WisPerMed), University of Duisburg-Essen, Germany.

References

Tanbir Ahmed, Md Momin Al Aziz, and Noman Mohammed. 2020. De-identification of electronic health record using neural network. *Scientific Reports*, 10(1):18600.

Emily Alsentzer, John Murphy, William Boag, Wei-Hung Weng, Di Jindi, Tristan Naumann, and Matthew McDermott. 2019. Publicly available clinical BERT embeddings. In *Proceedings of the 2nd Clinical Natural Language Processing Workshop*, pages 72–78, Minneapolis, Minnesota, USA. Association for Computational Linguistics.

Nicholas Carlini, Florian Tramer, Eric Wallace, Matthew Jagielski, Ariel Herbert-Voss, Katherine Lee, Adam Roberts, Tom Brown, Dawn Song, Ulfar Erlingsson, et al. 2021. Extracting training data from large language models. In *30th USENIX Security Symposium (USENIX Security 21)*, pages 2633–2650.

Branden Chan, Stefan Schweter, and Timo Möller. 2020. German's next language model. In *Proceedings of the 28th International Conference on Computational Linguistics*, pages 6788–6796, Barcelona, Spain (Online). International Committee on Computational Linguistics.

Alexis Conneau, Kartikay Khandelwal, Naman Goyal, Vishrav Chaudhary, Guillaume Wenzek, Francisco Guzmán, Edouard Grave, Myle Ott, Luke Zettlemoyer, and Veselin Stoyanov. 2020. Unsupervised cross-lingual representation learning at scale. In *Proceedings of the 58th Annual Meeting of the Association for Computational Linguistics*, pages 8440–8451, Online. Association for Computational Linguistics.

Jacob Devlin, Ming-Wei Chang, Kenton Lee, and Kristina Toutanova. 2019. BERT: Pre-training of deep bidirectional transformers for language understanding. In *Proceedings of the 2019 Conference of the North American Chapter of the Association for Computational Linguistics: Human Language Technologies, Volume 1 (Long and Short Papers)*, pages 4171–4186, Minneapolis, Minnesota. Association for Computational Linguistics.

Zi-Yi Dou and Graham Neubig. 2021. Word alignment by fine-tuning embeddings on parallel corpora. In *Proceedings of the 16th Conference of the European Chapter of the Association for Computational Linguistics: Main Volume*, pages 2112–2128, Online. Association for Computational Linguistics.

Rezarta Islamaj Doğan, Robert Leaman, and Zhiyong Lu. 2014. NCBI disease corpus: A resource for disease name recognition and concept normalization. *Journal of Biomedical Informatics*, 47:1–10.

Udo Hahn, Franz Matthies, Christina Lohr, and Markus Löffler. 2018. 3000pa - towards a national reference corpus of german clinical language. In *Building Continents of Knowledge in Oceans of Data: The Future of Co-Created eHealth - Proceedings of MIE 2018, Medical Informatics Europe, Gothenburg, Sweden, April 24-26, 2018*, volume 247 of *Studies in Health Technology and Informatics*, pages 26–30. IOS Press.

Masoud Jalili Sabet, Philipp Dufter, François Yvon, and Hinrich Schütze. 2020. SimAlign: High quality word alignments without parallel training data using static and contextualized embeddings. In *Findings of the Association for Computational Linguistics: EMNLP 2020*, pages 1627–1643, Online. Association for Computational Linguistics.

Alistair E.W. Johnson, Tom J. Pollard, Lu Shen, Liwei H. Lehman, Mengling Feng, Mohammad Ghassemi, Benjamin Moody, Peter Szolovits, Leo Anthony Celi, and Roger G. Mark. 2016. MIMIC-III, a freely accessible critical care database. *Scientific Data*, 3(1):160035.

Madeleine Kittner, Mario Lamping, Damian T Rieke, Julian Götze, Bariya Bajwa, Ivan Jelas, Gina Rüter, Hanjo Hautow, Mario Sänger, Maryam Habibi, Marit Zettwitz, Till de Bortoli, Leonie Ostermann, Jurica Ševa, Johannes Starlinger, Oliver Kohlbacher, Nisar P Malek, Ulrich Keilholz, and Ulf Leser. 2021. Annotation and initial evaluation of a large annotated German oncological corpus. *JAMIA Open*, 4(2).

Robert Leaman, Ritu Khare, and Zhiyong Lu. 2015. Challenges in clinical natural language processing for automated disorder normalization. *Journal of Biomedical Informatics*, 57:28–37.

Jinhyuk Lee, Wonjin Yoon, Sungdong Kim, Donghyeon Kim, Sunkyu Kim, Chan Ho So, and Jaewoo Kang. 2019. BioBERT: a pre-trained biomedical language representation model for biomedical text mining. *Bioinformatics*, 36(4):1234–1240.

Ilya Loshchilov and Frank Hutter. 2019. Decoupled weight decay regularization. In *7th International Conference on Learning Representations, ICLR 2019, New Orleans, LA, USA, May 6-9, 2019*. OpenReview.net.

Stephen Mayhew, Chen-Tse Tsai, and Dan Roth. 2017. Cheap translation for cross-lingual named entity recognition. In *Proceedings of the 2017 Conference on Empirical Methods in Natural Language Processing*, pages 2536–2545, Copenhagen, Denmark. Association for Computational Linguistics.

Nathan Ng, Kyra Yee, Alexei Baevski, Myle Ott, Michael Auli, and Sergey Edunov. 2019. Facebook FAIR's WMT19 news translation task submission. In *Proceedings of the Fourth Conference on Machine Translation (Volume 2: Shared Task Papers, Day 1)*, pages 314–319, Florence, Italy. Association for Computational Linguistics.

Aurélie Névéol, Hercules Dalianis, Sumithra Velupillai, Guergana Savova, and Pierre Zweigenbaum. 2018. Clinical natural language processing in languages other than english: opportunities and challenges. *Journal of biomedical semantics*, 9(1):12.

Matt Post. 2018. A call for clarity in reporting BLEU scores. In *Proceedings of the Third Conference on Machine Translation: Research Papers*, pages 186–191, Belgium, Brussels. Association for Computational Linguistics.

Phillip Richter-Pechanski, Nicolas A Geis, Christina Kiriakou, Dominic M Schwab, and Christoph Dieterich. 2021. Automatic extraction of 12 cardiovascular concepts from german discharge letters using pre-trained language models. *DIGITAL HEALTH*, 7:20552076211057662. PMID: 34868618.

Roland Roller, Laura Seiffe, Ammer Ayach, Sebastian Möller, Oliver Marten, Michael Mikhailov, Christoph Alt, Danilo Schmidt, Fabian Halleck, Marcel Naik, Wiebke Duettmann, and Klemens Budde. 2020. Information extraction models for german clinical text. In *2020 IEEE International Conference on Healthcare Informatics (ICHI)*, pages 1–2.

Elisa Terumi Rubel Schneider, João Vitor Andrioli de Souza, Julien Knafou, Lucas Emanuel Silva e Oliveira, Jenny Copara, Yohan Bonescki Gumiel, Lucas Ferro Antunes de Oliveira, Emerson Cabrera Paraiso, Douglas Teodoro, and Cláudia Maria Cabral Moro Barra. 2020. BioBERTpt - a Portuguese neural language model for clinical named entity recognition. In *Proceedings of the 3rd Clinical Natural Language Processing Workshop*, pages 65–72, Online. Association for Computational Linguistics.

Isabel Segura-Bedmar, Paloma Martínez, and Cesar de Pablo-Sánchez. 2011. Using a shallow linguistic kernel for drug–drug interaction extraction. *Journal of Biomedical Informatics*, 44(5):789–804.

Irena Spasić, Özlem Uzuner, and Li Zhou. 2020. Emerging clinical applications of text analytics. *International Journal of Medical Informatics*, 134:103974.

Yuqing Tang, Chau Tran, Xian Li, Peng-Jen Chen, Naman Goyal, Vishrav Chaudhary, Jiatao Gu, and Angela Fan. 2021. Multilingual translation from denoising pre-training. In *Findings of the Association for Computational Linguistics: ACL-IJCNLP 2021*, pages 3450–3466, Online. Association for Computational Linguistics.

Chau Tran, Shruti Bhosale, James Cross, Philipp Koehn, Sergey Edunov, and Angela Fan. 2021. Facebook AI's WMT21 news translation task submission. In *Proceedings of the Sixth Conference on Machine Translation*, pages 205–215, Online. Association for Computational Linguistics.

Özlem Uzuner, Brett R South, Shuying Shen, and Scott L DuVall. 2011. 2010 i2b2/VA challenge on concepts, assertions, and relations in clinical text. *Journal of the American Medical Informatics Association*, 18(5):552–556.

Stephen Wu, Kirk Roberts, Surabhi Datta, Jingcheng Du, Zongcheng Ji, Yuqi Si, Sarvesh Soni, Qiong Wang, Qiang Wei, Yang Xiang, Bo Zhao, and Hua Xu. 2019. Deep learning in clinical natural language processing: a methodical review. *Journal of the American Medical Informatics Association*, 27(3):457–470.

Jiateng Xie, Zhilin Yang, Graham Neubig, Noah A. Smith, and Jaime Carbonell. 2018. Neural cross-lingual named entity recognition with minimal resources. In *Proceedings of the 2018 Conference on Empirical Methods in Natural Language Processing*, pages 369–379, Brussels, Belgium. Association for Computational Linguistics.

Huijiong Yan, Tao Qian, Liang Xie, and Shanguang Chen. 2021. Unsupervised cross-lingual model transfer for named entity recognition with contextualized word representations. *PLOS ONE*, 16(9):1–17.

Vithya Yogarajan, Bernhard Pfahringer, and Michael Mayo. 2020. A review of automatic end-to-end de-identification: Is high accuracy the only metric? *Applied Artificial Intelligence*, 34(3):251–269.

What Do You See in this Patient?
Behavioral Testing of Clinical NLP Models

Betty van Aken **Sebastian Herrmann** **Alexander Löser**
Berliner Hochschule für Technik (BHT)
{bvanaken, aloeser}@bht-berlin.de
sebastianhe93@gmail.com

Abstract

Decision support systems based on clinical notes have the potential to improve patient care by pointing doctors towards overseen risks. Predicting a patient's outcome is an essential part of such systems, for which the use of deep neural networks has shown promising results. However, the patterns learned by these networks are mostly opaque and previous work revealed both reproduction of systemic biases and unexpected behavior for out-of-distribution patients. For application in clinical practice it is crucial to be aware of such behavior. We thus introduce a testing framework that evaluates clinical models regarding certain changes in the input. The framework helps to understand learned patterns and their influence on model decisions. In this work, we apply it to analyse the change in behavior with regard to the patient characteristics *gender*, *age* and *ethnicity*. Our evaluation of three current clinical NLP models demonstrates the concrete effects of these characteristics on the models' decisions. They show that model behavior varies drastically even when fine-tuned on the same data with similar AUROC score. These results exemplify the need for a broader communication of model behavior in the clinical domain.

1 Introduction

Outcome prediction from clinical notes. The use of automatic systems in the medical domain is promising due to their potential exposure to large amounts of data from earlier patients. This data can include information that helps doctors make better decisions regarding diagnoses and treatments of a patient at hand. Outcome prediction models take patient information as input and then output probabilities for all considered outcomes (Choi et al., 2018; Khadanga et al., 2019). We focus this work on outcome models using natural language in the form of clinical notes as an input, since they are a common source of patient information and contain a multitude of possible variables.

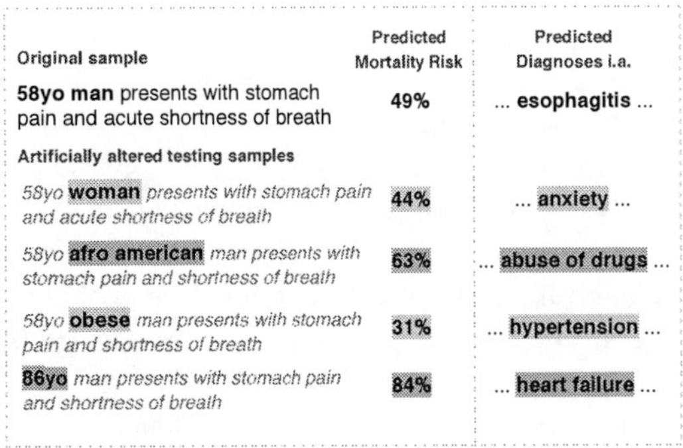

Figure 1: Minimal alterations to the patient description can have a large impact on outcome predictions of clinical NLP models. We introduce behavioral testing for the clinical domain to expose these impacts.

The problem of black box models for clinical predictions. Recent models show promising results on tasks such as mortality (Si and Roberts, 2019) and diagnosis prediction (Liu et al., 2018; Choi et al., 2018). However, since most of these models work as black boxes, it is unclear which features they consider important and how they interpret certain patient characteristics. From earlier work we know that highly parameterized models are prone to emphasize systemic biases in the data (Sun et al., 2019). Further, these models have high potential to disadvantage minority groups as their behavior towards out-of-distribution samples is often unpredictable. This behavior is especially dangerous in the clinical domain, since it can lead to underdiagnosis or inappropriate treatment (Straw, 2020). Thus, understanding models and allocative harms they might cause (Barocas et al., 2017) is an essential prerequisite for their application in clinical practice. We argue that more in-depth evaluations are needed to know whether models have learned medically meaningful patterns or not.

Behavioral testing for the clinical domain. As a step towards this goal, we introduce a novel test-

Proceedings of the 4th Clinical Natural Language Processing Workshop, pages 63 - 73
July 14, 2022

ing framework specifically for the clinical domain that enables us to examine the influence of certain patient characteristics on the model predictions. Our work is motivated by behavioral testing frameworks for general Natural Language Processing (NLP) tasks (Ribeiro et al., 2020) in which model behavior is observed under changing input data. Our framework incorporates a number of test cases and is further extendable to the needs of individual data sets and clinical tasks.

Influence of patient characteristics. As an initial case study we apply the framework to analyse the behavior of models trained on the widely used MIMIC-III database (Johnson et al., 2016). We analyse how sensitive these models are towards textual indicators of patient characteristics, such as *age*, *gender* and *ethnicity*, in English clinical notes. These characteristics are known to be affected by discrimination in health care (Stangl et al., 2019), on the other hand, they can represent important risk factors for certain diseases or conditions. That is why we consider it especially important to understand how these mentions affect model decisions.

Contributions. In summary, we present the following contributions in this work:
1) We introduce a behavioral testing framework specifically for clinical NLP models. We release the code for applying and extending the framework[1] to enable in-depth evaluations.
2) We present an analysis on the patient characteristics *gender*, *age* and *ethnicity* to understand the sensitivity of models towards textual cues regarding these groups and whether their predictions are medically plausible.
3) We show results of three state-of-the-art clinical NLP models and find that model behavior strongly varies depending on the applied pre-training. We further show that highly optimised models tend to overestimate the effect of certain patient characteristics leading to potentially harmful behavior.

2 Related Work

2.1 Clinical Outcome Prediction

Outcome prediction from clinical text has been studied regarding a variety of outcomes. The most prevalent being in-hospital mortality (Ghassemi et al., 2014; Jo et al., 2017; Suresh et al., 2018; Si and Roberts, 2019), diagnosis prediction (Tao et al., 2019; Liu et al., 2018, 2019a) and phenotyping (Liu et al., 2019b; Jain et al., 2019; Oleynik et al., 2019; Pfaff et al., 2020). In recent years, most approaches are based on deep neural networks due to their ability to outperform earlier methods in most settings. Most recently, Transformer-based models have been applied for prediction of patient outcomes with reported increases in performance (Huang et al., 2019; Zhang et al., 2020a; Tuzhilin, 2020; Zhao et al., 2021; van Aken et al., 2021; Rasmy et al., 2021). In this work we analyse three Transformer-based models due to their upcoming prevalence in the application of NLP in health care.

2.2 Behavioral Testing in NLP

Ribeiro et al. (2020) identify shortcomings of common model evaluation on held-out datasets, such as the occurrence of the same biases in both training and test set and the lack of broad testing scenarios in the held-out set. To mitigate these problems, they introduce CheckList, a behavioral testing framework for general NLP abilities. In particular, they highlight that such frameworks evaluate input-output behavior without any knowledge of internal structures of a system (Beizer, 1995). Building upon CheckList, Röttger et al. (2021) introduce a behavioral testing suite for the domain of hate speech detection to address the individual challenges of the task. Following their work, we create a behavioral testing framework for the domain of clinical outcome prediction, that comprise idiosyncratic data and respective challenges.

2.3 Analysing Clinical NLP Models

Zhang et al. (2020b) highlight the reproduction of systemic biases in clinical NLP models. They quantify such biases with the recall gap among patient groups and show that models trained on data from MIMIC-III inherit biases regarding gender, ethnicity, and insurance status–leading to higher recall values for majority groups. Log'e et al. (2021) further find disparities in pain treatment suggestions by language models for different races and genders. We take these findings as motivation to directly analyse the sensitivity of large pre-trained models with regard to patient characteristics. In contrast to earlier work and following Ribeiro et al. (2020), we want to eliminate the influence of existing data labels on our evaluation. Further, our approach simulates patient cases that are similar to real-life occurrences. It thus displays the actual impact of learned patterns on all analysed patient groups.

[1]URL: `https://github.com/bvanaken/clinical-behavioral-testing`

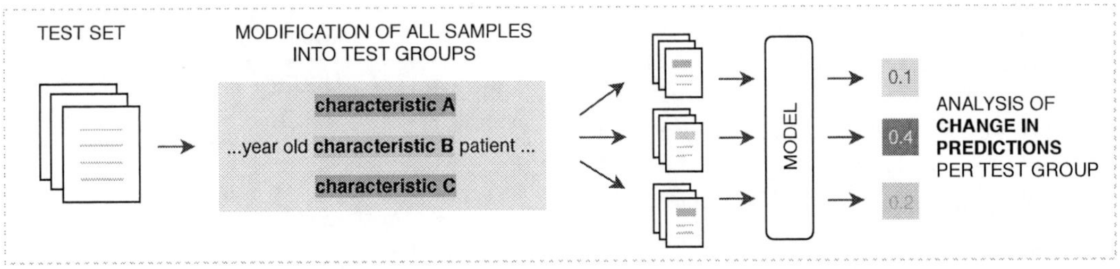

Figure 2: **Behavioral testing framework for the clinical domain.** Schematic overview of the introduced framework. From an existing test set we create test groups by altering specific tokens in the clinical note. We then analyse the change in predictions which reveals the impact of the mention on the clinical NLP model.

3 Behavioral Testing of Clinical NLP Models

Sample alterations. Our goal is to examine how clinical NLP models react to mentions of certain patient characteristics in text. Comparable to earlier approaches to behavioral testing we use sample alterations to artificially create different test groups. In our case, a test group is defined by one manifestation of a patient characteristic, such as *female* as the patient's gender. To ensure that we only measure the influence of this certain characteristic, we keep the rest of the patient case unchanged and apply the alterations to all samples in our test dataset. Depending on the original sample, the operations to create a certain test group thus include 1) changing a mention, 2) adding a mention or 3) keeping a mention unchanged (in case of a patient case that is already part of the test group at hand). This results in one newly created dataset per test group, all based on the same patient cases and only different in the patient characteristic under investigation.

Prediction analysis. After creating the test groups, we collect the models' predictions for all cases in each test group. Different from earlier approaches to behavioral testing we do not test whether predictions on the altered samples are true or false with regard to the ground truth. As van Aken et al. (2021) pointed out, clinical ground truth must be viewed critically, because the collected data does only show one possible pathway for a patient out of many. Further, existing biases in treatments and diagnoses are likely included in our testing data potentially leading to meaningless results. To prevent that, we instead focus on detecting how the model outputs change regardless of the original annotations. This way we can also evaluate very rare mentions (e.g. *transgender*) and observe their impact on the model predictions reliably. Figure 2 shows a schematic overview of the functioning of the framework.

Extensibility. In this study, we use the introduced framework to analyse model behavior with regard to patient characteristics as described in 4.2. However, it can also be used to test other model behavior like the ability to detect diagnoses when certain indicators are present in the text or the influence of stigmatizing language (cf. Goddu et al. (2018)). It is further possible to combine certain patient groups to test model behavior regarding intersectionality. While such analyses are beyond the scope of this paper, we include them in the published codebase as an example for further extensions.

4 Case Study: Patient Characteristics

4.1 Data

We conduct our analysis on data from the MIMIC-III database (Johnson et al., 2016). In particular we use the outcome prediction task setup by van Aken et al. (2021). The classification task includes 48,745 English admission notes annotated with the patients' clinical outcomes at discharge. We select the outcomes *diagnoses at discharge* and *in-hospital mortality* for this analysis, since they have the highest impact on patient care and present a high potential to disadvantage certain patient groups. We use three models (see 4.3) trained on the two *admission* to *discharge* tasks and conduct our analysis on the test set defined by the authors with 9,829 samples.

4.2 Considered Patient Characteristics

We choose three characteristics for the analysis in this work: *Age*, *gender* and *ethnicity*. While these characteristics differ in their importance as clinical risk factors, all of them are known to be subject to biases and stigmas in health care (Stangl et al.,

2019). Therefore, we want to test, whether the analysed models have learned medically plausible patterns or ones that might be harmful to certain patient groups. We deliberately also include groups that occur very rarely in the original dataset. We want to understand the impact of imbalanced input data especially on minority groups, since they are already disadvantaged by the health care system (Riley, 2012; Bulatao and Anderson, 2004).

When altering the samples in our test set, we utilize the fact that patients are described in a mostly consistent way in clinical notes. We collect all mention variations from the training set used to describe the different patient characteristics and alter the samples accordingly in an automated setup. Details regarding all applied variations can be found in the public repository linked in 1.

Age. The age of a patient is a significant risk factor for a number of clinical outcomes. Our test includes all ages between 18 and 89 and the [** Age over 90**] de-idenfitication label from the MIMIC-III database. By analysing the model behavior on changing age mentions we can get insights on how the models interpret numbers, which is considered challenging for current NLP models (Wallace et al., 2019).

Gender. A patient's gender is both a risk factor for certain diseases and also subject to unintended biases in healthcare. We test the model's behavior regarding gender by altering the gender mention and by changing all pronouns in the clinical note. In addition to *female* and *male*, we also consider *transgender* as a gender test group in our study. This group is extremely rare in clinical datasets like MIMIC-III, but since approximately 1.4 million people in the U.S. identify as transgender (Flores et al., 2016), it is important to understand how model predictions change when the characteristic is present in a clinical note.

Ethnicity. The ethnicity of a patient is only occasionally mentioned in clinical notes and its role in medical decision-making is controversial, since it can lead to disadvantages in patient care (Anderson et al., 2001; Snipes et al., 2011). Earlier studies have also shown that ethnicity in clinical notes is often incorrectly assigned (Moscou et al., 2003). We want to know how clinical NLP models interpret the mention of ethnicity in a clinical note and whether their behavior can cause unfair treatment. We choose *White*, *African American*, *Hispanic* and *Asian* as ethnicity groups for our evaluation, as they are the most frequent ethnicities in MIMIC-III.

	PubMedBERT	CORe	BioBERT
Diagnoses	**83.75**	83.54	82.81
Mortality	**84.28**	84.04	82.55

Table 1: Performance of three state-of-the-art models on the tasks *diagnoses* (multi-label) and *mortality prediction* (binary task) in % AUROC. PubMedBERT outperforms the other models in both tasks by a small margin.

4.3 Clinical NLP Models

In this study, we apply the introduced testing framework to three existing clinical models which are fine-tuned on the tasks of diagnosis and mortality prediction. We use public pre-trained model checkpoints and fine-tune all models on the same training data with the same hyperparameter setup[2]. The models are based on the BERT architecture (Devlin et al., 2019) as it presents the current state-of-the-art in predicting patient outcomes. Their performance on the two tasks is shown in Table 1. We deliberately choose three models based on the same architecture to investigate the impact of pre-training data while keeping architectural considerations aside. In general the proposed testing framework is model agnostic and works with any type of text-based outcome prediction model.

BioBERT. Lee et al. (2020) introduced BioBERT which is based on a pre-trained BERT Base (Devlin et al., 2019) checkpoint. They applied another language model fine-tuning step using biomedical articles from PubMed abstracts and full-text articles. BioBERT has shown improved performance on both medical and clinical downstream tasks.

CORe. Clinical Outcome Representations (CORe) by van Aken et al. (2021) are based on BioBERT and extended with a pre-training step that focuses on the prediction of patient outcomes. The pre-training data includes clinical notes, Wikipedia articles and case studies from PubMed. The tokenization is similar to the BioBERT model.

PubMedBERT. Gu et al. (2020) recently introduced PubMedBERT based on similar data as BioBERT. They use PubMed articles and abstracts but instead of extending a BERT Base model, they

[2]Batch size: 20; learning rate: 5e-05; dropout: 0.1; warmup steps: 1000; early stopping patience: 20.

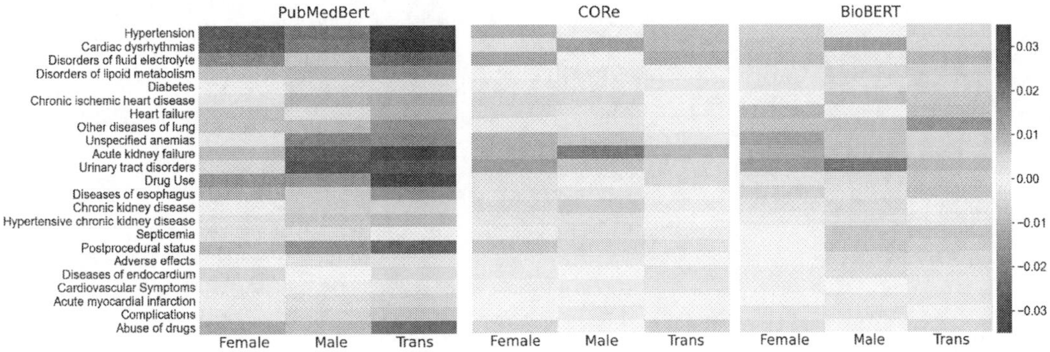

Figure 3: Influence of **gender** on predicted diagnoses. Blue: Predicted probability for diagnosis is below-average; red: predicted probability above-average. PubMedBERT shows highest sensitivity to gender mention and regards many diagnoses less likely if *transgender* is mentioned in the text. Graph shows deviation of probabilities on 24 most common diagnoses in test set.

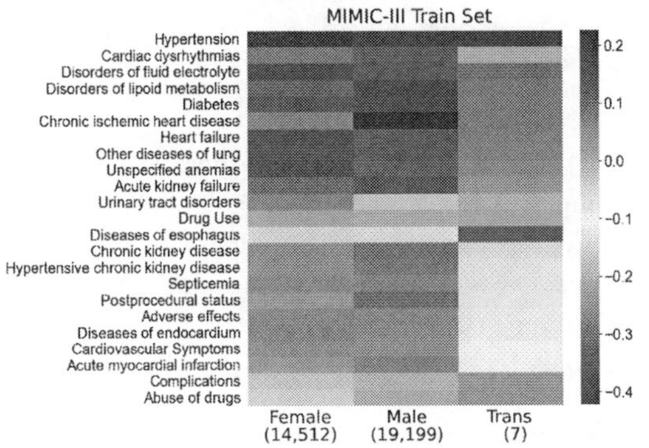

Figure 4: Original distribution of diagnoses per **gender** in MIMIC-III. Cell colors: Deviation from average probability. Numbers in parenthesis: Occurrences in the training set. Most diagnoses occur less often in transgender patients due to their very low sample count.

train PubMedBERT from scratch. The tokenization is adjusted to the medical domain accordingly. The model reaches state-of-the-art results on multiple medical NLP tasks and outperforms the other analysed models on the outcome prediction tasks.

5 Results

We present the results on all test cases by averaging the probabilities that a model assigns to each test sample. We then compare the averaged probabilities across test cases to identify which characteristics have a large impact on the model's prediction over the whole test set. The values per diagnosis in the heatmaps shown in Figure 3, 4, 7 and 8 are defined using the following formula:

$$c_i = p_i - \frac{\sum_j^N p_j}{N} \qquad (1)$$

where c_i is the value assigned to test group i, p is the (predicted) probability for a given diagnosis and N is the number of all test groups except i.

We choose this illustration based on the concept of partial dependence plots (Friedman, 2001) to highlight both positive and negative influence of a characteristic on model behavior. Since all test groups are based on the same patients and only differ regarding the characteristic at hand, even small differences in the averaged predictions can point towards general patterns that the model learned to associate with a characteristic.

5.1 Influence of Gender

Transgender mention leads to lower mortality and diagnoses predictions. Table 2 shows the mortality predictions of the three analysed models with regard to the gender assigned in the text. While the predicted mortality risk for female and male patients lies within a small range, all models predict the mortality risk of patients that are described as transgender as lower than non-transgender patients. This is probably due to the relative young age of most transgender patients

	PubMedBERT	CORe	BioBERT
Female	**0.335**	0.239	0.119
Male	0.333	**0.245**	**0.121**
Transgender	0.326	0.229	0.117

Table 2: Influence of **gender** on mortality predictions. PubMedBERT assigns highest risk to female, the other models to male patients. Notably, all models decrease their mortality prediction for transgender patients.

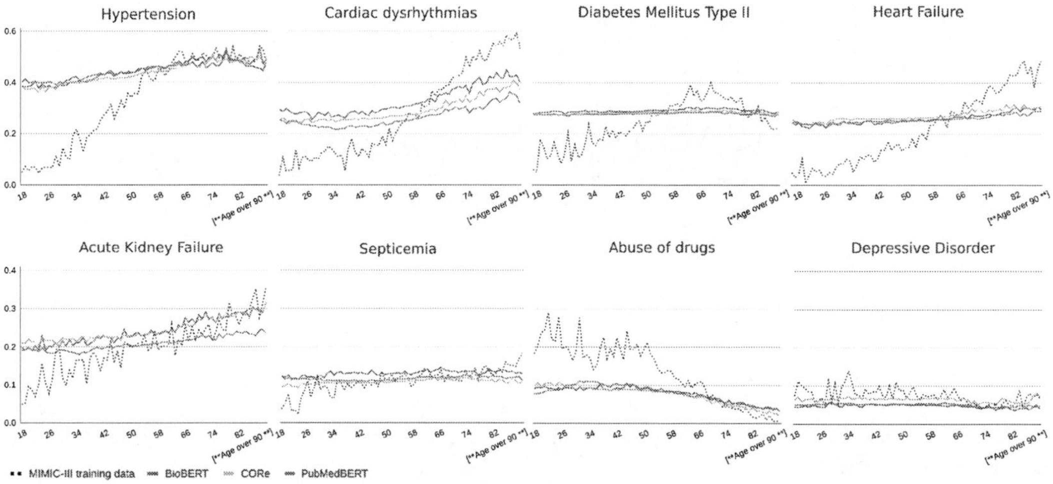

Figure 5: Influence of **age** on diagnosis predictions. The x-axis is the simulated age and the y-axis is the predicted probability of a diagnosis. All models follow similar patterns with some diagnosis risks increasing with age and some decreasing. The original training distributions (black dotted line) are mostly followed but attenuated.

in the MIMIC-III training data, but can be harmful to older patients identifying as transgender at inference time.

Sensitivity to gender mention varies per model. Figure 3 shows the change in model prediction for each diagnosis with regard to the gender mention. The cells of the heatmap are the deviations from the average score of the other test cases. Thus, a red cell indicates that the model assigns a higher probability to a diagnosis for this gender group. We see that PubMedBERT is highly sensitive to the change of the patient gender, especially regarding transgender patients. Except from few diagnoses such as *Cardiac dysrhythmias* and *Drug Use / Abuse*, the model predicts a lower probability to diseases if the patient letter contains the transgender mention. The CORe and BioBERT models are less sensitive in this regard. The most salient deviation of the BioBERT model is a drop in probability of *Urinary tract disorders* for male patients, which is medically plausible due to anatomic differences (Tan and Chlebicki, 2016).

Patterns in MIMIC-III training data are partially inherited. In Figure 4 we show the original distribution of diagnoses per gender in the training data. Note that the deviations are about 10 times larger than the ones produced by the model predictions in Figure 3. This indicates that the models take gender as a decision factor, but only among others. Due to the very rare occurrence of transgender mentions (only seven cases in the training data), most diagnoses are underrepresented for this group. This is partially reflected by the model predictions, especially by PubMedBERT, as described above. Other salient patterns such as the prevalence of *Chronic ischemic heart disease* in male patients are only reproduced faintly by the models.

5.2 Influence of Age

Mortality risk is differently influenced by age. Figure 6 shows the averaged predicted mortality per age for all models and the actual distribution from the training data (dotted line). We see that

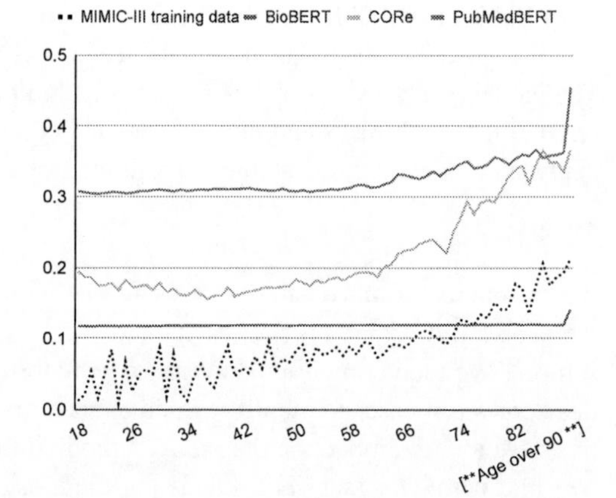

Figure 6: Influence of **age** on mortality predictions. X-axis: Simulated age; y-axis: predicted mortality risk. The three models are differently calibrated and only CORe is highly influenced by age.

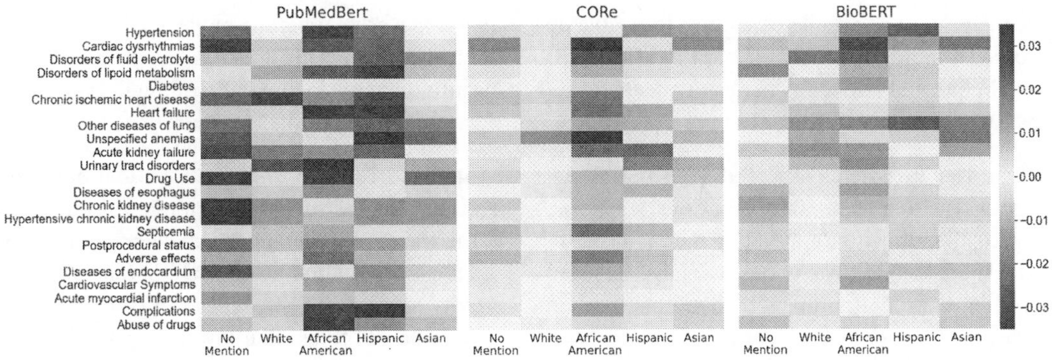

Figure 7: Influence of **ethnicity** on diagnosis predictions. Blue: Predicted probability for diagnosis is below-average; red: predicted probability above-average. PubMedBERT's predictions are highly influenced by ethnicity mentions, while CORe and BioBERT show smaller deviations, but also disparities on specific groups.

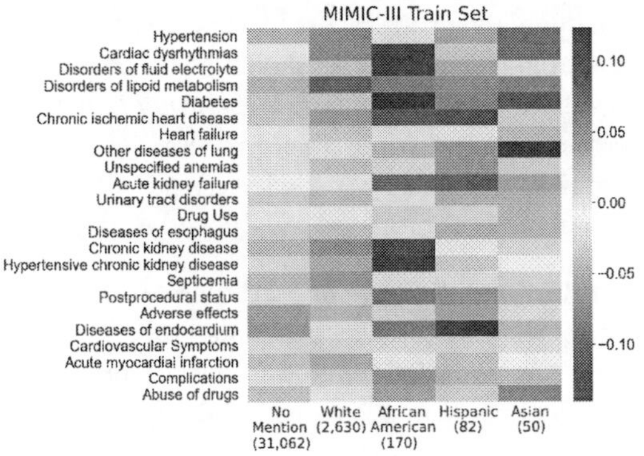

Figure 8: Original distribution of diagnoses per **ethnicity** in MIMIC-III. Cell colors: Deviation from average probability. Numbers in parenthesis: Occurrences in the training set. Both the distribution of samples and the occurrences of diagnoses are highly unbalanced in the training set.

BioBERT does not take age into account when predicting mortality risk except for patients over 90. PubMedBERT assigns a higher mortality risk to all age groups with a small increase for patients over 60 and an even steeper increase for patients over 90. CORe follows the training data the most while also inheriting peaks and troughs in the data.

Models are equally affected by age when predicting diagnoses. We exemplify the impact of age on diagnosis prediction on eight outcome diagnoses in Figure 5. The dotted lines show the distribution of the diagnosis within an age group in the training data. The change of predictions regarding age are similar throughout the analysed models with only small variations such as for *Cardiac dysrhythmias*. Some diagnoses are regarded more probable in older patients (e.g. *Acute Kidney Failure*) and others in younger patients (e.g. *Abuse of drugs*). The distributions per age group in the training data are more extreme, but follow the same tendencies as predicted by the models.

Peaks indicate lack of number understanding. From earlier studies we know that BERT-based models have difficulties dealing with numbers in text (Wallace et al., 2019). The peaks that we observe in some predictions support this finding. For instance, the models assign a higher risk of *Cardiac dysrhythmias* to patients aged 73 than to patients aged 74, because they do not capture that these are consecutive ages. Therefore, the influence of age on the predictions might solely be based on the individual age tokens observed in the training data.

5.3 Influence of Ethnicity

Mention of any ethnicity decreases prediction of mortality risk. Table 3 shows the mortality predictions when different ethnicities are mentioned and when there is no mention. We observe that

	PubMedBERT	CORe	BioBERT
No mention	**0.333**	**0.243**	**0.120**
White	0.329	0.235	0.119
African Amer.	0.329	0.239	0.116
Hispanic	0.331	0.237	0.118
Asian	0.330	0.238	0.118

Table 3: Influence of **ethnicity** on mortality predictions. The mention of an ethnicity decreases the predicted mortality risk. White and African American patients are assigned with the lowest mortality risk (gray-shaded).

the mention of any of the ethnicities leads to a decrease in mortality risk prediction in all models, with White and African American patients receiving the lowest probabilities.

Diagnoses predicted by PubMedBERT are highly sensitive to ethnicity mentions. Figure 7 depicts the influence of ethnicity mentions on the three models. Notably, the predictions of PubMedBERT are strongly influenced by ethnicity mentions. Multiple diagnoses such as *Chronic kidney disease* are more often predicted when there is no mention of ethnicity, while diagnoses like *Hypertension* and *Abuse of drugs* are regarded more likely in African American patients and *Unspecified anemias* in Hispanic patients. While the original training data in Figure 8 shows the same strong variance among ethnicities, this is not inherited the same way in the CORe and BioBERT models. However, we can also observe deviations regarding ethnicity in these models.

African American patients are assigned lower risk of diagnoses by CORe and BioBERT. The heatmaps showing predictions of CORe and BioBERT reveal a potentially harmful pattern in which the mention of *African American* in a clinical note decreases the predictions for a large number of diagnoses. This pattern is found more prominently in the CORe model, but also in BioBERT. Putting these models into clinical application could result in fewer diagnostic tests to be ordered by physicians and therefore lead to disadvantages in the treatment of African American patients. This is particularly critical as it would reinforce existing biases in health care (Nelson, 2002).

6 Discussion

Model behaviors show large variance. The results described in 5 reveal large differences in the influence of patient characteristics throughout models. The analysis shows that there is no overall *best* model, but each model has learned both useful patterns (e.g. age as a medical plausible risk factor) and potentially dangerous ones (e.g. decreases in diagnosis risks for minority groups). The large variance is surprising since the models have a shared architecture and are fine-tuned on the same data–they only differ in their pre-training. And while the reported AUROC scores for the models (Table 1) are close to each other, the variance in learned behavior show that we should consider in-depth analyses a crucial part of model evaluation in the clinical domain. This is especially important since harmful patterns in clinical NLP models are often fine-grained and difficult to detect.

Model scoring can obfuscate critical behavior. The analysis has shown that PubMedBERT which outperforms the other models in both mortality and diagnosis prediction by AUROC show larger sensitivity to mentions of gender and ethnicity in the text. Many of them–like lower diagnosis risk assignment to African American patients–might lead to undertreatment. This is alerting since it particularly affects minority groups which are already disadvantaged by the health care system. It also shows that instead of measuring clinical models regarding rather abstract scores, looking at their potential impact to patients should be further emphasized. To communicate model behavior to medical professionals one possible direction could be to use behavioral analysis results as a part of clinical model cards as proposed by Mitchell et al. (2019).

Limitations of the proposed framework. Unlike other behavioral testing setups (see 2.2), results of our framework cannot be easily categorized into *correct* and *false* behavior. While increased risk allocations can be beneficial to a patient group due to doctors running additional tests, they can also lead to mistreatment or other diagnoses being overlooked. Same holds for the influence of rare mentions, such as *transgender*: One could argue that based on only seven occurrences in the training set the characteristic should have less impact on model decisions overall. However, some features e.g. regarding rare diseases should be recognized as important even if very infrequent. Since our models often lack such judgement, the decision about which patient characteristic to consider a risk factor and their impact on outcome predictions is still best made by medical professionals. Nevertheless, decision support systems can be beneficial if their behavior is transparently communicated. With this framework we want to take a step towards improving this communication.

7 Conclusion

In this work, we introduced a behavioral testing framework for the clinical domain to understand the effects of textual variations on model predictions. We apply this framework to three current clinical NLP models to examine the impact of certain patient characteristics. Our results show that the models–even with very close AUROC scores–have learned very different behavioral patterns, some of them with high potential to disadvantage minority groups. With this work, we want to emphasize the importance of model evaluation beyond common metrics especially in sensitive areas like health care. We recommend to use the results of these evaluations for discussions with medical professionals. Being aware of specific model behavior and incorporating this knowledge into clinical decision making is a crucial step towards safe deployment of such models. For future work we consider iterative model fine-tuning with medical professionals in the loop a promising direction to teach models which patterns to stick to and which ones to discard.

Acknowledgments

We would like to thank Dr. med. Simon Ronicke for the valuable input. Our work is funded by the German Federal Ministry for Economic Affairs and Energy (BMWi) under grant agreement 01MD19003B (PLASS) and 01MK2008MD (Servicemeister).

References

Matthew Anderson, Susan Moscou, Celestine Fulchon, and Daniel Neuspiel. 2001. The role of race in the clinical presentation. *Family medicine*, 33:430–4.

Solon Barocas, Kate Crawford, Aaron Shapiro, and Hanna Wallach. 2017. The problem with bias: Allocative versus representational harms in machine learning. In *SIGCIS, Philadelphia, PA.*

Boris Beizer. 1995. *Black-box testing: techniques for functional testing of software and systems*. John Wiley & Sons, Inc.

Rodolfo A Bulatao and Norman B Anderson. 2004. Understanding racial and ethnic differences in health in late life: A research agenda. *National Academies Press (US)*.

Edward Choi, Cao Xiao, Walter F. Stewart, and Jimeng Sun. 2018. Mime: Multilevel medical embedding of electronic health records for predictive healthcare. In *Advances in Neural Information Processing Systems 31: Annual Conference on Neural Information Processing Systems 2018, NeurIPS 2018, December 3-8, 2018, Montréal, Canada*, pages 4552–4562.

Jacob Devlin, Ming-Wei Chang, Kenton Lee, and Kristina Toutanova. 2019. BERT: Pre-training of deep bidirectional transformers for language understanding. In *Proceedings of the 2019 Conference of the North American Chapter of the Association for Computational Linguistics: Human Language Technologies, Volume 1 (Long and Short Papers)*, pages 4171–4186, Minneapolis, Minnesota. Association for Computational Linguistics.

A.R. Flores, J.L. Herman, G.J. Gates, and T.N.T. Brown. 2016. How many adults identify as transgender in the united states? *Los Angeles, CA: The Williams Institute*.

Jerome H Friedman. 2001. Greedy function approximation: a gradient boosting machine. *Annals of statistics*, pages 1189–1232.

Marzyeh Ghassemi, Tristan Naumann, Finale Doshi-Velez, Nicole Brimmer, Rohit Joshi, Anna Rumshisky, and Peter Szolovits. 2014. Unfolding physiological state: mortality modelling in intensive care units. In *The 20th ACM SIGKDD International Conference on Knowledge Discovery and Data Mining, KDD '14, New York, NY, USA - August 24 - 27, 2014*, pages 75–84. ACM.

Anna Goddu, Katie O'Conor, Sophie Lanzkron, Mustapha Saheed, Somnath Saha, Carlton Haywood, and Mary Catherine Beach. 2018. Do words matter? stigmatizing language and the transmission of bias in the medical record. *Journal of General Internal Medicine*, 33.

Yu Gu, Robert Tinn, Hao Cheng, Michael Lucas, Naoto Usuyama, Xiaodong Liu, Tristan Naumann, Jianfeng Gao, and Hoifung Poon. 2020. Domain-specific language model pretraining for biomedical natural language processing.

Kexin Huang, Jaan Altosaar, and Rajesh Ranganath. 2019. Clinicalbert: Modeling clinical notes and predicting hospital readmission. *arXiv preprint arXiv:1904.05342*.

Sarthak Jain, Ramin Mohammadi, and Byron C. Wallace. 2019. An analysis of attention over clinical notes for predictive tasks. In *Proceedings of the 2nd Clinical Natural Language Processing Workshop*, pages 15–21, Minneapolis, Minnesota, USA. Association for Computational Linguistics.

Yohan Jo, Lisa Lee, and Shruti Palaskar. 2017. Combining lstm and latent topic modeling for mortality prediction. *arXiv preprint arXiv:1709.02842*.

Alistair EW Johnson, Tom J Pollard, Lu Shen, H Lehman Li-Wei, Mengling Feng, Mohammad Ghassemi, Benjamin Moody, Peter Szolovits, Leo Anthony Celi, and Roger G Mark. 2016. MIMIC-III, a Freely Accessible Critical Care Database. *Scientific Data*, 3(1):1–9.

Swaraj Khadanga, Karan Aggarwal, Shafiq Joty, and Jaideep Srivastava. 2019. Using clinical notes with time series data for ICU management. In *Proceedings of the 2019 Conference on Empirical Methods* in Natural Language Processing and the 9th International Joint Conference on Natural Language Processing (EMNLP-IJCNLP)*, pages 6432–6437, Hong Kong, China. Association for Computational Linguistics.

Jinhyuk Lee, Wonjin Yoon, Sungdong Kim, Donghyeon Kim, Sunkyu Kim, Chan Ho So, and Jaewoo Kang. 2020. Biobert: a pre-trained biomedical language representation model for biomedical text mining. *Bioinformatics*, 36(4):1234–1240.

Dianbo Liu, Dmitriy Dligach, and Timothy Miller. 2019a. Two-stage federated phenotyping and patient representation learning. In *Proceedings of the 18th BioNLP Workshop and Shared Task*, pages 283–291, Florence, Italy. Association for Computational Linguistics.

Dianbo Liu, Dmitriy Dligach, and Timothy Miller. 2019b. Two-stage federated phenotyping and patient representation learning. In *Proceedings of the 18th BioNLP Workshop and Shared Task*, pages 283–291, Florence, Italy. Association for Computational Linguistics.

Jingshu Liu, Zachariah Zhang, and Narges Razavian. 2018. Deep EHR: chronic disease prediction using medical notes. In *Proceedings of the Machine Learning for Healthcare Conference, MLHC 2018, 17-18 August 2018, Palo Alto, California*, volume 85 of *Proceedings of Machine Learning Research*, pages 440–464. PMLR.

C'ecile Log'e, Emily L. Ross, David Yaw Amoah Dadey, Saahil Jain, Adriel Saporta, Andrew Y. Ng, and Pranav Rajpurkar. 2021. Q-pain: A question answering dataset to measure social bias in pain management. *ArXiv*, abs/2108.01764.

Margaret Mitchell, Simone Wu, Andrew Zaldivar, Parker Barnes, Lucy Vasserman, Ben Hutchinson, Elena Spitzer, Inioluwa Deborah Raji, and Timnit Gebru. 2019. Model cards for model reporting. In *Proceedings of the Conference on Fairness, Accountability, and Transparency*, FAT* '19, page 220–229, New York, NY, USA. Association for Computing Machinery.

Susan Moscou, Matthew R Anderson, Judith B Kaplan, and Lisa Valencia. 2003. Validity of racial/ethnic classifications in medical records data: an exploratory study. *American journal of public health*, 93(7):1084–1086.

Alan Nelson. 2002. Unequal treatment: confronting racial and ethnic disparities in health care. *Journal of the national medical association*, 94(8):666.

Michel Oleynik, Amila Kugic, Zdenko Kasáč, and Markus Kreuzthaler. 2019. Evaluating shallow and deep learning strategies for the 2018 n2c2 shared task on clinical text classification. *Journal of the American Medical Informatics Association*, 26(11):1247–1254.

Emily R Pfaff, Miles Crosskey, Kenneth Morton, and Ashok Krishnamurthy. 2020. Clinical annotation research kit (clark): Computable phenotyping using machine learning. *JMIR medical informatics*, 8(1):e16042.

Laila Rasmy, Yang Xiang, Ziqian Xie, Cui Tao, and Degui Zhi. 2021. Med-bert: pretrained contextualized embeddings on large-scale structured electronic health records for disease prediction. *NPJ digital medicine*, 4(1):1–13.

Marco Tulio Ribeiro, Tongshuang Wu, Carlos Guestrin, and Sameer Singh. 2020. Beyond accuracy: Behavioral testing of NLP models with CheckList. In *Proceedings of the 58th Annual Meeting of the Association for Computational Linguistics*, pages 4902–4912, Online. Association for Computational Linguistics.

Wayne J Riley. 2012. Health disparities: gaps in access, quality and affordability of medical care. *Transactions of the American Clinical and Climatological Association*, 123:167.

Paul Röttger, Bertie Vidgen, Dong Nguyen, Zeerak Waseem, Helen Margetts, and Janet Pierrehumbert. 2021. HateCheck: Functional tests for hate speech detection models. In *Proceedings of the 59th Annual Meeting of the Association for Computational Linguistics and the 11th International Joint Conference on Natural Language Processing (Volume 1: Long Papers)*, pages 41–58, Online. Association for Computational Linguistics.

Yuqi Si and Kirk Roberts. 2019. Deep patient representation of clinical notes via multi-task learning for mortality prediction. *AMIA Joint Summits on Translational Science proceedings. AMIA Joint Summits on Translational Science*, 2019:779–788.

Shedra Snipes, Sherrill Sellers, Adebola Tafawa, Lisa Cooper, Julie Fields, and Vence Bonham. 2011. Is race medically relevant? a qualitative study of physicians' attitudes about the role of race in treatment decision-making. *BMC health services research*, 11:183.

Anne L Stangl, Valerie A Earnshaw, Carmen H Logie, Wim van Brakel, Leickness C Simbayi, Iman Barré, and John F Dovidio. 2019. The health stigma and discrimination framework: a global, crosscutting framework to inform research, intervention development, and policy on health-related stigmas. *BMC medicine*, 17(1):1–13.

Isabel Straw. 2020. The automation of bias in medical artificial intelligence (AI): decoding the past to create a better future. *Artif. Intell. Medicine*, 110:101965.

Tony Sun, Andrew Gaut, Shirlyn Tang, Yuxin Huang, Mai ElSherief, Jieyu Zhao, Diba Mirza, Elizabeth Belding, Kai-Wei Chang, and William Yang Wang. 2019. Mitigating gender bias in natural language processing: Literature review. In *Proceedings of the*

57th Annual Meeting of the Association for Computational Linguistics, pages 1630–1640, Florence, Italy. Association for Computational Linguistics.

Harini Suresh, Jen J. Gong, and John V. Guttag. 2018. Learning tasks for multitask learning: Heterogenous patient populations in the ICU. In *Proceedings of the 24th ACM SIGKDD International Conference on Knowledge Discovery & Data Mining, KDD 2018, London, UK, August 19-23, 2018*, pages 802–810. ACM.

Chee Tan and Maciej Chlebicki. 2016. Urinary tract infections in adults. *Singapore Medical Journal*, 57:485–490.

Yifeng Tao, Bruno Godefroy, Guillaume Genthial, and Christopher Potts. 2019. Effective feature representation for clinical text concept extraction. In *Proceedings of the 2nd Clinical Natural Language Processing Workshop*, pages 1–14, Minneapolis, Minnesota, USA. Association for Computational Linguistics.

Alexander Tuzhilin. 2020. Predicting clinical diagnosis from patients electronic health records using bert-based neural networks. In *Artificial Intelligence in Medicine: 18th International Conference on Artificial Intelligence in Medicine, AIME 2020, Minneapolis, MN, USA, August 25-28, 2020, Proceedings*, volume 12299, page 111. Springer Nature.

Betty van Aken, Jens-Michalis Papaioannou, Manuel Mayrdorfer, Klemens Budde, Felix Gers, and Alexander Loeser. 2021. Clinical outcome prediction from admission notes using self-supervised knowledge integration. In *Proceedings of the 16th Conference of the European Chapter of the Association for Computational Linguistics: Main Volume*, pages 881–893, Online. Association for Computational Linguistics.

Eric Wallace, Yizhong Wang, Sujian Li, Sameer Singh, and Matt Gardner. 2019. Do NLP models know numbers? probing numeracy in embeddings. In *Proceedings of the 2019 Conference on Empirical Methods in Natural Language Processing and the 9th International Joint Conference on Natural Language Processing (EMNLP-IJCNLP)*, pages 5307–5315, Hong Kong, China. Association for Computational Linguistics.

Dongyu Zhang, Jidapa Thadajarassiri, Cansu Sen, and Elke Rundensteiner. 2020a. Time-aware transformer-based network for clinical notes series prediction. In *Machine Learning for Healthcare Conference*, pages 566–588. PMLR.

Haoran Zhang, Amy X Lu, Mohamed Abdalla, Matthew McDermott, and Marzyeh Ghassemi. 2020b. Hurtful words: quantifying biases in clinical contextual word embeddings. In *Proceedings of the ACM Conference on Health, Inference, and Learning*, pages 110–120.

Yun Zhao, Qinghang Hong, Xinlu Zhang, Yu Deng, Yuqing Wang, and Linda Petzold. 2021. Bertsurv: Bert-based survival models for predicting outcomes of trauma patients. *arXiv preprint arXiv:2103.10928*.

Learning to Ask Like a Physician

Eric Lehman[1,2,*], Vladislav Lialin[3], Katelyn Y. Legaspi[5], Anne Janelle R. Sy[4], Patricia Therese S. Pile[4], Nicole Rose I. Alberto[5], Richard Raymund R. Ragasa[5], Corinna Victoria M. Puyat[5], Isabelle Rose I. Alberto[5], Pia Gabrielle I. Alfonso[5], Marianne Taliño[6], Dana Moukheiber[1], Byron C. Wallace[7], Anna Rumshisky[3], Jennifer J. Liang[2,8], Preethi Raghavan[1,9], Leo Anthony Celi[1,10], Peter Szolovits[1,2]

[1]MIT, [2]MIT-IBM Watson AI Lab, [3]University of Massachusetts Lowell, [4]UERM Memorial Medical Center [5]University of the Philippines, [6]ASMPH, [7]Northeastern University, [8]IBM Research, [9]Fidelity Investments, [10]Beth Israel Deaconess Medical Center

Abstract

Existing question answering (QA) datasets derived from electronic health records (EHR) are artificially generated and consequently fail to capture realistic physician information needs. We present **Di**scharge **S**ummary **C**linical **Q**uestions (DiSCQ), a newly curated question dataset composed of 2,000+ questions paired with the snippets of text (*triggers*) that prompted each question. The questions are generated by medical experts from 100+ MIMIC-III discharge summaries. We analyze this dataset to characterize the types of information sought by medical experts. We also train baseline models for trigger detection and question generation (QG), paired with unsupervised answer retrieval over EHRs. Our baseline model is able to generate high quality questions in over 62% of cases when prompted with human selected triggers. We release this dataset (and all code to reproduce baseline model results) to facilitate further research into realistic clinical QA and QG. [1]

His past medical history is significant for prostate cancer, benign prostatic hypertrophy, hypothyroidism, status post radiation for non Hodgkin's lymphoma, chronic painless hematuria, degenerative joint disease and history of a murmur.

(1) prostate cancer, benign prostatic hypertrophy
Date of diagnosis? Any interventions done (RT, surgery)?

(2) hypothyroidism
Maintenance medications?

Figure 1: Example of an annotated discharge summary section. The highlighted portion shows the "trigger" for the questions.

1 Introduction

Physicians often query electronic health records (EHR) to make fully informed decisions about patient care (Demner-Fushman et al., 2009). However, D'Alessandro et al. (2004) found that it takes an average of 8.3 minutes to answer a single question, even when physicians are trained to retrieve information from an EHR platform. Natural language technologies such as automatic question answering (QA) may partially address this problem.

There have been several dataset collection efforts that aim to facilitate the training and evaluation of clinical QA models (Pampari et al., 2018; Yue et al., 2021; Raghavan et al., 2021; Kell et al., 2021). However, template-based (Pampari et al., 2018; Raghavan et al., 2021) and other kinds of automated generation (Yue et al., 2021) methods are by nature brittle and have limited evidence of producing questions that medical professionals ask.

Datasets such as emrQA (Pampari et al., 2018) and emrKBQA (Raghavan et al., 2021) attempt to simulate physician queries by defining templates derived from actual questions posed by physicians and then performing slot-filling with clinical entities. This method yields questions that are structurally realistic, but not consistently medically relevant. Yue et al. (2020) found that sampling just 5% of the emrQA questions was sufficient for training a model. They further note that 96% of the questions in a subsection of emrQA contain key phrases that overlap with those in the selected answer.

In follow-up work, Yue et al. (2021) provide a new dataset of 975 questions generated using a diverse question generation model with a human-in-the-loop and 312 questions generated by medical experts from scratch, with the caveat that they must be answerable on the given discharge summary. However, a random sample of 100 questions from the former reveals that 96% of the 975 questions were slot-filled templates directly from emrQA. A

* lehmer16@mit.edu

[1] https://github.com/elehman16/discq

Proceedings of the 4th Clinical Natural Language Processing Workshop, pages 74 - 86
July 14, 2022 ©2022 Association for Computational Linguistics

separate random sample of 100 questions from the latter set reveals that 54% of the questions also use the same slot-filled templates from emrQA. Similarly, we find that 85% of the machine-generated questions and 75% of the human-generated questions contain the exact same key phrases as in the selected answer. Although Yue et al. (2020) does not discuss how they prompt physician questions, our analysis strongly suggests that even in the case of questions "written" by physicians, answer spans are likely identified in advance; this significantly constrains the set of questions a medical professional can ask.

To address this paucity of natural, clinically relevant questions, we collect queries that might plausibly be asked by healthcare providers during patient handoff (i.e., transitions of care). We use patient discharge summaries from the Medical Information Mart for Intensive Care III (MIMIC-III) English dataset (Johnson et al., 2016) to mimic the handoff process. We expect this process to produce more natural questions than prior work. We work with 10 medical experts of varying skill levels. We ask them to review a given discharge summary as the receiving physician in a patient handoff and record any questions they have as well as the piece of text within the discharge summary (trigger) that prompted the question. A sample of questions and corresponding triggers can be seen in Figure 1.

We train question trigger detection and question generation (QG) models on DiSCQ, paired with unsupervised answer retrieval over the EHR. Finally, we propose a new set of guidelines for human evaluation of clinical questions and evaluate the performance of our pipeline using these guidelines. Concretely, our contributions are summarized as follows:

- We work with 10 medical experts to compile DiSCQ, a new dataset of 2000+ questions and 1000+ triggers from over 100+ discharge summaries, providing an important new resource for research in clinical NLP.
- We demonstrate the dataset's utility by training baseline models for trigger detection and question generation.
- We develop novel guidelines for human evaluation of clinical questions. Our experiments show that widely used automated QG metrics do not correlate with human-evaluated question quality.

2 Related Work

2.1 Clinical Question Datasets

Clinical information retrieval, and in particular clinical question answering, is a challenging research task with direct potential applications in clinical practice. Several dataset collection efforts gather consumer health questions and pair them with answers from sources like WebMD and PubMED (Yu et al., 2007; Cao et al., 2011; Abacha and Zweigenbaum, 2015; Abacha et al., 2017; Zahid et al., 2018; Demner-Fushman et al., 2020; Savery et al., 2020; Zhu et al., 2020; Abacha et al., 2019). Likewise, Suster and Daelemans (2018) automatically generate 100,000+ information retrieval queries from over 11,000+ BMJ Case Reports. While these resources are helpful in testing a model's understanding and information retrieval ability on biomedical texts, these datasets consist of broad medical questions asked by the general population. Doctors will not only ask more specific and targeted questions, but also query the EHR to make fully informed decisions about patient care.

The number of publicly available QA datasets derived from EHR systems is quite limited due to the labor intensiveness and high skill requirement needed to create such a dataset. As mentioned previously, to help alleviate this dearth of clinical questions, Pampari et al. (2018) introduced emrQA, a QA dataset constructed from templatized physician queries slot-filled with n2c2 annotations.[2] Fan (2019) extended emrQA by explicitly focusing on "why" questions. Soni et al. (2019) introduced a novel approach for constructing clinical questions that can be slot-filled into logical-forms. Yue et al. (2021) applied an emrQA-trained question generation model paired with a human-in-the-loop to collect 1287 questions conditioned on and answerable from the given context.

In contrast, in our data collection process we do not restrict the medical expert to ask only questions answerable from a particular part of the discharge summary. This leads to more diverse and natural questions. Additionally, in DiSCQ each question is associated with a span of text that triggered the question.

2.2 Question Generation

Question Generation (QG) is a challenging task that requires a combination of reading comprehen-

[2] https://www.i2b2.org/NLP/DataSets/

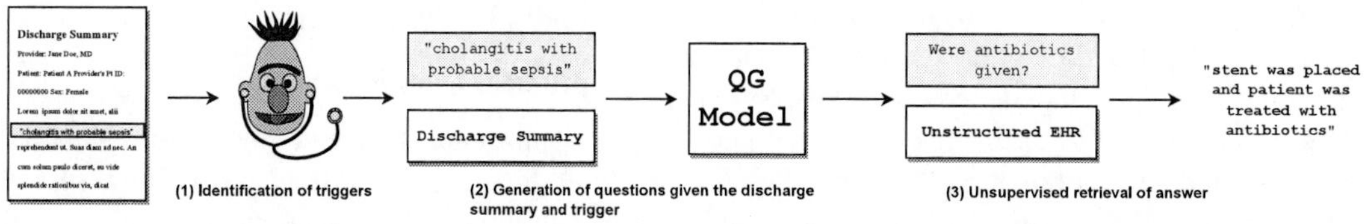

Figure 2: Schematic of the pipeline process used to generate and answer questions.

sion and text generation. Successful QG models may aid in education (Heilman and Smith, 2010; Du et al., 2017), creating dialogue systems or chatbots (Shang et al., 2015; Mostafazadeh et al., 2016; Shum et al., 2018), building datasets (Duan et al., 2017) or improving question answering models through data augmentation (Tang et al., 2017; Dong et al., 2019; Puri et al., 2020; Yue et al., 2021).

Most QG approaches can be broken down into either rule-based or neural methods. Rule-based approaches often involve slot filling templatized questions (Heilman and Smith, 2010; Mazidi and Nielsen, 2014; Labutov et al., 2015; Chali and Hasan, 2015; Pampari et al., 2018). While often effective at generating numerous questions, these methods are very rigid, as virtually any domain change requires a new set of rules. This problem is particularly important in medical QG, as different types of practices may focus on varying aspects of a patient and therefore ask different questions.

Compared to rule-based methods, sequence-to-sequence models (Serban et al., 2016; Du et al., 2017) and more recently transformer-based models (Dong et al., 2019; Qi et al., 2020; Lelkes et al., 2021; Murakhovs'ka et al., 2021; Luo et al., 2021) allow for generation of more diverse questions and can potentially mitigate the problem of domain generalization via large-scale pre-training (Brown et al., 2020) or domain adaptation techniques. We choose to train both BART (Lewis et al., 2020) and T0 (Sanh et al., 2021) models for the task of question generation due to their high performance and ability to generalize to new tasks.

3 DiSCQ Dataset

We work with 10 medical experts of varying skill levels, ranging from senior medical students to practicing MDs, to construct a dataset of 2029 questions over 100+ discharge summaries from MIMIC-III (Johnson et al., 2016).

3.1 Dataset Collection

The goal of our question collection is to gather questions that may be asked by healthcare providers during patient handoff (i.e., transitions of care). We use the patient discharge summary to simulate the handoff process,[3] where the discharge summary is the communication from the previous physician regarding the patient's care, treatment and current status. Annotators are asked to review the discharge summary as the receiving physician and ask any questions they may have as the physician taking over the care of this patient.

Annotators are instructed to read the discharge summary line-by-line and record (1) any questions that may be important with respect to the patient's future care, and, (2) the text within the note that triggered the question. This may mean that questions asked early on may be answered later in the discharge summary. Annotators are permitted to go back and ask questions if they feel the need to do so. To capture the annotators' natural thought processes, we purposely provide only minimal guidance to annotators on how to select a trigger or what type of questions to ask. We only ask that annotators use the minimum span of text when specifying a trigger.[4]

We also encourage all questions to be asked in whatever format they feel appropriate. This leads to many informal queries, in which questions are incomplete or grammatically incorrect (Figure 1). Further, we encourage all types of questions to be asked, regardless of whether they could be answered based on the EHR. We also allow the annotators to ask an arbitrary number of questions. This allows for annotators to skip discharge summaries entirely should they not have any questions.

3.2 Dataset Statistics

The trigger/question pairs are generated over entire discharge summaries. We instruct annotators

[3]We discard any records pertaining to neonatal or deceased patients.

[4]Instructions given to annotators will be available here.

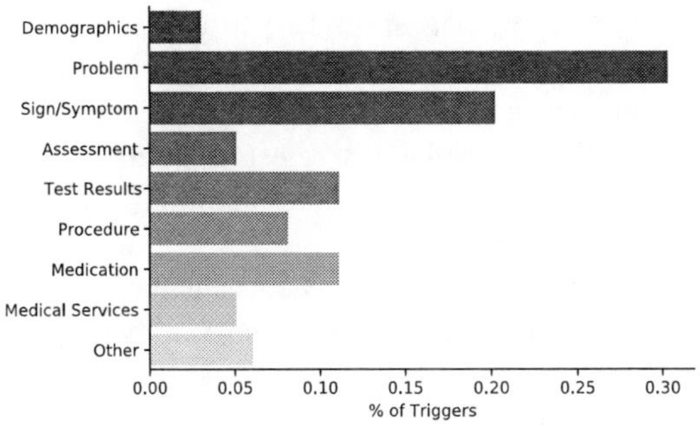

Figure 3: We randomly sample 100 gold triggers and have one of the authors, a physician, categorize the type of information that the trigger contains.

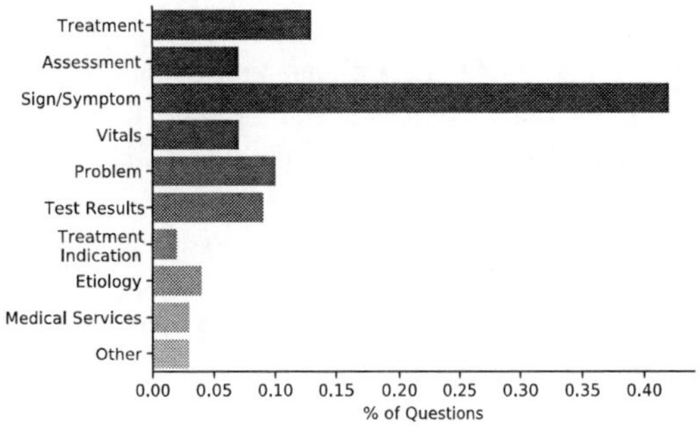

Figure 4: We randomly sample 100 questions and have one of the authors, a physician, categorize what type of information the question is asking for.

to select the minimum span that they used as the trigger to their question; this leads to triggers of length 5.0 ± 14.1 tokens. We additionally find that there are 1.86 ± 1.56 questions per trigger. As mentioned previously, we encourage our medical experts to ask questions however they feel most comfortable. This led to a wide variety in how questions were asked, with some entirely self-contained (46%), others requiring the trigger for understanding (46%), and some requiring the entire sentence containing the trigger to comprehend (8%).[5] We also observe that 59% of the bi-grams in our questions are unique (i.e., over half of all bi-grams that appear in one question are not seen in any other question), demonstrating the diversity of how our questions are asked (Table 1).

We additionally examine where in the discharge summary annotators tend to select triggers from. We find that a majority of triggers are selected from the `Hospital Course` (13%) and `History of Present Illness` (39%) sections. This is unsurprising, as these are the narrative sections of the note where the patient's history prior to admission and their medical care during hospitalization are described. Further, we find that a majority of triggers selected are either a `Problem` or `Sign/Symptom` (Figure 3). This aligns with our intuition, as clinicians are often trained to organize patient information from a problem-oriented perspective. Moreover, developing a differential diagnosis usually begins with gathering details of the patient's clinical presentation.

In Figure 4, we examine the types of information needs exhibited by our questions. We find that 83% and 80% of the questions categorized as `Sign/Symptom` and `Problem`, respectively, stem from the same category of trigger. `Sign/Symptom` questions generated from `Sign/Symptom` triggers are usually asking about associated symptoms (e.g., Trigger: *dysuria*; Question: *Any perineal rash or irritation?*) or additional details about the trigger (e.g., onset, timing). Similarly, `Problem` questions generated from `Problem` triggers are usually asking about associated comorbid conditions or additional details of a diagnosis (e.g., date of diagnosis, severity). We interestingly find that 62% of the `Treatment` questions and 56% of the `Test Results` questions are derived from triggers of type `Problem`. This can be attributed to diagnostic tests being used to monitor disease progression and treatment questions asking about how a problem is managed.

Characteristics	emrQA	CliniQG4QA	DiSCQ
Total Articles	2,425	36	114
Total Questions	455,837	1287	2029
Questions / Article	187	35.8	17.8
Article Length	3828	2644	1481
Question Length	7.8	8.7	4.4
Unique Question Bi-grams	-	24%	59%
Physician Generated	0%	24%	100%
Indicates Question Motivation	No	No	Yes

Table 1: Comparison of emrQA, CliniQG4QA and our dataset. Question and article length scale given in tokens. Unique question bi-grams is given as a ratio.

As a soundness check, we randomly sample 100 questions from our dataset and find that only 22% of them directly map to emrQA templates. Of the 22 that match, 17 of them map directly to `|problem|?` and `|test|?`. Additionally, we sample 100 questions to determine where a physician would hypothetically search the EHR should

[5] Based on a sample of 100 questions.

they choose to find the answers to these questions.[6] We find that one of the authors, a physician, would search external resources 3% of the time, the structured data 20% of the time and both the structured and unstructured data 21% of the time. The remaining 56% of questions would be answered solely from unstructured EHR data. This differs significantly from both emrQA and CliniQG4QA, in which all questions are answerable using unstructured EHR data.

As mentioned previously, we provide only minimal guidance on how to select a trigger or what type of question to ask, in order to capture the annotators' natural thought processes. The task is purposely presented in an open-ended fashion to encourage natural questions. This may lead to situations in which two annotators examining the same discharge summary focus on entirely different aspects of the patient. Such a scenario is likely to be common, as if most experts agree that a piece of information is important, then it would likely already be in the discharge summary. We can attempt to measure this variation between medical experts by calculating trigger level agreement in documents annotated by two different annotators (roughly 50% of discharge summaries in DiSCQ). We find a Cohen Kappa of 0.08.[7]

This lower agreement can be expected, as different spans can express the same information due to information redundancy in clinical notes. Furthermore, clinical reasoning is not a linear process; therefore, different triggers can lead to the same question. For example, an expression of elevated blood pressure (*"blood pressure of 148 to 162/45 to 54"*) and a diagnosis of hypertension (*"Hypertension"*) led two annotators to both ask about the patient's normal blood pressure range. We do not measure agreement of questions asked, as this is an inherently subjective task and questions are asked *because* of differences between medical experts.

4 Task Setup

We consider the task of generating questions that are relevant to a patient's care, given a discharge summary and a trigger. Afterwards, we attempt to find answers to these generated questions (Figure 2). We also examine model performance for when the trigger is not provided and must instead be predicted. The task of generating questions without triggers can be viewed similarly to answer-agnostic question generation. We take a similar approach to (Subramanian et al., 2018), in which we implement a pipeline system that first selects key phrases from the passage and then generates questions about the selected key phrases.

While a majority of past works attempt to ensure that the generated question is answerable (Nema et al., 2019; Pan et al., 2020; Wang et al., 2020a; Huang et al., 2021), we do not impose this constraint. In fact, we argue that the ability to generate unanswerable questions is necessary for real-world applications, as a question answering system should be able to identify such questions. These questions can be used as hard-negatives to train and calibrate QA systems.

5 Models

Pre-trained transformers have become ubiquitous in many natural language processing tasks (Devlin et al., 2019; Raffel et al., 2020; Sanh et al., 2021), including natural language generation (Lewis et al., 2020; Bao et al., 2020). Additionally, large-scale transformers have demonstrated the importance of parameter count for both upstream (Kaplan et al., 2020) and downstream tasks, especially in low-resource settings (Brown et al., 2020; Sanh et al., 2021). As these results were mainly shown in non-clinical general domains, we find it important to evaluate both medium-sized and large models.

We formulate trigger detection as a tagging problem, for which we fine-tune ClinicalBERT (Alsentzer et al., 2019). For question generation, we experiment with both BART (406M parameters) (Lewis et al., 2020) and T0 (11B parameters) (Sanh et al., 2021). Question generation is formulated as a conditional generation problem and modelled via a sequence-to-sequence approach. During evaluation, we use greedy sampling to produce generated text.

Reducing context size Due to memory constraints and the limited sequence length of pre-trained models, we only select the part of the discharge summary containing the trigger. This is done in two possible ways: (1) extracting the sentence[8] with the trigger or multiple sentences if a trigger spans across sentence boundaries or (2) extracting a chunk of size 512 containing the trigger in it. To check if this context is actually used by

[6]We use the same sample of 100 questions as before.

[7]This is calculated on a per-token level.

[8]Sentence splitting is performed using ScispaCy's `en_core_sci_md`.

the models we also fine-tune BART without extra discharge summary context (trigger text only).

Handling multiple questions 41% of the DiSCQ examples have multiple questions per trigger. Sometimes the questions depend on each other:

- *What meds was used? dosage? and route of administration?*
- *Any culture done? What were the findings?*

For this reason, we train and evaluate models in two different setups: split questions (by the `?`-symbol) and combined questions. While the split-questions format might be more comparable to pre-existing work, the combined-questions setting likely models more realistic behavior of medical professionals.

Prompting Schick and Schütze (2021) demonstrate that adding natural language instructions to the model input can significantly improve model quality. The area of prompting has recently gained widespread popularity (Liu et al., 2021) and has had particular success in low-supervision scenarios (Schick and Schütze, 2021). T0 (Sanh et al., 2021) is a fine-tuned T5 (Raffel et al., 2020) model trained on 64 datasets and prompts from the Public Pool of Prompts (Bach et al., 2022). Given a trigger and some context from the discharge summary, we fine-tune T0++ and BART with the following prompt: "`{context}`After reading the above EMR, what question do you have about "`{trigger}`"? Question:".

6 Results

We split 2029 questions into train (70%), validation (10%) and test (20%) sets[9] and fine-tune the models as described in Section 5. To evaluate trigger detection, we use token-level precision, recall and F1 score. For automated evaluation of question generation we use ROUGE-L (Lin, 2004), METEOR (Banerjee and Lavie, 2005) and BERTScore (Zhang et al., 2020) metrics. To monitor the diversity of generated questions, we measure the fraction of unique questions on the evaluation set. As the question generation task has high variability of plausible generations, the utility of automatic metrics is debatable due to poor correlation with human evaluation (Callison-Burch et al., 2006; Novikova et al., 2017; Elliott and Keller, 2014; Zhang et al., 2020; Bhandari et al., 2020). For this reason, we additionally perform human evaluation (Section 7).

[9]We use a document level split.

6.1 Trigger detection

As mentioned in Section 3, we collect triggers for each question asked. We train a simple ClinicalBERT model to predict whether or not each token-piece is a trigger. To ground these results, we additionally use ScispaCy Large (Neumann et al., 2019) to tag and classify all clinical entities as triggers. Results are shown in Table 2.

Model	Recall	Precision	F1
ScispaCy	0.186	0.033	0.056
ClinicalBERT	0.184	0.196	0.190

Table 2: Trigger detection results on the test set.

We see that our model exhibits poor performance likely due to the fact that there is low agreement between annotators about which spans to highlight when asking questions.

6.2 Question generation

Automated metrics for question generation experiments are available in Table 4. While generation diversity changes significantly between different models, ranging from 30% of unique questions to 79%, METEOR, ROUGE-L and BERTScore show very similar and low performance across the board.

However, upon observation, many of the generated questions seem reasonable (Table 3), suggesting that these metrics might not fit the task. We hypothesize that this is caused by two reasons: (1) the short length of our questions and (2) a high number of potentially reasonable questions that could be generated. As we observe during the data collection process, different annotators seem to ask different questions despite citing the same trigger. For these reasons, human evaluation (Section 7) might be a more appropriate approach for testing the quality of these models.

6.3 Answer Selection

In addition to identifying triggers and generating questions, we attempt to find answers to these questions. We only consider the unstructured portion of the EHR data. We train a ClinicalBERT model on emrQA augmented with unanswerable questions via negative sampling (Liang et al., 2022). Due to the question's frequent dependency on the trigger, given a trigger and a question, we prompt the model with the following text: "With respect to `{trigger}`, `{question}`?". We first query the remainder of the discharge summary that the question was generated from. If we are unable to find

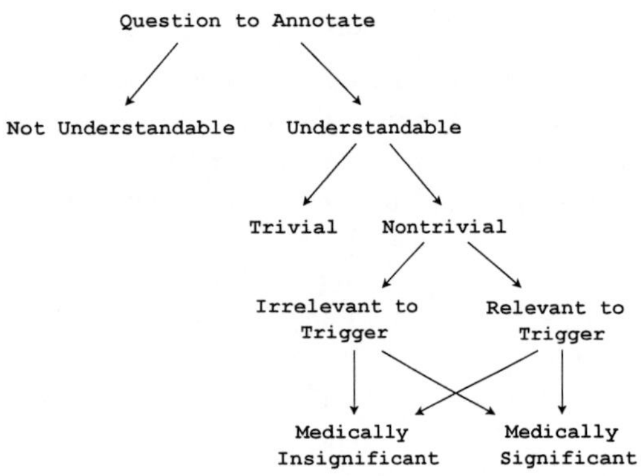

Figure 5: A breakdown of how questions are annotated.

an answer with probability above some threshold[10], we query the model on prior patient notes. We then select the highest probability span and expand it to a sentence level prediction. We always return a prediction even in cases where all sentences are equally unlikely to be the answer.

7 Human Evaluation

Human evaluation is still the most reliable way to compare generative models for diverse tasks like question generation. Common categories for question generation to consider are grammar, difficulty, answerability and fluency (Nema et al., 2019; Tuan et al., 2019; Wang et al., 2020b; Huang et al., 2021). However, not all of these categories are relevant to *clinical* question generation. We evaluate questions generated using our pipeline, as well as gold standard questions on the following four categories (binary scale):

Understandability Can an individual familiar with medical/clinical language understand the information needs expressed, even if the question is not a complete sentence or contains grammar/spelling errors?

Nontriviality Is the question unanswerable with respect to the sentence it was triggered/generated from? A question that would be considered *trivial* would be "Did the patient have a fever?" if the context presented was "The patient had a fever".

Relevancy to trigger Is the trigger or the sentence containing the trigger related to the question?

[10]This threshold was chosen manually by examining question-answer pairs on a validation set.

Clinical meaningfulness Will the answer to this question be helpful for further treatment of this patient or understanding the patient's current condition? Or alternatively, is it reasonable that a medical professional would ask this question given the provided context?

Annotations were divided evenly between medical experts. Each question is scored independently by two different annotators. However, due to time constraints, there are no discussions between annotators about their decisions. We also ensure that annotators did not receive discharge summaries that they had seen previously. Lastly, it is important to note that annotations were assigned blindly. Annotators were informed that they would be scoring both human and machine generated questions, but were not informed about (1) where the question was generated from (i.e., human or machine) and (2) the proportion of human:machine generated questions.

We score questions using the tree presented in Figure 5. In cases in which the question is both understandable and nontrivial, we additionally ask medical experts to determine whether or not the proposed answer fully answers, partially answers or is irrelevant to the question. Results can be seen in Table 5 and Table 6.

8 Discussion

We evaluate performance of both the best BART and T0 model with respect to ROUGE-L score. We select 400 questions generated from each model, half of which are generated with gold triggers and the other half with predicted triggers, as described in Section 6.1. Two medical experts score each question. Due to the subjective nature of the task, we find moderate agreement between annotators with respect to scoring questions ($\kappa = 0.46$) and scoring answer sufficiency ($\kappa = 0.47$). We use the "Satisfies All" column (i.e., satisfies all four human evaluation categories) to calculate agreement between questions.

Results show that the T0 model prompted with gold triggers successfully generates a high-quality question 62.5% of the time (Table 5). This model significantly outperforms BART when given gold-standard triggers. However, the performance significantly drops when the triggers are no longer provided. We find that T0 produces a large number of *trivial* questions when given a predicted trigger. More testing and investigation is needed to further

Context	Generated Question	Trigger Type	Question Type
Pt reports that he noticed a *right neck mass* last October	Size, outline (asymmetry), color, elevation, evolving?	sign/symptom	sign/symptom
She was also significantly *tachypneic*	were there interventions done to address this?	sign/symptom	treatment
According to Dr. <name>, she has had stable deficits for many years *without any flare-like episodes*.	How is her vision now?	assessment	sign/symptom
Her bicarb began to drop and she developed an *anion gap acidosis*	confusion? confusion? agitation? hand tremors? bounding pulses?	problem	sign/symptom

Table 3: Example T0 model generations, cherry-picked. This model examines single sentences and is trained with combined questions. Trigger phrases are *italicized*.

Model Type	Context	Split Qs	Unique Question Ratio	METEOR	BERTScore	ROUGE-L
BART	Trigger	N	0.301	3.6	0.856	10.2
BART	Trigger	Y	0.037	0.1	0.838	3.4
BART	Sentence	N	0.526	6.1	0.860	10.2
BART	Sentence	Y	0.468	7.8	0.858	12.0
BART	Chunk	N	0.741	7.9	0.861	11.9
BART	Chunk	Y	0.619	7.2	0.861	11.6
T0-11B	Sentence	N	**0.779**	3.9	0.861	11.9
T0-11B	Sentence	Y	0.410	**8.4**	**0.884**	12.2
T0-11B	Chunk	N	0.398	3.7	0.860	**12.4**
T0-11B	Chunk	Y	0.400	6.7	0.879	10.9

Table 4: Automated metrics for baseline models on the question generation task. *Sentence* and *Chunk* contexts include both the text surrounding the trigger and the trigger itself. *Trigger* context only includes trigger text. Split Qs means splitting multiple questions for a trigger into multiple examples (unique question ratio of these models should not be compared). Results given on dev set.

understand this large drop in performance, as we do not observe this same behavior with BART.

As human evaluation demonstrates, despite low automatic metric scores, both BART and T0 achieve reasonable success in generating coherent, relevant and clinically interesting questions. To evaluate if the automated metrics can capture the quality of generated questions, we calculate the Spearman's Rank Correlation Coefficient between human evaluation and automatic metrics. We find extremely low and statistically insignificant correlation for ROUGE-L (-0.09), METEOR (-0.04) and BERTScore (-0.04). This is unsurprising, as these automatic metrics are not designed to capture the categories we examine during human evaluation.

We also score the answers selected by our ClinicalBERT model trained on emrQA (Section 6.3). Interestingly, we find that of the answers the model successfully recovers, 44% are extracted from the remainder of the discharge summary used to generate the question. The remaining 56% come from nursing notes, Radiology/ECG reports and previous discharge summaries. However, for a majority of the questions, we are unable to recover a sufficient answer (Table 6). We sample 50 gold standard questions whose suggested answers were marked as invalid, in order to determine if this was due to the model's poor performance. We find that 36% of the questions do in fact have answers in the EHR, thus demonstrating the need for improved clinical QA resources and models.

9 Conclusion

We present **Di**scharge **S**ummary **C**linical **Q**uestions (DiSCQ), a new human-generated clinical question dataset composed of 2000+ questions paired with the snippets of text that prompted each question. We train baseline models for trigger detection and question generation. We find that despite poor performance on automatic metrics, we are

Model	Triggers	Understandable	Nontrivial	Relevant	Clinically Meaningful	Satisfies All
Gold	-	93.8%	86.0%	83.3%	82.3%	80.5%
BART	Gold	81.5%	59.8%	52.3%	54.8%	47.8%
T0	Gold	85.8%	72.3%	68.0%	66.5%	**62.5%**
BART	Predicted	78.3%	57.3%	49.3%	49.8%	41.8%
T0	Predicted	76.8%	49.0%	45.0%	44.5%	41.0%

Table 5: We present results of human evaluation on generated questions. Gold refers to questions generated by medical experts. We do not annotate whether or not a question is nontrivial, relevant and clinically meaningful if it is not understandable, thus lowering the number of questions that satisfy these categories.

Model	Triggers	Partially	Fully
Gold	-	15.0%	7.50%
BART	Gold	13.75%	7.75%
T0	Gold	11.5%	6.00%
BART	Predicted	14.5%	6.25%
T0	Predicted	9.75%	3.25%

Table 6: Percent of the time that the answer retrieved by our model partially answers and fully answers the question.

able to produce reasonable questions in a majority of cases when given triggers selected by medical experts. However, we find that performance significantly drops when given machine predicted triggers. Further, we find that baseline models trained on emrQA are insufficient for recovering answers to both human and machine generated questions. Our results demonstrate that existing machine learning systems, including large-scale neural networks, struggle with the tasks we propose. We encourage the community to improve on our baseline models. We release this dataset and our code to facilitate further research into realistic clinical question answering and generation here.

10 Acknowledgements

This work was supported and sponsored by the MIT-IBM Watson AI Lab. The authors would like to thank Sierra Tseng for feedback on a draft of this manuscript, as well as Melina Young and Maggie Liu for their help in designing some of the figures.

References

Asma Ben Abacha, Eugene Agichtein, Yuval Pinter, and Dina Demner-Fushman. 2017. Overview of the medical question answering task at trec 2017 liveqa. In *TREC*.

Asma Ben Abacha, Yassine Mrabet, Mark E. Sharp, Travis R. Goodwin, Sonya E. Shooshan, and Dina Demner-Fushman. 2019. Bridging the gap between consumers' medication questions and trusted answers. *Studies in health technology and informatics*, 264:25–29.

Asma Ben Abacha and Pierre Zweigenbaum. 2015. Means: A medical question-answering system combining nlp techniques and semantic web technologies. *Inf. Process. Manag.*, 51:570–594.

Emily Alsentzer, John Murphy, William Boag, Wei-Hung Weng, Di Jindi, Tristan Naumann, and Matthew McDermott. 2019. Publicly available clinical BERT embeddings. In *Proceedings of the 2nd Clinical Natural Language Processing Workshop*, pages 72–78, Minneapolis, Minnesota, USA. Association for Computational Linguistics.

Stephen H. Bach, Victor Sanh, Zheng-Xin Yong, Albert Webson, Colin Raffel, Nihal V. Nayak, Abheesht Sharma, Taewoon Kim, M Saiful Bari, Thibault Fevry, Zaid Alyafeai, Manan Dey, Andrea Santilli, Zhiqing Sun, Srulik Ben-David, Canwen Xu, Gunjan Chhablani, Han Wang, Jason Alan Fries, Maged S. Al-shaibani, Shanya Sharma, Urmish Thakker, Khalid Almubarak, Xiangru Tang, Dragomir Radev, Mike Tian-Jian Jiang, and Alexander M. Rush. 2022. Promptsource: An integrated development environment and repository for natural language prompts.

Satanjeev Banerjee and Alon Lavie. 2005. METEOR: An automatic metric for MT evaluation with improved correlation with human judgments. In *Proceedings of the ACL Workshop on Intrinsic and Extrinsic Evaluation Measures for Machine Translation and/or Summarization*, pages 65–72, Ann Arbor, Michigan. Association for Computational Linguistics.

Hangbo Bao, Li Dong, Furu Wei, Wenhui Wang, Nan Yang, Xiaodong Liu, Yu Wang, Songhao Piao, Jianfeng Gao, Ming Zhou, and Hsiao-Wuen Hon. 2020. Unilmv2: Pseudo-masked language models for unified language model pre-training. In *ICML*.

Manik Bhandari, Pranav Narayan Gour, Atabak Ashfaq, Peng fei Liu, and Graham Neubig. 2020. Re-evaluating evaluation in text summarization. *ArXiv*, abs/2010.07100.

Tom Brown, Benjamin Mann, Nick Ryder, Melanie Subbiah, Jared D Kaplan, Prafulla Dhariwal, Arvind Neelakantan, Pranav Shyam, Girish Sastry, Amanda Askell, Sandhini Agarwal, Ariel Herbert-Voss, Gretchen Krueger, Tom Henighan, Rewon Child, Aditya Ramesh, Daniel Ziegler, Jeffrey Wu, Clemens Winter, Chris Hesse, Mark Chen, Eric Sigler, Mateusz Litwin, Scott Gray, Benjamin Chess, Jack Clark, Christopher Berner, Sam McCandlish, Alec Radford, Ilya Sutskever, and Dario Amodei. 2020. Language models are few-shot learners. In *Advances in Neural Information Processing Systems*, volume 33, pages 1877–1901. Curran Associates, Inc.

Chris Callison-Burch, Miles Osborne, and Philipp Koehn. 2006. Re-evaluating the role of Bleu in machine translation research. In *11th Conference of the European Chapter of the Association for Computational Linguistics*, pages 249–256, Trento, Italy. Association for Computational Linguistics.

Yonggang Cao, F. Liu, Pippa M Simpson, Lamont D. Antieau, Andrew S. Bennett, James J. Cimino, John W. Ely, and Hong Yu. 2011. Askhermes: An online question answering system for complex clinical questions. *Journal of biomedical informatics*, 44 2:277–88.

Nicholas Carlini, Florian Tramèr, Eric Wallace, Matthew Jagielski, Ariel Herbert-Voss, Katherine Lee, Adam Roberts, Tom B. Brown, Dawn Xiaodong Song, Úlfar Erlingsson, Alina Oprea, and Colin Raffel. 2021. Extracting training data from large language models. In *USENIX Security Symposium*.

Yllias Chali and Sadid A. Hasan. 2015. Towards topic-to-question generation. *Computational Linguistics*, 41(1):1–20.

Donna D'Alessandro, Clarence Kreiter, and Michael Peterson. 2004. An evaluation of information-seeking behaviors of general pediatricians. *Pediatrics*, 113:64–9.

Dina Demner-Fushman, Wendy Chapman, and Clement Mcdonald. 2009. What can natural language processing do for clinical decision support? *Journal of biomedical informatics*, 42:760–72.

Dina Demner-Fushman, Yassine Mrabet, and Asma Ben Abacha. 2020. Consumer health information and question answering: helping consumers find answers to their health-related information needs. *Journal of the American Medical Informatics Association : JAMIA*.

Jacob Devlin, Ming-Wei Chang, Kenton Lee, and Kristina Toutanova. 2019. BERT: Pre-training of deep bidirectional transformers for language understanding. In *Proceedings of the 2019 Conference of the North American Chapter of the Association for Computational Linguistics: Human Language Technologies, Volume 1 (Long and Short Papers)*, pages 4171–4186, Minneapolis, Minnesota. Association for Computational Linguistics.

Li Dong, Nan Yang, Wenhui Wang, Furu Wei, Xiaodong Liu, Yu Wang, Jianfeng Gao, Ming Zhou, and Hsiao-Wuen Hon. 2019. Unified language model pre-training for natural language understanding and generation.

Xinya Du, Junru Shao, and Claire Cardie. 2017. Learning to ask: Neural question generation for reading comprehension. *CoRR*, abs/1705.00106.

Nan Duan, Duyu Tang, Peng Chen, and Ming Zhou. 2017. Question generation for question answering. In *Proceedings of the 2017 Conference on Empirical Methods in Natural Language Processing*, pages 866–874, Copenhagen, Denmark. Association for Computational Linguistics.

Desmond Elliott and Frank Keller. 2014. Comparing automatic evaluation measures for image description. In *Proceedings of the 52nd Annual Meeting of the Association for Computational Linguistics (Volume 2: Short Papers)*, pages 452–457, Baltimore, Maryland. Association for Computational Linguistics.

Jungwei Fan. 2019. Annotating and characterizing clinical sentences with explicit why-QA cues. In *Proceedings of the 2nd Clinical Natural Language Processing Workshop*, pages 101–106, Minneapolis, Minnesota, USA. Association for Computational Linguistics.

Michael Heilman and Noah A. Smith. 2010. Good question! statistical ranking for question generation. In *Human Language Technologies: The 2010 Annual Conference of the North American Chapter of the Association for Computational Linguistics*, pages 609–617, Los Angeles, California. Association for Computational Linguistics.

Qingbao Huang, Mingyi Fu, Linzhang Mo, Yi Cai, Jingyun Xu, Pijian Li, Qing Li, and Ho-fung Leung. 2021. Entity guided question generation with contextual structure and sequence information capturing. *Proceedings of the AAAI Conference on Artificial Intelligence*, 35(14):13064–13072.

Alistair EW Johnson, Tom J Pollard, Lu Shen, H Lehman Li-wei, Mengling Feng, Mohammad Ghassemi, Benjamin Moody, Peter Szolovits, Leo Anthony Celi, and Roger G Mark. 2016. Mimic-iii, a freely accessible critical care database. *Scientific data*, 3:160035.

Jared Kaplan, Sam McCandlish, T. J. Henighan, Tom B. Brown, Benjamin Chess, Rewon Child, Scott Gray, Alec Radford, Jeff Wu, and Dario Amodei. 2020. Scaling laws for neural language models. *ArXiv*, abs/2001.08361.

Gregory Kell, Iain Marshall, Byron Wallace, and Andre Jaun. 2021. What would it take to get biomedical QA systems into practice? In *Proceedings of the 3rd*

Workshop on Machine Reading for Question Answering, pages 28–41, Punta Cana, Dominican Republic. Association for Computational Linguistics.

Igor Labutov, Sumit Basu, and Lucy Vanderwende. 2015. Deep questions without deep understanding. In *Proceedings of the 53rd Annual Meeting of the Association for Computational Linguistics and the 7th International Joint Conference on Natural Language Processing (Volume 1: Long Papers)*, pages 889–898, Beijing, China. Association for Computational Linguistics.

Eric P. Lehman, Sarthak Jain, Karl Pichotta, Yoav Goldberg, and Byron C. Wallace. 2021. Does bert pretrained on clinical notes reveal sensitive data? *ArXiv*, abs/2104.07762.

Adam D. Lelkes, Vinh Q. Tran, and Cong Yu. 2021. Quiz-style question generation for news stories.

Mike Lewis, Yinhan Liu, Naman Goyal, Marjan Ghazvininejad, Abdelrahman Mohamed, Omer Levy, Veselin Stoyanov, and Luke Zettlemoyer. 2020. BART: Denoising sequence-to-sequence pre-training for natural language generation, translation, and comprehension. In *Proceedings of the 58th Annual Meeting of the Association for Computational Linguistics*, pages 7871–7880, Online. Association for Computational Linguistics.

Jennifer J. Liang, Eric Lehman, Ananya S. Iyengar, Diwakar Mahajan, Preethi Raghavan, Cindy Y. Chang, and Peter Szolovits. 2022. Towards generalizable methods for automating risk score calculation. In *Proceedings of the 21st SIGBioMed Workshop on Biomedical Language Processing*. Association for Computational Linguistics.

Chin-Yew Lin. 2004. ROUGE: A package for automatic evaluation of summaries. In *Text Summarization Branches Out*, pages 74–81, Barcelona, Spain. Association for Computational Linguistics.

Pengfei Liu, Weizhe Yuan, Jinlan Fu, Zhengbao Jiang, Hiroaki Hayashi, and Graham Neubig. 2021. Pretrain, prompt, and predict: A systematic survey of prompting methods in natural language processing.

Hongyin Luo, Seunghak Yu, Shang-Wen Li, and James R. Glass. 2021. Cooperative learning of zero-shot machine reading comprehension. *ArXiv*, abs/2103.07449.

Karen Mazidi and Rodney D. Nielsen. 2014. Linguistic considerations in automatic question generation. In *Proceedings of the 52nd Annual Meeting of the Association for Computational Linguistics (Volume 2: Short Papers)*, pages 321–326, Baltimore, Maryland. Association for Computational Linguistics.

Nasrin Mostafazadeh, Nathanael Chambers, Xiaodong He, Devi Parikh, Dhruv Batra, Lucy Vanderwende, Pushmeet Kohli, and James Allen. 2016. A corpus and cloze evaluation for deeper understanding of commonsense stories. In *Proceedings of the 2016 Conference of the North American Chapter of the Association for Computational Linguistics: Human Language Technologies*, pages 839–849, San Diego, California. Association for Computational Linguistics.

Lidiya Murakhovs'ka, Chien Sheng Wu, Tong Niu, Wenhao Liu, and Caiming Xiong. 2021. Mixqg: Neural question generation with mixed answer types. *ArXiv*, abs/2110.08175.

Preksha Nema, Akash Kumar Mohankumar, Mitesh M. Khapra, Balaji Vasan Srinivasan, and Balaraman Ravindran. 2019. Let's ask again: Refine network for automatic question generation. *ArXiv*, abs/1909.05355.

Mark Neumann, Daniel King, Iz Beltagy, and Waleed Ammar. 2019. Scispacy: Fast and robust models for biomedical natural language processing. *ArXiv*, abs/1902.07669.

Jekaterina Novikova, Ondřej Dušek, Amanda Cercas Curry, and Verena Rieser. 2017. Why we need new evaluation metrics for NLG. In *Proceedings of the 2017 Conference on Empirical Methods in Natural Language Processing*, pages 2241–2252, Copenhagen, Denmark. Association for Computational Linguistics.

Anusri Pampari, Preethi Raghavan, Jennifer Liang, and Jian Peng. 2018. emrqa: A large corpus for question answering on electronic medical records.

Liangming Pan, Yuxi Xie, Yansong Feng, Tat-Seng Chua, and Min-Yen Kan. 2020. Semantic graphs for generating deep questions. In *Proceedings of the 58th Annual Meeting of the Association for Computational Linguistics*, pages 1463–1475, Online. Association for Computational Linguistics.

F. Pedregosa, G. Varoquaux, A. Gramfort, V. Michel, B. Thirion, O. Grisel, M. Blondel, P. Prettenhofer, R. Weiss, V. Dubourg, J. Vanderplas, A. Passos, D. Cournapeau, M. Brucher, M. Perrot, and E. Duchesnay. 2011. Scikit-learn: Machine learning in Python. *Journal of Machine Learning Research*, 12:2825–2830.

Raul Puri, Ryan Spring, Mohammad Shoeybi, Mostofa Patwary, and Bryan Catanzaro. 2020. Training question answering models from synthetic data. In *Proceedings of the 2020 Conference on Empirical Methods in Natural Language Processing (EMNLP)*, pages 5811–5826, Online. Association for Computational Linguistics.

Weizhen Qi, Yu Yan, Yeyun Gong, Dayiheng Liu, Nan Duan, Jiusheng Chen, Ruofei Zhang, and Ming Zhou. 2020. ProphetNet: Predicting future n-gram for sequence-to-SequencePre-training. In *Findings of the Association for Computational Linguistics: EMNLP 2020*, pages 2401–2410, Online. Association for Computational Linguistics.

Colin Raffel, Noam Shazeer, Adam Roberts, Katherine Lee, Sharan Narang, Michael Matena, Yanqi Zhou, Wei Li, and Peter J. Liu. 2020. Exploring the limits of transfer learning with a unified text-to-text transformer. *Journal of Machine Learning Research*, 21(140):1–67.

Preethi Raghavan, Jennifer J Liang, Diwakar Mahajan, Rachita Chandra, and Peter Szolovits. 2021. emrKBQA: A clinical knowledge-base question answering dataset. In *Proceedings of the 20th Workshop on Biomedical Language Processing*, pages 64–73, Online. Association for Computational Linguistics.

Victor Sanh, Albert Webson, Colin Raffel, Stephen H. Bach, Lintang Sutawika, Zaid Alyafeai, Antoine Chaffin, Arnaud Stiegler, Teven Le Scao, Arun Raja, Manan Dey, M Saiful Bari, Canwen Xu, Urmish Thakker, Shanya Sharma Sharma, Eliza Szczechla, Taewoon Kim, Gunjan Chhablani, Nihal Nayak, Debajyoti Datta, Jonathan Chang, Mike Tian-Jian Jiang, Han Wang, Matteo Manica, Sheng Shen, Zheng Xin Yong, Harshit Pandey, Rachel Bawden, Thomas Wang, Trishala Neeraj, Jos Rozen, Abheesht Sharma, Andrea Santilli, Thibault Fevry, Jason Alan Fries, Ryan Teehan, Stella Biderman, Leo Gao, Tali Bers, Thomas Wolf, and Alexander M. Rush. 2021. Multitask prompted training enables zero-shot task generalization.

Max E. Savery, Asma Ben Abacha, Soumya Gayen, and Dina Demner-Fushman. 2020. Question-driven summarization of answers to consumer health questions. *Scientific Data*, 7.

Timo Schick and Hinrich Schütze. 2021. It's not just size that matters: Small language models are also few-shot learners. *ArXiv*, abs/2009.07118.

Iulian Vlad Serban, Tim Klinger, Gerald Tesauro, Kartik Talamadupula, Bowen Zhou, Yoshua Bengio, and Aaron C. Courville. 2016. Multiresolution recurrent neural networks: An application to dialogue response generation. *CoRR*, abs/1606.00776.

Lifeng Shang, Zhengdong Lu, and Hang Li. 2015. Neural responding machine for short-text conversation. *CoRR*, abs/1503.02364.

Heung-Yeung Shum, Xiaodong He, and Di Li. 2018. From eliza to xiaoice: Challenges and opportunities with social chatbots.

Sarvesh Soni, Meghana Gudala, Daisy Zhe Wang, and Kirk Roberts. 2019. Using fhir to construct a corpus of clinical questions annotated with logical forms and answers. *AMIA ... Annual Symposium proceedings. AMIA Symposium*, 2019:1207–1215.

Sandeep Subramanian, Tong Wang, Xingdi Yuan, Saizheng Zhang, Adam Trischler, and Yoshua Bengio. 2018. Neural models for key phrase extraction and question generation. In *Proceedings of the Workshop on Machine Reading for Question Answering*, pages 78–88, Melbourne, Australia. Association for Computational Linguistics.

Simon Suster and Walter Daelemans. 2018. Clicr: a dataset of clinical case reports for machine reading comprehension. In *NAACL*.

Duyu Tang, Nan Duan, Tao Qin, and Ming Zhou. 2017. Question answering and question generation as dual tasks. *CoRR*, abs/1706.02027.

Luu Anh Tuan, Darsh J Shah, and Regina Barzilay. 2019. Capturing greater context for question generation.

Bingning Wang, Xiaochuan Wang, Ting Tao, Qi Zhang, and Jingfang Xu. 2020a. Neural question generation with answer pivot. *Proceedings of the AAAI Conference on Artificial Intelligence*, 34(05):9138–9145.

Liuyin Wang, Zihan Xu, Zibo Lin, Haitao Zheng, and Ying Shen. 2020b. Answer-driven deep question generation based on reinforcement learning. In *Proceedings of the 28th International Conference on Computational Linguistics*, pages 5159–5170, Barcelona, Spain (Online). International Committee on Computational Linguistics.

Thomas Wolf, Lysandre Debut, Victor Sanh, Julien Chaumond, Clement Delangue, Anthony Moi, Pierric Cistac, Tim Rault, Rémi Louf, Morgan Funtowicz, and Jamie Brew. 2019. Huggingface's transformers: State-of-the-art natural language processing. *ArXiv*, abs/1910.03771.

Hong Yu, Minsuk Lee, David R. Kaufman, John W. Ely, Jerome A. Osheroff, George Hripcsak, and James J. Cimino. 2007. Development, implementation, and a cognitive evaluation of a definitional question answering system for physicians. *Journal of biomedical informatics*, 40 3:236–51.

Xiang Yue, Bernal Jimenez Gutierrez, and Huan Sun. 2020. Clinical reading comprehension: A thorough analysis of the emrQA dataset. In *Proceedings of the 58th Annual Meeting of the Association for Computational Linguistics*, pages 4474–4486, Online. Association for Computational Linguistics.

Xiang Yue, Xinliang Frederick Zhang, Ziyu Yao, Simon Lin, and Huan Sun. 2021. Cliniqg4qa: Generating diverse questions for domain adaptation of clinical question answering.

M. A. H. Zahid, Ankush Mittal, Ramesh Chandra Joshi, and Gowtham Atluri. 2018. Cliniqa: A machine intelligence based clinical question answering system. *ArXiv*, abs/1805.05927.

Tianyi Zhang, Varsha Kishore, Felix Wu, Kilian Q. Weinberger, and Yoav Artzi. 2020. Bertscore: Evaluating text generation with bert.

Ming Zhu, Aman Ahuja, Da-Cheng Juan, Wei Wei, and Chandan K. Reddy. 2020. Question answering with long multiple-span answers. In *Findings of the Association for Computational Linguistics: EMNLP 2020*, pages 3840–3849, Online. Association for Computational Linguistics.

A Appendix

A.1 Model and Metric Implementation

To run BART and T0, we make use of the Huggingface implementations (Wolf et al., 2019). We additionally calculate automated metrics for question generation using Huggingface. For calculating Cohen Kappa, precision, recall, and F1 score, we use sklearn (Pedregosa et al., 2011).

A.2 Model Hyperparameters

We use a majority of the default settings provided by the Huggingface library (Wolf et al., 2019). However, we do experiment with varying learning rates (2e-5, 2e-4, 3e-4, 4e-4), warm up steps (100, 200), and weight-decay (0, 1e-6, 1e-3, 1e-1). For the best BART model, we find that using a learning rate of 2e-4, warm up steps of 200, and weight decay of 1e-6 led to the best model. For the T0 model, we find that using a learning rate of 3e-4, running for 100 warmup steps and using a weight-decay of 0.1 led to the best performance. We run for 50 epochs on the BART model and 30 epochs on the T0 model. We use the best epoch with respect to evaluation loss. In our dev set evaluation, we use a beam search width of 5. We use a gradient accumulation step of 32 and 16 for our BART model and T0 model, respectively,

A.3 GPUs and Run Time

For the BART models, we run on 4 GeForce GTX TITAN X. Due to the limited size of these GPUs, we only use a batch size of 1 per GPU. The BART style models take roughly 8 hours to finish training.

For the T0 models, we train using eight V100 GPUs. We set batch size to be 2 per GPU. These models take roughly 24 hours to train.

A.4 Risk of Patient Privacy

We will release our code and data under MIMIC-III access. Carlini et al. (2021) warns against training large-scale transformer models (particularly ones for generation) on sensitive data. Although MIMIC-III notes consist of deidentified data, we will not release our model weights to the general public. With respect to the trigger detection system, there is less risk in releasing the model weights, as BERT has not been pretrained with generation tasks (Lehman et al., 2021). We caution all follow up work to take these privacy concerns into account.

Clinical Flair: A Pre-Trained Language Model for Spanish Clinical Natural Language Processing

Matías Rojas[1,3], Jocelyn Dunstan[2,3,4], and Fabián Villena[1,3]
[1]Department of Computer Sciences, University of Chile.
[2]Initiative for Data & Artificial Intelligence, University of Chile.
[3]Center for Mathematical Modeling - CNRS IRL 2807, University of Chile.
[4]Millenium Institute for Intelligent Healthcare Engineering, ANID, Chile.
matias.rojas.g@ug.uchile.cl
{jdunstan, fabian.villena}@uchile.cl

Abstract

Word embeddings have been widely used in Natural Language Processing (NLP) tasks. Although these representations can capture the semantic information of words, they cannot learn the sequence-level semantics. This problem can be handled using contextual word embeddings derived from pre-trained language models, which have contributed to significant improvements in several NLP tasks. Further improvements are achieved when pre-training these models on domain-specific corpora. In this paper, we introduce Clinical Flair, a domain-specific language model trained on Spanish clinical narratives. To validate the quality of the contextual representations retrieved from our model, we tested them on four named entity recognition datasets belonging to the clinical and biomedical domains. Our experiments confirm that incorporating domain-specific embeddings into classical sequence labeling architectures improves model performance dramatically compared to general-domain embeddings, demonstrating the importance of having these resources available.

1 Introduction

Word embeddings are dense, semantically meaningful vector representations of a word. This method has proven to be a fundamental building block when constructing neural network-based architectures. However, the main drawback of using these embeddings is that they provide only a single representation of a given word across many documents. This is not optimal in practice, as the representation depends on the sentence in which the word appears. Contextual word embeddings address this problem by capturing syntactic and semantic information at the sentence level to represent words according to their context.

Contextualized embeddings are commonly retrieved from language models trained on giant text corpora. These models are usually composed of sequential or attention neural networks, which allows obtaining sentence-level semantics. This method has contributed to major advances in several NLP tasks such as named entity recognition, text classification, and relation extraction. Classic examples of contextual representation models are Flair (Akbik et al., 2018), ELMo (Peters et al., 2018), and BERT (Devlin et al., 2019).

Regarding specific domains such as clinical and biomedical, there are widely used models for the English language, such as BioBERT (Lee et al., 2020), BioELMo (Jin et al., 2019), and the PubMed version of Flair. These studies have shown that incorporating domain-specific contextual word embeddings contributes to a significant improvement in the performance of the models. However, although unstructured clinical texts are abundant in Spanish, there is still a significant lack of language models. Most of the domain-specific contextual representation models available for Spanish focus on data obtained from scientific articles and not from texts written in a more realistic context.

To fill this gap, we trained and publicly released Clinical Flair[1], a character-level language model trained on a corpus with real diagnoses in Spanish. To measure the potential impact of using these representations, we provide an empirical study of the effects of using language models trained on domain-specific against general-domain corpora. We evaluated the effectiveness of the proposed embeddings on four named entity recognition datasets belonging to the clinical and biomedical domain in Spanish. The results suggest that the embeddings obtained from our model contribute to achieving a better model performance compared to the general-domain contextualized embeddings by a wide margin.

[1]https://github.com/plncmm/spanish-clinical-flair

Proceedings of the 4th Clinical Natural Language Processing Workshop, pages 87 - 92
July 14, 2022

2 Related Work

Language models allow us to generate high-quality representations of words based on their surrounding context, better known as contextual word embeddings. These models are usually trained with large corpora, either general-domain or domain-specific. Most of the available models have been trained with English resources, where the most popular ones are BERT (Devlin et al., 2019), ELMo (Peters et al., 2018), GPT-2 (Radford et al., 2019), and Flair (Akbik et al., 2018).

As pointed out in Lee et al. (2020), building domain-specific language models allows to improve models performance compared to general-domain language models. In relation to biomedical information retrieval (IR) tasks in English, the most well-known architectures are BioBERT (Lee et al., 2020), Clinical BERT (Alsentzer et al., 2019), SciBERT (Beltagy et al., 2019), Pubmed BERT (Gu et al., 2022), BioELMo (Jin et al., 2019) and Pubmed Flair.

Regarding the clinical domain in Spanish, we found the models Biomedical Roberta (Carrino et al., 2022) and SciELO Flair (Akhtyamova et al., 2020). In the first case, the main difference with our model is that Biomedical Roberta was trained on a corpus formed by several biomedical and clinical corpora, while we only used clinical narratives. In the case of SciELO Flair, a point of differentiation is that they used data obtained from medical publications, whereas our data comes from primary care diagnoses. Moreover, they only tested their model on the PharmaCoNER corpus, created from the same data source they trained SciELO Flair. In contrast, we tested the effectiveness of our model using four clinical and biomedical datasets.

3 Methods

This section describes the clinical dataset used to train our language model, the details of the training process, and, finally, the task and datasets used in our experiments.

3.1 Clinical Flair

Flair (Akbik et al., 2018) is a character-level language model, which represents words as sequences of characters contextualized by the surrounded text. Flair authors created a method to obtain contextualized representations by retrieving the internal states of a bidirectional character-level LSTM. Specifically, the embedding is created by concatenating the output of the hidden state after the last character and before the first character of the word. This process allows obtaining the word context in the sentence in both directions.

We decided to use Flair instead of BERT because the character-level language model is beneficial for handling misspelled and out-of-vocabulary words, which are abundant in clinical and biomedical texts. This is because BERT is limited to a predefined vocabulary used to perform the tokenization. When a word is outside the vocabulary, the BERT model combines the embeddings of its subwords to compute the final representation, which may decrease the quality of the embeddings. This does not occur in the case of Flair, where each word has an embedding independent of its subword embeddings.

To create our clinical version of Flair, we used as a starting point the existing language models *es-forward* and *es-backward*. These models trained on a large corpus obtained from the Spanish Wikipedia are freely available in the Flair framework (Akbik et al., 2019). To incorporate key information from the clinical context, we fine-tuned these models on the Chilean Waiting List corpus (Báez et al., 2020), which is a clinical corpus created from real diagnoses from the Chilean public healthcare system.

The Chilean Waiting List corpus consists of $5,157,902$ free-text diagnostic suspicions comprising $14,057,401$ sentences and $68,541,727$ tokens. Although the general purpose of this dataset was to be a new resource for named entity recognition, it has also been used to obtain static word embeddings from the clinical domain (Villena et al., 2021b). These representations have boosted the model's performance in several clinical NLP tasks such as tumor encoding (Villena et al., 2021a) and named entity recognition (Báez et al., 2022).

We did not perform any pre-processing of the data for training our language model. The corpus was divided into 60% for training, 20% for validation, and 20% for testing. According to the suggestions of Flair authors, we set the maximum sentence length to 250, the mini-batches to 100 sentences, the maximum training epochs to $1,000$, and the learning rate to 20. The experiments were performed with a Tesla V100 GPU and 192 GB RAM. After one week of training, we reached a final perplexity value of 1.61 and 1.63 for our *es-clinical-forward* and *es-clinical-backward* models, respectively.

	CANTEMIST			PharmaCoNER			Clinical Trials			NUBes		
	Train	Test	Dev	Train	Test	Dev	Train	Test	Dev	Train	Test	Dev
Tokens	442,097	240,326	396,457	210,778	104,201	100,147	208,188	68,994	69,319	255,897	51,233	35,416
Sentences	19,397	11,168	18,165	8,177	3,976	3,790	12,555	4,506	4,550	13,802	2,762	1,840
Avg sentence length	22.8	21.5	21.8	25.8	26.2	26.4	16.6	15.3	15.3	18.5	18.6	19,2
Entities	6,347	3,596	5,948	3,821	1,876	1,926	24,224	7,717	8,258	17,122	3,548	2,293
Avg entity length	2.4	2.3	2.3	1.4	1.4	1.4	2.0	2.0	2.0	2.6	2.6	2.6

Table 1: Statistics of the NER datasets used in our experiments.

3.2 Datasets

To evaluate the quality of our contextual representations, we used the Named Entity Recognition (NER) task, which seeks to identify spans of text expressing references to predefined categories. Specifically, we performed our experiments on four NER corpora belonging to the clinical and biomedical domains. The statistics for each corpus are shown in Table 1.

- **CANTEMIST[2] (Miranda-Escalada et al., 2020)**: An open annotated corpus that comprises 1,301 oncologic clinical case reports written in Spanish and manually annotated by clinical experts with mentions of tumor morphology. It contains a total of 48,730 sentences and 15,891 entity mentions.
- **PharmaCoNER[3] (Gonzalez-Agirre et al., 2019)**: Biomedical corpus created for recognizing chemical and protein entities. It consists of 1,000 clinical cases with 7,623 entity mentions, corresponding to four entity types.
- **Clinical Trials[4] (Campillos-Llanos et al., 2021)**: It consists of 1,200 texts collected from 500 abstracts of journal articles about clinical trials and 700 announcements of trial protocols. It comprises a total of 40,199 entity mentions, which belong to a subset of semantic groups from the Unified Medical Language System (UMLS).
- **NUBes[5] (Lima Lopez et al., 2020)**: Biomedical corpus obtained from anonymized health records annotated with negation and uncertainty. It consists of 18,404 sentences, including 22,963 mentions of negation and uncertainty.

[2]https://zenodo.org/record/3978041

[3]https://zenodo.org/record/4270158

[4]http://www.lllf.uam.es/ESP/nlpmedterm_en

[5]https://github.com/Vicomtech/NUBes-negation-uncertainty-biomedical-corpus

Parameter	Value
max epochs	150
optimizer	SGD
batch size	32
initial learning rate	0.1
word dropout	0.05
BiLSTM layers	1
BiLSTM hidden size	256

Table 2: Hyperparameters used in our experiments.

3.3 NER Model

To solve the NER task, we used the LSTM-CRF approach proposed by Lample et al. (2016), which is one of the most widely used architectures for sequence labeling tasks. The model consists of three main modules: the embedding layer, the encoding layer with a BiLSTM, and the classification layer, where the most likely sequence of labels is obtained using the CRF algorithm. Our contextualized embeddings were incorporated in the first layer, replacing traditional representations such as word and character-level embeddings.

To compare the performance of our language model, we used two baselines: the Spanish Flair model trained on the general domain using Wikipedia articles and the SciELO Flair model, which was trained over a subset of SciELO text.

In addition, it is worth mentioning that some of the datasets had nested entities, i.e., entities contained within other entity mentions (Finkel and Manning, 2009). Since traditional sequence labeling architectures cannot address this problem, we followed the simplifications made in previous work, keeping only the outermost entities in each nesting.

3.4 Settings

To select the best hyperparameters, we performed the random search strategy, which selects the best values by exhaustively testing different combinations of hyperparameters over a range of values. We measured the performance using the validation partition to establish the best combination.

	Spanish Flair			SciELO Flair			Clinical Flair		
Dataset	P	R	F1	P	R	F1	P	R	F1
CANTEMIST	0.827 (0.002)	0.842 (0.003)	0.834 (0.001)	0.850 (0.001)	0.864 (0.001)	0.857 (0.001)	0.857 (0.004)	0.867 (0.001)	**0.862 (0.002)**
PharmaCoNER	0.876 (0.002)	0.849 (0.001)	0.862 (0.001)	0.905 (0.001)	0.889 (0.002)	**0.897 (0.001)**	0.901 (0.001)	0.875 (0.002)	0.888 (0.001)
Clinical Trials	0.809 (0.003)	0.815 (0.001)	0.812 (0.001)	0.814 (0.005)	0.832 (0.001)	0.823 (0.002)	0.836 (0.002)	0.834 (0.003)	**0.835 (0.001)**
NUBes	0.887 (0.002)	0.901 (0.003)	0.894 (0.001)	0.888 (0.002)	0.905 (0.001)	0.896 (0.001)	0.905 (0.002)	0.897 (0.001)	**0.901 (0.001)**

Table 3: Overall results on four clinical and biomedical NER datasets. Data shown are mean (SD).

In Table 2, we list the main hyperparameters used throughout our experiments, which were the ones that gave us the best results in most of the datasets. We trained the NER models using the SGD optimizer to a maximum of 150 epochs, with mini-batches of size 32 and a learning rate of 0.1. To control overfitting, we used the early stopping strategy and a dropout regularization of 0.05 after the embedding layer.

Performance was evaluated using precision, recall, and micro F1-score, which is the standard metric used in NER. This metric is strict since an entity is considered correct when both entity types and boundaries are predicted correctly. Three rounds of evaluation were computed using different seeds, reporting the mean and standard deviation. All the experiments were performed using the Flair framework, and the source code is available to reproduce our experiments[6].

4 Results

Table 3 shows the overall performance of the NER model comparing contextualized embeddings retrieved from our Clinical Flair model, Spanish Flair, and SciELO Flair. We can see that across all datasets, the performance of our model is superior to the model trained on a general domain, demonstrating the importance of incorporating contextualized embeddings trained on domain-specific corpora.

On the other hand, although we did not train our model on biomedical corpora, we observe that it is also beneficial for solving NER on those datasets. Although we did not outperform the SciELO Flair model in PharmaCoNER, we obtained competitive results. However, as mentioned in their paper, they selected a subset of SciELO texts to train the language model in line with the PharmaCoNER corpus. Therefore, we expected that their results would be superior.

Compared with Spanish Flair, the major difference occurs in CANTEMIST, reaching an average difference of $+0.028$, while the slightest difference is observed in NUBes with $+0.007$ according to the F1 measure. One possible reason for the similar performance between our model and Spanish Flair in NUBes is that, although the dataset belongs to the biomedical domain, the task aims to identify entities associated with negations and uncertainties; therefore, the target labels are general-domain and distant from the original corpus on which we trained our model.

Finally, and as expected, in both corpora belonging to the clinical domain CANTEMIST and Clinical Trials, our model outperforms both Spanish Flair and SciELO Flair. In the case of Clinical Trials, we reached an average difference of $+0.023$ and $+0.012$ compared to both models, respectively, while in the case of CANTEMIST, we obtained improvements of $+0.028$ and $+0.005$ according to the F1 measure.

5 Conclusions and Future Work

Despite the growing interest of the NLP research community in contextualized embeddings, there is still a lack of language models for the Spanish language, a gap that increases even more concerning domain-specific texts. To address this issue, this paper introduced Clinical Flair, a character-level language model for clinical NLP in Spanish. Specifically, we used a general-domain language model as a starting point and then fine-tuned it on Chilean clinical narratives. Our experimental results on four clinical and biomedical NER datasets show that incorporating our domain-specific embeddings outperforms by a wide margin the results obtained with general-domain embeddings, demonstrating the importance of having these resources available for languages not as widely explored.

Future work includes extending our study to other NLP tasks and using different combinations of embeddings, such as concatenating Word2vec or character-level embeddings. In addition, to provide a variety of contextual representation models for clinical texts, we are training a clinical version of BERT in Spanish. Although preliminary

[6]https://github.com/plncmm/clinical-flair

results have been inferior to those obtained with our Clinical Flair model, we expect to collect a larger clinical corpus to improve performance.

Acknowledgements

This work was funded by ANID Chile: Basal Funds for Center of Excellence FB210005 (CMM), Millennium Science Initiative Program ICN2021_004 (iHealth), and Fondecyt grant 11201250. This research was partially supported by the supercomputing infrastructure of the NLHPC (ECM-02) and the Patagón supercomputer of Universidad Austral de Chile (FONDEQUIP EQM180042). We also acknowledge the help received from Kinan Martin and the reviewers.

References

Alan Akbik, Tanja Bergmann, Duncan Blythe, Kashif Rasul, Stefan Schweter, and Roland Vollgraf. 2019. FLAIR: An easy-to-use framework for state-of-the-art NLP. In *Proceedings of the 2019 Conference of the North American Chapter of the Association for Computational Linguistics (Demonstrations)*, pages 54–59, Minneapolis, Minnesota. Association for Computational Linguistics.

Alan Akbik, Duncan Blythe, and Roland Vollgraf. 2018. Contextual string embeddings for sequence labeling. In *Proceedings of the 27th International Conference on Computational Linguistics*, pages 1638–1649, Santa Fe, New Mexico, USA. Association for Computational Linguistics.

Liliya Akhtyamova, Paloma Martínez, Karin Verspoor, and John Cardiff. 2020. Testing contextualized word embeddings to improve ner in spanish clinical case narratives. *IEEE Access*, 8:164717–164726.

Emily Alsentzer, John Murphy, William Boag, Wei-Hung Weng, Di Jindi, Tristan Naumann, and Matthew McDermott. 2019. Publicly available clinical BERT embeddings. In *Proceedings of the 2nd Clinical Natural Language Processing Workshop*, pages 72–78, Minneapolis, Minnesota, USA. Association for Computational Linguistics.

Pablo Báez, Felipe Bravo-Marquez, Jocelyn Dunstan, Matías Rojas, and Fabián Villena. 2022. Automatic extraction of nested entities in clinical referrals in spanish. *ACM Trans. Comput. Healthcare*, 3(3).

Pablo Báez, Fabián Villena, Matías Rojas, Manuel Durán, and Jocelyn Dunstan. 2020. The Chilean waiting list corpus: a new resource for clinical named entity recognition in Spanish. In *Proceedings of the 3rd Clinical Natural Language Processing Workshop*, pages 291–300, Online. Association for Computational Linguistics.

Iz Beltagy, Kyle Lo, and Arman Cohan. 2019. SciBERT: A pretrained language model for scientific text. In *Proceedings of the 2019 Conference on Empirical Methods in Natural Language Processing and the 9th International Joint Conference on Natural Language Processing (EMNLP-IJCNLP)*, pages 3615–3620, Hong Kong, China. Association for Computational Linguistics.

Leonardo Campillos-Llanos, Ana Valverde-Mateos, Adrián Capllonch-Carrión, and Antonio Moreno-Sandoval. 2021. A clinical trials corpus annotated with umls entities to enhance the access to evidence-based medicine. *BMC Medical Informatics and Decision Making*, 21.

Casimiro Pio Carrino, Joan Llop, Marc Pàmies, Asier Gutiérrez-Fandiño, Jordi Armengol-Estapé, Joaquín Silveira-Ocampo, Alfonso Valencia, Aitor Gonzalez-Agirre, and Marta Villegas. 2022. Pretrained biomedical language models for clinical NLP in Spanish. In *Proceedings of the 21st Workshop on Biomedical Language Processing*, pages 193–199, Dublin, Ireland. Association for Computational Linguistics.

Jacob Devlin, Ming-Wei Chang, Kenton Lee, and Kristina Toutanova. 2019. BERT: Pre-training of deep bidirectional transformers for language understanding. In *Proceedings of the 2019 Conference of the North American Chapter of the Association for Computational Linguistics: Human Language Technologies, Volume 1 (Long and Short Papers)*, pages 4171–4186, Minneapolis, Minnesota. Association for Computational Linguistics.

Jenny Rose Finkel and Christopher D. Manning. 2009. Nested named entity recognition. In *Proceedings of the 2009 Conference on Empirical Methods in Natural Language Processing*, pages 141–150, Singapore. Association for Computational Linguistics.

Aitor Gonzalez-Agirre, Montserrat Marimon, Ander Intxaurrondo, Obdulia Rabal, Marta Villegas, and Martin Krallinger. 2019. PharmaCoNER: Pharmacological substances, compounds and proteins named entity recognition track. In *Proceedings of The 5th Workshop on BioNLP Open Shared Tasks*, pages 1–10, Hong Kong, China. Association for Computational Linguistics.

Yu Gu, Robert Tinn, Hao Cheng, Michael Lucas, Naoto Usuyama, Xiaodong Liu, Tristan Naumann, Jianfeng Gao, and Hoifung Poon. 2022. Domain-specific language model pretraining for biomedical natural language processing. *ACM Transactions on Computing for Healthcare*, 3(1):1–23.

Qiao Jin, Bhuwan Dhingra, William Cohen, and Xinghua Lu. 2019. Probing biomedical embeddings from language models. In *Proceedings of the 3rd Workshop on Evaluating Vector Space Representations for NLP*, pages 82–89, Minneapolis, USA. Association for Computational Linguistics.

Guillaume Lample, Miguel Ballesteros, Sandeep Subramanian, Kazuya Kawakami, and Chris Dyer. 2016.

Neural architectures for named entity recognition. In *Proceedings of the 2016 Conference of the North American Chapter of the Association for Computational Linguistics: Human Language Technologies*, pages 260–270, San Diego, California. Association for Computational Linguistics.

Jinhyuk Lee, Wonjin Yoon, Sungdong Kim, Donghyeon Kim, Sunkyu Kim, Chan Ho So, and Jaewoo Kang. 2020. Biobert: A pre-trained biomedical language representation model for biomedical text mining. *Bioinformatics*, 36(4):1234–1240.

Salvador Lima Lopez, Naiara Perez, Montse Cuadros, and German Rigau. 2020. NUBes: A corpus of negation and uncertainty in Spanish clinical texts. In *Proceedings of the 12th Language Resources and Evaluation Conference*, pages 5772–5781, Marseille, France. European Language Resources Association.

A Miranda-Escalada, E Farré, and M Krallinger. 2020. Named entity recognition, concept normalization and clinical coding: Overview of the cantemist track for cancer text mining in spanish, corpus, guidelines, methods and results. In *Proceedings of the Iberian Languages Evaluation Forum (IberLEF 2020), CEUR Workshop Proceedings*.

Matthew E. Peters, Mark Neumann, Mohit Iyyer, Matt Gardner, Christopher Clark, Kenton Lee, and Luke Zettlemoyer. 2018. Deep contextualized word representations. In *Proceedings of the 2018 Conference of the North American Chapter of the Association for Computational Linguistics: Human Language Technologies, Volume 1 (Long Papers)*, pages 2227–2237, New Orleans, Louisiana. Association for Computational Linguistics.

Alec Radford, Jeff Wu, Rewon Child, David Luan, Dario Amodei, and Ilya Sutskever. 2019. Language models are unsupervised multitask learners. *OpenAI blog*, 1(8):9.

Fabián Villena, Pablo Báez, Sergio Peñafiel, Matías Rojas, Inti Paredes, and Jocelyn Dunstan. 2021a. Automatic support system for tumor coding in pathology reports in spanish. *SSRN Electronic Journal*.

Fabian Villena, Jorge Perez, Rene Lagos, and Jocelyn Dunstan. 2021b. Supporting the classification of patients in public hospitals in chile by designing, deploying and validating a system based on natural language processing. *BMC Medical Informatics and Decision Making*, 21(1):1–11.

An exploratory data analysis: the performance differences of a medical code prediction system on different demographic groups

Heereen Shim[1,2,3], Dietwig Lowet[3], Stijn Luca[4] and Bart Vanrumste[1,2]
[1]Campus Group T, e-Media Research Lab, KU Leuven, Leuven, Belgium
[2]Department of Electrical Engineering (ESAT), STADIUS, KU Leuven, Leuven, Belgium
[3]Philips Research, Eindhoven, the Netherlands
[4]Department of Data Analysis and Mathematical Modelling, Ghent University, Ghent, Belgium
{heereen.shim, bart.vanrumste}@kuleuven.be
{dietwig.lowet}@philips.com
{stijn.luca}@ugent.be

Abstract

Recent studies show that neural natural processing models for medical code prediction suffer from a label imbalance issue. This study aims to investigate further imbalance in a medical code prediction dataset in terms of demographic variables and analyse performance differences in demographic groups. We use sample-based metrics to correctly evaluate the performance in terms of the data subject. Also, a simple label distance metric is proposed to quantify the difference in the label distribution between a group and the entire data. Our analysis results reveal that the model performs differently towards different demographic groups: significant differences between age groups and between insurance types are observed. Interestingly, we found a weak positive correlation between the number of training data of the group and the performance of the group. However, a strong negative correlation between the label distance of the group and the performance of the group is observed. This result suggests that the model tends to perform poorly in the group whose label distribution is different from the global label distribution of the training data set. Further analysis of the model performance is required to identify the cause of these differences and to improve the model building.

1 Introduction

Medical coding is the process of assigning standard codes, such as The International Classification of Diseases (ICD) codes, to each clinical document for documenting records and medical billing purposes. Even though medical coding is an important process in the healthcare system, it is expensive, time-consuming, and error-prone (O'malley et al., 2005).

Researchers have investigated approaches for automated ICD coding systems and there has been great progress with neural network architectures (Kalyan and Sangeetha, 2020). However, current state-of-the-art models still suffer from data imbalance issues: since the benchmark dataset is imbalanced in terms of assigned ICD codes, the model performances differ across ICD codes (Mullenbach et al., 2018; Li and Yu, 2020; Kim and Ganapathi, 2021; Vu et al., 2021; Ji et al., 2021). Moreover, a recent study argues that the performances of models tend to decrease when the ICD codes have fewer training instances (Ji et al., 2021).

Based on this observation from the literature (i.e., imbalanced ICD code distribution results in the performance imbalance between the ICD codes), the goal of this paper is to investigate the effect of the imbalance of different demographic groups in the training data set on the performances of the demographic groups. More specifically, we study the following questions: 1) Is a benchmark dataset for medical code prediction imbalance in terms of the data subject's demographic variables (i.e., age, gender, ethnicity, socioeconomic status)?; 2) If so, would it result in performance differences between demographic groups? To answer these questions, we analyse the benchmark dataset, reproduce one of the state-of-the-art models (Li and Yu, 2020), and analyse the performance of the model. To the best of our knowledge, this is the first attempt to study the demographic imbalance of the medical code prediction benchmark dataset and analyse the performance differences between demographic groups.

Our contribution is three-fold. Firstly, we analysed the medical code prediction benchmark dataset to investigate the underlying imbalance in the dataset (Section 4.1) and reproduced one of the state-of-the-art medical code prediction models proposed by Li and Yu (2020). Secondly, we propose sample-based evaluation metrics (Section. 3.4) to identify potential biases inside a model and potential risk of the bias (Section. 4.2). Thirdly, we propose a simple label distance metric to quantify the

Proceedings of the 4th Clinical Natural Language Processing Workshop, pages 93 - 102
July 14, 2022

differences in the label distribution between each group and the global data (Section. 3.2) and found that the label distance metric is strongly correlated with the performance negatively (Section. 4.3). We expect that these analytic results could provide a valuable insight to the natural language processing (NLP) research community working for clinical applications.

2 Data

This section includes the information on the benchmark dataset used and the details of pre-processing steps taken for preparing data for the experiments. Note that we followed the previous approach to reproduce the result from the literature. More details are explained in the following subsections.

2.1 MIMIC-III dataset

We used Medical Information Mart for Intensive Care (MIMIC-III v1.4.) dataset (Johnson et al., 2016)[1] for the experiments. MIMIC-III is the benchmark dataset that has been widely used to build a system for automated medical code prediction (Shi et al., 2017; Mullenbach et al., 2018; Li and Yu, 2020; Kim and Ganapathi, 2021). For medical code prediction, discharge summary texts[2] are used as inputs and corresponding ICD-9 codes[3] are used as output of a system. In other words, the medical code prediction is formulated as a multi-label classification where the ground truth of the given input includes one or more ICD-9 codes.

For benchmarking purposes, Mullenbach et al. (2018) provides script codes that pre-process the discharge summary text data and splits the dataset by patient IDs into training, validation, and testing sets[4]. Also, Mullenbach et al. (2018) creates two benchmark sets, with full ICD codes as well as with the top 50 most frequent ICD codes, which are denoted as `MIMIC-III full` and `MIMIC-III 50`, respectively. The `MIMIC-III full` dataset contains 52,728 discharge summaries with 8,921 unique ICD codes and the `MIMIC-III 50` dataset contains 11,368 discharge summaries with 50 unique ICD codes.

In this paper, we only consider the `MIMIC-III 50` dataset. Following the previous works (Li and Yu, 2020; Kim and Ganapathi, 2021; Vu et al., 2021), we used Mullenbach et al. (2018)'s scripts to split the data which results in 8,066 discharge summaries for training, 1,573 for validation, and 1,729 for testing. Additionally, we extracted patients' demographic information from the MIMIC-III dataset, including gender, age, ethnicity, and insurance type as a socioeconomic proxy.

2.2 Data pre-processing

Discharge Summary texts One of our objectives is to reproduce the results by Li and Yu (2020) and analyse the performance. Therefore, we followed the Li and Yu (2020)'s pre-processing steps which are the same as the work by Mullenbach et al. (2018). Data cleaning and pre-processing include the following steps: the discharge summary texts were tokenized, tokens that contain no alphabetic characters were removed, and all tokens were lowercased. All documents are truncated to a maximum length of 2500 tokens. More details can be found in the original paper (Mullenbach et al., 2018).

Demographic data In the MIMIC-III dataset, each unique hospital visit for a patient is assigned with a unique admission ID. Therefore we used admission ID to extract the demographic information of patients. The following steps were taken to pre-process the demographic data: firstly, age values are computed based on the date of birth data and the admission time data[5]. Secondly, the four most frequent values in ethnicity data, including 'WHITE', 'BLACK', 'ASIAN', 'HISPANIC', are being kept, whereas the remaining values are combined into one group and labelled as 'OTHER'. Thirdly, the three most frequent values in insurance type data, including 'Medicare', 'Private', 'Medicaid', are being kept, whereas the other values are combined into one group 'Other'.

3 Methods

3.1 Data analysis

We analysed the size, as well absolute as relative, of each group and investigated relationships between variables. Also, we analysed the length of discharge summary notes and the number of assigned ICD codes per note to investigate relation-

[1]https://physionet.org/content/mimiciii/1.4/

[2]A discharge summary is a note that summarises information about a hospital stay

[3]MIMIC-III dataset includes both diagnoses and procedures which occurred during the patient's stay

[4]https://github.com/jamesmullenbach/caml-mimic

[5]The date of birth data of patients older than 89 have been shifted and the original values cannot be recovered. Therefore, we assigned the same age value of 90 to all patients who are older than 89.

ships between the length of notes and demographic variables and between the number of ICD codes per note and demographic variables. We also calculate the differences in the ICD code label distributions between the entire data and each group.

3.2 Label distribution distance metric

To calculate the differences in the ICD code label distributions between the entire data and each group, we used cosine distance[6] between ICD code label representations, each of which is a multi-hot vector $\mathbb{R}^{1\times 50}$. Specifically, we compute the average distances between the globally averaged label vector and the label vector of each data point in groups, which is defined as:

$$D_k = \frac{1}{N_k}\sum_{i}^{N_k} 1 - \frac{\boldsymbol{u}\cdot\boldsymbol{v_i}}{||\boldsymbol{u}||_2||\boldsymbol{v_i}||_2} \quad (1)$$

where $\boldsymbol{u}$ is the globally averaged label vector of the entire data and $\boldsymbol{v_i}$ is a label vector of a single data point in the group k that contains N_k of data points. A low distance score means the group contains patients whose label set is close to the global label distribution of the entire data.

3.3 Medical code prediction model

In this study, we study one of the state-of-the-art medical code prediction models proposed by Li and Yu (2020). There are three important architectural details in Li and Yu (2020)'s model: firstly, it uses a convolutional layer with multiple filters where each filter has a different kernel size (Kim, 2014). This multi-filter convolutional layer allows a model to capture various text patterns with different word lengths. Secondly, residual connections (He et al., 2016) are used on top of each filter in the multi-filter convolutional layer. This residual convolutional layer enlarges the receptive field of the model. Thirdly, the label attention layer (Mullenbach et al., 2018) is deployed after the multi-filter convolutional layer. More details on the model architecture can be found in the original paper (Li and Yu, 2020). For implementation, we re-trained a model by using a script[7] and followed the same hyperparameter setting except the early-stopping setting: we used a macro-averaged F1 score as an early-stopping criterion with a patience value 10.

[6]We used cosine distance because it is widely used to calculate the similarity between high-dimensional vectors and the distance is always normalised between 0 and 1.

[7]https://github.com/foxlf823/Multi-Filter-Residual-Convolutional-Neural-Network

3.4 Evaluation metrics

Performance metrics To evaluate the model's performance, micro-and macro-averaged F1 scores are widely used in the literature (Shi et al., 2017; Mullenbach et al., 2018; Li and Yu, 2020). Micro-averaged scores are calculated by treating each <text input, code label> pair as a separate prediction. Macro-averaged scores are calculated by averaging metrics computed per label. For recall, the metrics are computed as follows:

$$\text{Micro-R} = \frac{\sum_{l=1}^{L}\text{TP}_l}{\sum_{l=1}^{L}\text{TP}_l + \text{FN}_l} \quad (2)$$

$$\text{Macro-R} = \frac{1}{|L|}\sum_{l=1}^{L}\frac{\text{TP}_l}{\text{TP}_l + \text{FN}_l} \quad (3)$$

where TP_l and FN_l, denote true positive examples and false negative examples for a specific ICD-9 code label l, respectively. Since we use `MIMIC-III 50` dataset, $|L|$ equals 50

Since we focus on performance differences in terms of data subject's demographics, we additionally use sample-averaged F1 scores. Sample-averaged scores are calculated by computing scores at the instance level and averaging over all instances in the data set. For sample-averaged recall, the metric is computed as follows:

$$\text{Sample-R} = \frac{1}{|N|}\sum_{n=1}^{N}\frac{|\boldsymbol{y_n}\cap\hat{\boldsymbol{y_n}}|}{|\boldsymbol{y_n}|} \quad (4)$$

where $\boldsymbol{y_n}$ and $\hat{\boldsymbol{y_n}}$ denote the ground truth labels and the predicted labels for the n-th test example, respectively and N denotes the total number of test samples. Precision is computed in a similar manner.

For statistical analysis, we conducted the Kruskal-Wallis tests to investigate differences between the average performance scores of each group. Also, we computed the Pearson correlation coefficient and p-value for testing the correlation between the training data size of the group and the model performance on the group and between label distance of the group and the model performance on the group. All statistical tests were done by using sample-F1 scores.

Error metrics Following previous studies (Hardt et al., 2016; Chouldechova, 2017), we consider two metrics to quantify the error of a trained model: false negative rate (FNR) and false positive rate

	Count (n)	Percentage (%)
Total	8066	
Gender		
F	3593	44.5
M	4473	55.5
Age		
0-17	440	5.5
18-29	300	3.7
30-49	1148	14.2
50-69	2931	36.3
70-89	2817	34.9
90+	430	5.3
Ethnicity		
WHITE	5651	70.1
OTHER	1097	13.6
BLACK	799	9.9
HISPANIC	311	3.9
ASIAN	208	2.6
Insurance		
Medicare	4440	55.0
Private	2636	32.7
Medicaid	709	8.8
Other	281	3.5

Table 1: Sample size (absolute and relative) of the groups of gender, age, ethnicity, and insurance type.

(FPR) in the sample level. FNR is the fraction of ICD codes that are failed to be predicted by a system but included in a ground truth label set. FPR is the fraction of ICD codes that are erroneously predicted by a system but not included in a ground truth label set. High FNR scores imply low recall scores and high FPR implies low precision scores. Two metrics are computed as follows:

$$\text{FNR} = \frac{1}{|N|}\sum_{n=1}^{N} 1 - \frac{|\boldsymbol{y}_n \cap \hat{\boldsymbol{y}_n}|}{|\boldsymbol{y}_n|} \quad (5)$$

$$\text{FPR} = \frac{1}{|N|}\sum_{n=1}^{N} 1 - \frac{|\boldsymbol{y}_n \cap \hat{\boldsymbol{y}_n}|}{|\hat{\boldsymbol{y}_n}|} \quad (6)$$

To assess the risk of errors, we use the worst-case comparison method (Ghosh et al., 2021). Also, we conducted Mann–Whitney U tests to investigate the differences between the error scores of the best and the error scores of the worst models.

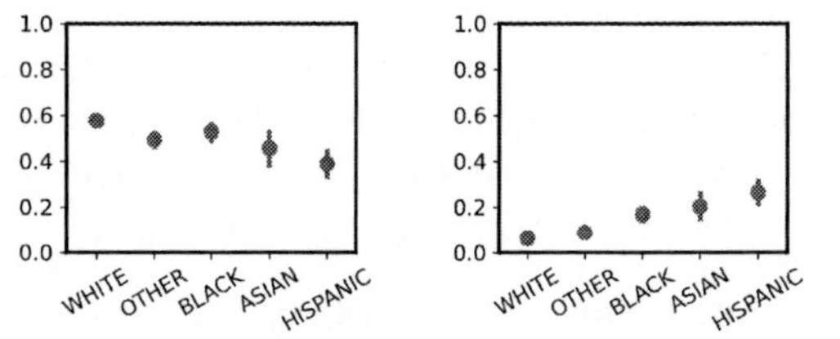

(a) Percentage of Medicare within each ethnic group

(b) Percentage of Medicaid within each ethnic group

Figure 1: Relationship between insurance and demographic variables. 95% confidence intervals are illustrated by lines.

4 Results

4.1 Data analysis results

Table 1 summarizes the sample sizes of the data set. It is shown that only gender variables are well-balanced. For age groups, patients who are 50-89 take up to 71.2% of the data. Also, the data set includes more White patients than patients from other ethnic groups. Also, more than half of the entire patients in the data set are patients with Medicare insurance and only 8.8% of patients are with Medicaid insurance.

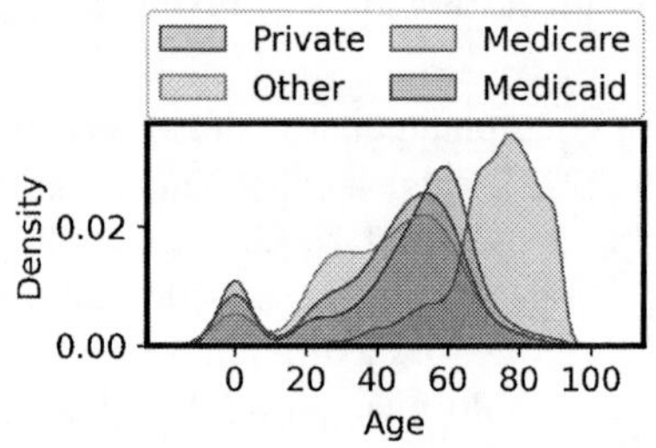

Figure 2: Kernel density estimate plot for visualising the age distribution of each insurance type

Figure 1 shows the relationship between insurance types, Medicare and Medicaid, and ethnicity variables. It is observed that insurance type has a certain relationship with the patient's race: 57.7% of White patients are paying with Medicare, whereas 38.9% of Hispanic patients are paying with Medicare. On the other hand, 26.4% of Hispanic patients are paying with Medicaid, whereas only 0.63% of White patients are paying with Medicaid.

Figure 2 illustrate the age distribution of each insurance type. Medicare and Medicaid are two separate, government-run insurance in the United States. Medicare is available for people age 65 or above and younger people with severe illnesses and

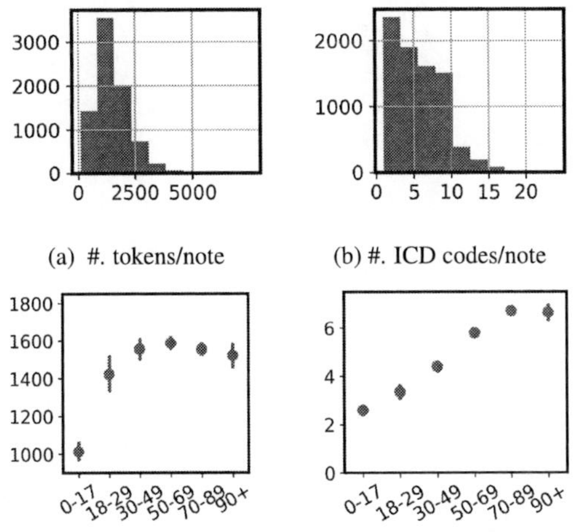

(a) #. tokens/note (b) #. ICD codes/note

(c) #. tokens/note (d) #. ICD codes/note

Figure 3: The distribution of the length of a discharge summary note (a) and the number of ICD codes assigned per note (d). Relationship between the length of notes and age groups (c) and between the number of ICD codes per note and age groups (d). X-axes indicate the average number of tokens in a note (a, c) and the average number of ICD codes per note (b,d). 95% confidence intervals are illustrated by lines.

	Distance
Gender	
F	0.613 (0.137)
M	0.615 (0.133)
Age	
0-17	0.737 (0.097)
18-29	0.746 (0.111)
30-49	0.684 (0.133)
50-69	0.610 (0.129)
70-89	0.564 (0.116)
90+	0.560 (0.118)
Ethnicity	
WHITE	0.610 (0.135)
OTHER	0.607 (0.131)
BLACK	0.633 (0.135)
HISPANIC	0.646 (0.135)
ASIAN	0.626 (0.143)
Insurance	
Medicare	0.579 (0.124)
Private	0.653 (0.135)
Medicaid	0.658 (0.136)
Other	0.691 (0.139)

Table 2: Average label distribution distances between each group and the global data. Standard deviations are added in parentheses.

Medicaid is available to low-income individuals under the age of 65 and their families. Because of the eligibility criteria for Medicare, Medicare includes more older patients compared to other insurance types, as we can see from the Figure 2.

Figure 3a and Figure 3b show the distribution of the length of a discharge summary note and the number of ICD codes assigned per note, respectively. The average length is 1529.7 (std=754.9) and the average number of codes per note is 5.7 (std=3.3). Figure 3c and Figure 3d illustrate relationship between patients age and the length of note and the number of codes per note, respectively. From Figure 3c, it is observed that the length of note tends to increase until age group 50-69 and starts to decrease afterwards. From Figure 3d, positive correlations between age and the number of ICD codes per note are observed. Other noticeable patterns are not observed in other demographic variables (i.e., gender, insurance, ethnicity) with the respect to the length of a discharge summary note and the number of ICD codes assigned per note.

Figure 4 illustrates ICD code distributions. Figure 4a shows the entire data set has long-tail distribution. Between female and male patient groups, no noticeable difference between the label distributions is not observed. In terms of insurance type and ethnicity, each group shows slightly different ICD code distributions. Clear differences are observed between age groups: patients whose ages are younger than 30 (0-17, 18-29) show less spread ICD code distributions with fewer ICD codes than other age groups. The label distribution distances between each group and the global data are summarised in Table 2. Similar to the observations from Figure 4, age groups 0-17 and 18-29 have the bigger distance scores.

4.2 Performance & error analysis results

Table 3 summarises the prediction results on the test set. It is observed that a re-trained model slight underperforms compared to the original model (Li and Yu, 2020). The different early-stopping settings might cause this difference. Both models achieve higher scores in micro-averaged metrics than macro-averaged metrics, which means the model's performance on rare labels is worse than on frequent labels. The sample-averaged metrics are higher than macro-averaged metrics but lower than micro-averaged metrics.

Noticeable performance differences are observed between age groups, especially between patients

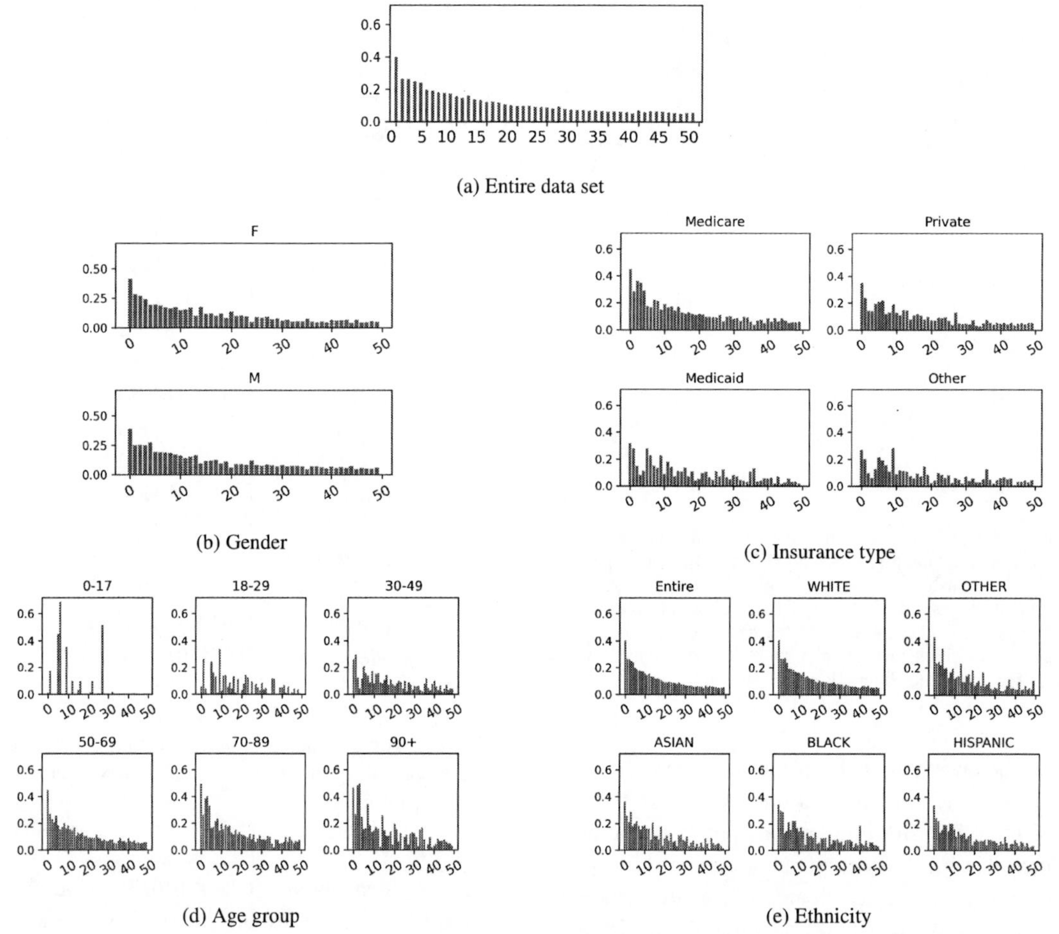

(a) Entire data set

(b) Gender

(c) Insurance type

(d) Age group

(e) Ethnicity

Figure 4: ICD code distribution. X-axis indicates the sorted ICD code class label and Y-axis indicate the percentage of labels observed in the training set.

younger than 30 years (18-29) and older than 90 (90+). The percentages of both groups in the training set are low but patients younger than 30 years get distinctively worse predictions in terms of all F-1 scores. Between different ethnic groups, it is observed that Hispanic and Asian patients get worse predictions compared to other patients. Between insurance types, it is also observed that patients with other types of insurance and Medicaid insurance get worse predictions compared to patients with Medicare and Private insurance in sample-averaged F-1 scores.

As the result of the Kruskal-Wallis test, we found statistically significant differences in sample-averaged F1 scores according to age group (H(4)=46.57, p<0.001) and insurance type (H(3)=18.58, p<0.001), separately. Close to being statistically significant is found according to gender (H(1)=3.65, p=0.056) and no statistically significant difference is found according to ethnicity (H(4)=2.657, p=0.657).

Error metrics per group are summarised in Table 4. Error metrics between groups show a similar trend as the performance metrics: differences between age groups are the most pronounced. It is observed that FNR scores tend to decrease as age increases. However, the largest difference between age groups is not significant (p=0.06). FPR also tends to increase as the age increases in the age groups under 90 and the largest difference between the younger group (18-29) and the older group (70-89) is significant (p<0.001). Patients with other types of insurance take significantly worse scores compared to Medicare patients in terms of FNR scores. Interestingly, FPR shows different patterns. For example, patients with Medicare get the worst FPR scores and patients with Private insurance get the best FPR scores.

	F-1 (%)		
	Micro	**Macro**	**Sample**
Total			
Li and Yu (2020)	67.3†	60.8†	-
Reproduced	64.4	59.2	60.6
Gender			
F (44.5)	<u>63.2</u>	<u>58.1</u>	<u>59.7</u>
M (55.5)	**65.3**	**59.4**	**61.4**
Age			
18-29 (3.7)	<u>53.9</u>	<u>36.1</u>	<u>48.2</u>
30-49 (14.2)	58.9	58.2	52.4
50-69 (36.3)	64.2	57.7	60.9
70-89 (34.9)	65.6	**59.2**	63.6
90+ (5.3)	**67.1**	55.9	**65.0**
Ethnicity			
WHITE (70.1)	64.3	59.2	60.8
OTHER (13.6)	64.3	**60.9**	60.7
BLACK (9.9)	**66.2**	60.2	**61.7**
HISPANIC (3.9)	<u>62.0</u>	54.6	<u>56.0</u>
ASIAN (2.6)	64.7	<u>51.2</u>	59.3
Insurance			
Medicare (55.0)	**65.3**	58.4	**62.5**
Private (32.7)	63.4	58.8	59.0
Medicaid (8.8)	62.9	**59.3**	57.8
Other (3.5)	<u>56.0</u>	<u>49.3</u>	<u>50.5</u>

Table 3: Performances on the MIMIC-III 50 test set. † indicates performances reported in the paper by Li and Yu (2020). Other results are obtained from a reproduced model. The percentage of training samples (%) is added in parentheses after the group labels. Best performances are boldfaced and worst performances are underlined.

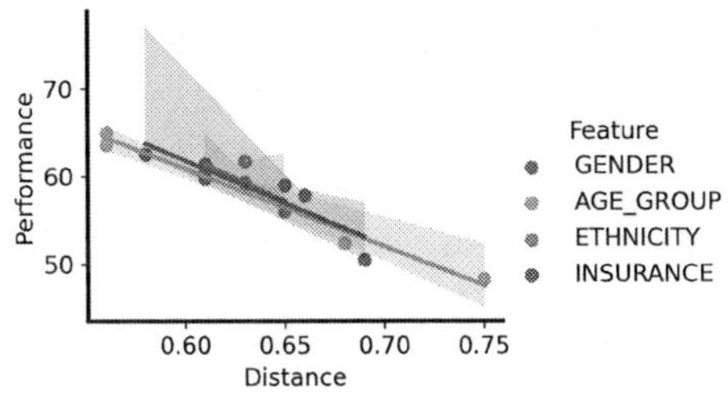

Figure 5: Label distance of each group and the model performance on each group. Linear relationships are illustrated by lines determined through linear regression.

4.3 Correlation test result.

As the result of correlation tests, we found a weak positive correlation (0.43, p=0.09) between training set size and performance. This result shows that even though the model performs well for groups with more training data in general, the relationship is not statistically significant. Contrary to this result, we found a very strong negative correlation (-0.95, p<0.001) between label distance and performance. This result implies that the model performs poorly in the groups containing many patients whose label set is different from the global label distribution of the entire data. The group-specific correlations between label distances and the performances are illustrated in Figure 5. It is observed that the negative correlation is much more pronounced between different age groups than in other groups.

	FNR (%)	**FPR (%)**
Total	40.6	3.8
Gender		
F (44.5)	<u>39.7</u>	<u>4.3</u>
M (55.5)	**38.0**	**4.2**
largest diff. (↓)	1.7	0.1
smallest ratio (%) (↑)	95.8	98.2
Age		
18-29 (3.7)	<u>46.2</u>	**2.9**
30-49 (14.2)	45.9	3.3
50-69 (36.3)	39.5	3.9
70-89 (34.9)	35.7	<u>5.0</u>
90+ (5.3)	**34.1**	4.4
largest diff. (↓)	12.2	2.1***
smallest ratio (%) (↑)	73.7	57.7
Ethnicity		
WHITE (70.1)	38.7	4.2
OTHER (13.6)	39.3	<u>4.5</u>
BLACK (9.9)	**37.0**	4.2
HISPANIC (3.9)	<u>42.5</u>	4.2
ASIAN (2.6)	40.3	**3.8**
largest diff. (↓)	5.4	0.8
smallest ratio (%) (↑)	87.2	83.3
Insurance		
Medicare (55.0)	**37.0**	<u>4.7</u>
Private (32.7)	40.7	**3.4**
Medicaid (3.5)	41.0	3.6
Other (8.8)	<u>46.9</u>	4.2
largest diff. (↓)	9.8*	1.3***
smallest ratio (%) (↑)	79.0	71.5

Table 4: Errors on the MIMIC-III 50 test set. The percentage of training samples (%) is added in parentheses. Best performances are boldfaced and worst performances are underlined. * and *** indicate the error of the worst model is greater than the error of the best with statistical significance of p=0.05 and p=0.001 (Mann–Whitney U test), respectively.

5 Discussion

Impact of the study. The MIMIC-II dataset for medical code prediction provides opportunities to develop and benchmark models and facilitates natural language processing research in the clinical domain. Since it is one of the most frequently used benchmark datasets for medical code prediction, it has a huge impact on the quality of the developed models. For example, previous studies (Mullenbach et al., 2018; Li and Yu, 2020; Kim and Ganapathi, 2021; Vu et al., 2021; Ji et al., 2021) have shown that the ICD code distribution in the MIMIC-III dataset is imbalanced and it results in performance differences between ICD codes. In this study, we investigated the data imbalance of the MIMIC-III 50 data, in terms of the data subject's demographic factors, and its effect on the model performance for ICD code prediction.

Evaluation metrics for fairness. In this paper, we proposed metrics that can correctly evaluate the model's performance in terms of individual patients' benefits and potential harms. Especially, we formulated the medical code prediction task as a multi-label classification task. From a machine learning perspective, sample-based metrics and label-based metrics are used to evaluate the performance of a model in a multi-label classification task (Zhang and Zhou, 2013). Sample-based and label-based metrics focus on different aspects of model performance, one in sample-wise performance and the other in label-wise performance. However, label-based metrics are more frequently used in the literature (Xiao et al., 2018; Mullenbach et al., 2018; Li and Yu, 2020; Kim and Ganapathi, 2021; Vu et al., 2021; Ji et al., 2021). Considering a healthcare application setting where all patients are expected to receive an equal quality of service, we argue that using sample-based metrics is required to evaluate the model performance. Also, we propose to use disaggregated metrics (Barocas et al., 2021), which are metrics evaluated on each group of data, to ensure that a model is equally accurate for patients from different demographic groups (Rajkomar et al., 2018; Gichoya et al., 2021).

Correlation between demographic variables We analysed the MIMIC-III dataset to identify the underlying data imbalance of demographic variables. Our data analysis results show that the MIMIC-III dataset is imbalanced in terms of the data subject's demographics. However, we also found a correlation between demographic variables. For example, age is correlated with insurance type: patients older than 65 are likely to be insured with Medicare. This confounding factor across demographic variables makes it complicated to interpret the main effects of the data subject's demographics on the model performance.

Correlation between label distance and performance Based on the previous study arguing the performances of models tend to decrease when the ICD codes have fewer training samples (Ji et al., 2021), we hypothesised that the performance of the model on a demographic group is correlated with the number of data of that group in the training data set. However, the analysis results do not support this hypothesis: even though the performance differences are observed across some demographic groups (i.e., across age groups and insurance types), the correlation between the number of training data of the group and the performance of the group is weak. Instead, we found that the label distance of the group is negatively correlated with the performance of the group. This result suggests that when the group contains patients whose label set is different from the global label distribution of the entire data, it is likely that the model performs poorly in that group.

In terms of machine learning perspective, this issue can be seen as a label shift: the train and test label distribution is different while the feature distribution remains the same (Lipton et al., 2018; Guo et al., 2020). To address this issue, one interesting area for future work may be in re-training the classifier with adjusted training sample weights (Lipton et al., 2018) or adapting the predictions of a pre-trained classifier (Saerens et al., 2002; Du Plessis and Sugiyama, 2014; Alexandari et al., 2020).

Limitations and future directions There are several limitations to this study. Firstly, we used a subset of MIMIC-III data with the top 50 most frequent ICD codes to simplify the analysis. Since the full MIMIC-III dataset contains more than 47,000 ICD codes, further study is required. Secondly, we only studied the model proposed by Li and Yu (2020). One potential direction is to investigate the performance of models using pre-trained language models (Zhang et al., 2020; Ji et al., 2021). Thirdly, we found an issue of confounding across demographic variables, which makes it complicates the interpretation of the main effects of the data subject's demographic factors on the model performance. To address this issue, further analysis of multiple intersectional groups or causal analysis is required. In future work, we will also investigate how to build a model that can perform equally well on across all demographic groups.

6 Conclusion

In this study, we performed an empirical analysis to investigate the data imbalance of the MIMIC-III 50 dataset and its effect on the model performance for ICD code prediction. We found that demographic imbalance exists in the MIMIC-III 50 dataset and a medical code prediction model performs differently across some demographic groups. Interestingly, the correlation between the number of training data of the group and the performance of the group is weak. Instead, we found a negative correlation between the label distance of the group and the performance of the group. This result suggests that the model tends to perform poorly in the group whose label distribution is different from the global label distribution. Potential future research direction includes further analysis of the main effects of the data subject's demographic factors on the model performance and investigation of building a robust and fair model that can perform equally well across demographic groups with different label distributions.

Acknowledgements

We thank anonymous reviewers for providing valuable feedback on this work. Data processing activities were conducted by the first author and the other authors did not involve in the raw data processing. This project has received funding from the European Union's Horizon 2020 research and innovation programme under the Marie Skłodowska-Curie grant agreement No 766139. This article reflects only the author's view and the REA is not responsible for any use that may be made of the information it contains.

References

Amr Alexandari, Anshul Kundaje, and Avanti Shrikumar. 2020. Maximum likelihood with bias-corrected calibration is hard-to-beat at label shift adaptation. In *International Conference on Machine Learning*, pages 222–232. PMLR.

Solon Barocas, Anhong Guo, Ece Kamar, Jacquelyn Krones, Meredith Ringel Morris, Jennifer Wortman Vaughan, W Duncan Wadsworth, and Hanna Wallach. 2021. Designing disaggregated evaluations of ai systems: Choices, considerations, and tradeoffs. In *Proceedings of the 2021 AAAI/ACM Conference on AI, Ethics, and Society*, pages 368–378.

Alexandra Chouldechova. 2017. Fair prediction with disparate impact: A study of bias in recidivism prediction instruments. *Big data*, 5(2):153–163.

Marthinus Christoffel Du Plessis and Masashi Sugiyama. 2014. Semi-supervised learning of class balance under class-prior change by distribution matching. *Neural Networks*, 50:110–119.

Avijit Ghosh, Lea Genuit, and Mary Reagan. 2021. Characterizing intersectional group fairness with worst-case comparisons. In *Artificial Intelligence Diversity, Belonging, Equity, and Inclusion*, pages 22–34. PMLR.

Judy Wawira Gichoya, Liam G McCoy, Leo Anthony Celi, and Marzyeh Ghassemi. 2021. Equity in essence: a call for operationalising fairness in machine learning for healthcare. *BMJ Health & Care Informatics*, 28(1).

Jiaxian Guo, Mingming Gong, Tongliang Liu, Kun Zhang, and Dacheng Tao. 2020. Ltf: A label transformation framework for correcting label shift. In *International Conference on Machine Learning*, pages 3843–3853. PMLR.

Moritz Hardt, Eric Price, and Nati Srebro. 2016. Equality of opportunity in supervised learning. *Advances in neural information processing systems*, 29.

Kaiming He, Xiangyu Zhang, Shaoqing Ren, and Jian Sun. 2016. Deep residual learning for image recognition. In *Proceedings of the IEEE conference on computer vision and pattern recognition*, pages 770–778.

Shaoxiong Ji, Matti Hölttä, and Pekka Marttinen. 2021. Does the magic of BERT apply to medical code assignment? A quantitative study. *Computers in Biology and Medicine*, 139.

Alistair EW Johnson, Tom J Pollard, Lu Shen, Li-wei H Lehman, Mengling Feng, Mohammad Ghassemi, Benjamin Moody, Peter Szolovits, Leo Anthony Celi, and Roger G Mark. 2016. Mimic-iii, a freely accessible critical care database. *Scientific data*, 3(1):1–9.

Katikapalli Subramanyam Kalyan and Sivanesan Sangeetha. 2020. Secnlp: A survey of embeddings in clinical natural language processing. *Journal of biomedical informatics*, 101:103323.

Byung-Hak Kim and Varun Ganapathi. 2021. Read, Attend, and Code: Pushing the Limits of Medical Codes Prediction from Clinical Notes by Machines. *Proceedings of Machine Learning Research*, 149:1–12.

Yoon Kim. 2014. Convolutional neural networks for sentence classification. In *Proceedings of the 2014 Conference on Empirical Methods in Natural Language Processing (EMNLP)*, pages 1746–1751, Doha, Qatar. Association for Computational Linguistics.

Fei Li and Hong Yu. 2020. ICD coding from clinical text using multi-filter residual convolutional neural network. In *AAAI 2020 - 34th AAAI Conference on Artificial Intelligence*, volume 34, pages 8180–8187. AAAI press.

Zachary Lipton, Yu-Xiang Wang, and Alexander Smola. 2018. Detecting and correcting for label shift with black box predictors. In *International conference on machine learning*, pages 3122–3130. PMLR.

James Mullenbach, Sarah Wiegreffe, Jon Duke, Jimeng Sun, and Jacob Eisenstein. 2018. Explainable prediction of medical codes from clinical text. In *NAACL HLT 2018 - 2018 Conference of the North American Chapter of the Association for Computational Linguistics: Human Language Technologies - Proceedings of the Conference*, volume 1, pages 1101–1111.

Kimberly J O'malley, Karon F Cook, Matt D Price, Kimberly Raiford Wildes, John F Hurdle, and Carol M Ashton. 2005. Measuring diagnoses: Icd code accuracy. *Health services research*, 40(5p2):1620–1639.

Alvin Rajkomar, Michaela Hardt, Michael D Howell, Greg Corrado, and Marshall H Chin. 2018. Ensuring fairness in machine learning to advance health equity. *Annals of internal medicine*, 169(12):866–872.

Marco Saerens, Patrice Latinne, and Christine Decaestecker. 2002. Adjusting the outputs of a classifier to new a priori probabilities: a simple procedure. *Neural computation*, 14(1):21–41.

Haoran Shi, Pengtao Xie, Zhiting Hu, Ming Zhang, and Eric P Xing. 2017. Towards automated icd coding using deep learning. *arXiv preprint arXiv:1711.04075*.

Thanh Vu, Dat Quoc Nguyen, and Anthony Nguyen. 2021. A label attention model for icd coding from clinical text. In *Proceedings of the Twenty-Ninth International Conference on International Joint Conferences on Artificial Intelligence*, pages 3335–3341.

Cao Xiao, Edward Choi, and Jimeng Sun. 2018. Opportunities and challenges in developing deep learning models using electronic health records data: a systematic review. *Journal of the American Medical Informatics Association*, 25(10):1419–1428.

Min-Ling Zhang and Zhi-Hua Zhou. 2013. A review on multi-label learning algorithms. *IEEE transactions on knowledge and data engineering*, 26(8):1819–1837.

Zachariah Zhang, Jingshu Liu, and Narges Razavian. 2020. Bert-xml: Large scale automated icd coding using bert pretraining. In *Proceedings of the 3rd Clinical Natural Language Processing Workshop*, pages 24–34.

Ensemble-based Fine-Tuning Strategy for Temporal Relation Extraction from the Clinical Narrative

Lijing Wang[1], Timothy Miller[1], Steven Bethard[2], Guergana Savova[1]
[1]Boston Children's Hospital and Harvard Medical School
[2]University of Arizona
[1]{first.last}@childrens.harvard.edu
[2]bethard@email.arizona.edu

Abstract

In this paper, we investigate ensemble methods for fine-tuning transformer-based pretrained models for clinical natural language processing tasks, specifically temporal relation extraction from the clinical narrative. Our experimental results on the THYME data show that ensembling as a fine-tuning strategy can further boost model performance over single learners optimized for hyperparameters. Dynamic snapshot ensembling is particularly beneficial as it fine-tunes a wide array of parameters and results in a 2.8% absolute improvement in F1 over the base single learner.

1 Introduction

The clinical narrative in electronic medical records (EMRs) can provide critical information for improving quality of care, patient outcomes, and safety. Extracting information from EMRs has been an active area of research in recent years due to the advances in natural language processing (NLP) techniques. As transformer-based neural language models, such as Bidirectional Encodings Representations from Transformers (BERT) (Devlin et al., 2019), have achieved state-of-the-art performance for a variety of NLP tasks they have gained increased prominence in clinical NLP.

However, in the clinical domain, data is often sparsely labeled and not shareable as it is guarded by patient confidentiality provisions. Building large transformer-based models from scratch using such data is thus often infeasible. A common approach has been to take models pretrained on large general domain corpora, and continue pretraining them on clinical corpora to derive domain-specific language models (Lee et al., 2020; Alsentzer et al., 2019; Beltagy et al., 2019; Lin et al., 2021).

The weights of pretrained models are adjusted for a specific clinical NLP task through the process of *fine-tuning*. This process often involves searching for optimal hyperparameters while continuing to train the pretrained model on a domain-specific dataset. The search is challenging due to the high dimensionality of the search space, which includes random seed, initial learning rate, batch size, etc. Given the limited computing resources available in practice, only a small number of values for each hyperparameter can be explored, and often only a subset of hyperparameters can be fine-tuned. Are we able to retain the benefits from the existing search efforts and to further improve model performance for the same task or new tasks without too much extra effort? Ensemble methods have been successful in boosting predictive performance of single learners (Wang et al., 2003; CireşAn et al., 2012; Xie et al., 2013) and thus are promising. In this paper, we will investigate ensemble-based fine-tuning methods to answer this question.

Another downside of the limited search capability is that some hyperparameters are unexplored in past efforts. For example, learning rate schedules have rarely been explored in previous efforts of fine-tuning. One promising approach is training with cyclical learning rates (e.g., cosine annealing learning rate and slanted triangular learning rate), which have been shown to achieve improved classification accuracy in fewer iterations (Loshchilov and Hutter, 2016; Smith, 2017). We will explore the impact of cyclical learning rates in fine-tuning methods in the context of an ensemble algorithm.

Major contributions: In this work, (1) we use ensembles to investigate the impact of various hyperparameters for fine-tuning pretrained transformer-based models for the clinical domain by focusing on one critical task – temporal relation extraction; (2) we conduct comprehensive experiments and the empirical findings show that training epoch, random initialization, and data order have potentially significant influence; (3) we explore multiple hyperparameters in a single framework with the aim of building computationally efficient fine-tuning strategies to boost model performance on top of

Proceedings of the 4th Clinical Natural Language Processing Workshop, pages 103 - 108
July 14, 2022 ©2022 Association for Computational Linguistics

any given base setting.

2 Temporal Relation Extraction in Clinical Narratives

We explore the ensemble-based fine-tuning methods within the context of temporal relation extraction from the EMR clinical narrative. Temporal relation extraction and reasoning in the clinical domain continues to be a primary area of interest due to the potential impact on disease understanding and, ultimately, patient care. A significant body of text available for this purpose is the THYME (Temporal Histories of Your Medical Events) corpus (Styler IV et al., 2014), consisting of 594 de-identified clinical and pathology notes on colon cancer patients and 600 radiology, oncology and clinical notes on brain cancer patients, all from the EMR of a leading US medical center. This dataset has previously undergone a variety of annotation efforts, most notably temporal annotation (Styler IV et al., 2014). It has been part of several SemEval shared tasks such as Clinical TempEval (Bethard et al., 2017) where state-of-the-art results have been established. We use the THYME++ version of the corpus and the train/dev/test splits as described by Wright-Bettner et al. (2020).

3 Ensemble-based Fine-Tuning and Experimental Setup

Our intuition behind using ensembles for fine-tuning is to leverage models from local optima to obtain greater coverage of the feature space, and get consensus for the predictions so that the ensemble learner can reduce the overall risk of making a poor selection. In this section, we first describe our setting and implementation of a base model based on the state-of-the-art setting described by Lin et al. (2021). Then we discuss fine-tuning several hyperparameters during training and their potential impact on model performance. Based on these discussions, we then introduce the bagging ensemble method (Breiman, 1996) and the dynamic snapshot ensemble method (Wang et al., 2020) and apply them to the fine-tuning process.

3.1 Base setting and implementation

To set up an ensemble learning method, we first need to set up a base setting as a starting point. Based on the results and discussions of Lin et al. (2021), we choose `PubmedBERTbase-MimicBig-EntityBERT`[1] as our pretrained model. The fine-tuning setting in that work includes random seed 42, batch size 32, epoch number 3, learning rate 4e-5, learning rate scheduler *linear*, max sequence length 100, and gradient accumulation steps 2. We adopt the same setting in our base implementation. We use an NVIDIA Titan RTX GPU cluster of 7 nodes for fine-tuning experiments through HuggingFace's Transformer API (Wolf et al., 2020) version 4.13.0. We leverage the `run_glue.py` pytorch version as our fine-tuning script. Unless specified, default settings are used in our experiments. Due to differences in the fine-tuning script and some missing settings, we were unable to reproduce the exact scores reported in Lin et al. (2021). Results with our implementation are reported as BASE. We use our implementation as the starting point to conduct the ensemble experiment and compare ensemble results with BASE.

3.2 Hyperparameters in fine-tuning

There are more than a hundred hyperparameters in the fine-tuning process. Among those hyperparameters, not every one has a major impact on model performance. Some of them are preset with default values that have been shown to be robust in empirical experiments, such as the default values of β_1, β_2, and ϵ for AdamW optimizer. In our work, we investigate several hyperparameters which potentially have high impact on model performance. We apply ensemble learning on the following hyperparameters to reduce the variance of predictions and reduce generalization error:

Random seed is set at the beginning of training. It impacts the initialization of models and trainers, as well as the convergence of scholastic learning algorithms. We run base fine-tuning 5 times but with 5 random seed values (42, 52, 62, 72, 82).

Learning rate scheduler is the scheduling algorithm for changing the learning rate during training. In the previous fine-tuning works, the *linear* scheduler is used by default. We run base fine-tuning with 3 different learning rate schedulers: *linear*, *cosine with restarts*, and *polynomial*.

Epoch number is the number of passes over the data that the training process takes. A small epoch number may lead to underfitting while a large epoch number tends to cause overfitting to

[1] `https://physionet.org/content/entity-bert/1.0.0/`

the domain-specific training data. We run the base fine-tuning with 5 epoch numbers (3, 6, 9, 12, 15).

Pretrained model is the model checkpoint from which fine-tuning begins. The PubMedBERT model (Gu et al., 2021) has been shown to outperform other BERT-based models for temporal relation extraction in clinical narratives (Lin et al., 2021). In our experiments, we leverage the three PubMedBERT models released by Lin et al. (2021): `PubmedBERTbase-MimicBig-EntityBERT`, `PubmedBERTbase-MimicSmall-EntityBERT`, and `PubmedBERTbase-MimicBig-RandMask`.

Random shuffling of training and validation data can avoid selecting models that overfit to a single validation set during fine-tuning. In contrast to traditional random shuffling of training instances during training, the random shuffling in this work refers to mixing training and validation datasets and then resampling train/validation datasets with the same size and class distribution from the mix pool. We generate 5 different samplings of splits using random seeds (42, 52, 62, 72, 82). We then run base fine-tuning 5 times with different samplings.

3.3 Bagging ensemble

Bagging ensemble is the simple and straightforward thus is commonly used in various tasks. Component learners are trained independently in parallel and are combined following some kind of combination method. We leverage bagging ensemble and use majority voting for generating ensemble predictions on each hyperparameter variable. For example, for the random seed variable, we combine predictions from 5 fine-tuned models trained with different random seeds using majority voting, denoted as Seed-ENS. We report the ensemble performance regarding each hyperparameter variable in Table 1 together with BASE.

3.4 Dynamic snapshot ensemble

We also explore dynamic snapshot ensembles first proposed in (Wang et al., 2020), which we call DynSnap-ENS in this paper. The DynSnap-ENS framework allows a pretrained model to be fine-tuned multiple times (i.e., multiple training runs) sequentially with different random seeds and data samplings of train/validation splits. It uses a cyclic annealing schedule and cyclic snapshot strategy to periodically save the best model during each training run. After each training run, a dynamic pruning algorithm is applied to select a few single learners

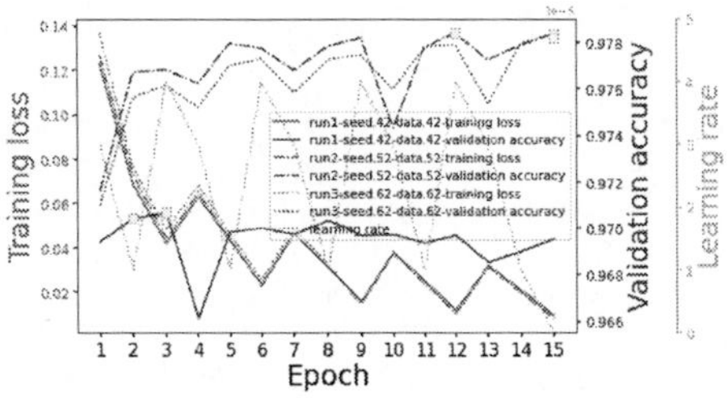

Figure 1: Training history of DynSnap-ENS on learning rate, training loss, and validation accuracy along epochs. Ensemble size is 5. The sequential training runs are run1-run2-run3. The selected single learners are highlighted with yellow squares.

from the saved ones which can lead to better performance of the ensemble learner with theoretical guarantees. The sequential training runs stop when the accumulated number of selected single learners reaches a preset ensemble size. The total amount of training runs is a dynamic value rather than a preset value, which is determined by the snapshot strategy and pruning factor during the sequential training. Take Figure 1 as an example. The preset ensemble size is 5, and training epoch is 15. Training run1 is set with random seed 42 and a data split. After the training, top 4 models are saved based on validation accuracy, and among those 2 models are selected as ensemble components after pruning. Since 2 is smaller than 5, training run2 is triggered with random seed 52 and another data split. This process will repeat until the accumulated number of ensemble components reaches the ensemble size. More details of the learning algorithm can be found in the original paper.

We are the first to apply DynSnap-ENS to solve challenges in clinical text classifications. It enables diversity in data and model parameters through a cyclic learning rate, multiple random seeds, epoch numbers, and training and validation datasets. These hyperparameters are explored in one learning framework, which is computationally efficient compared to independent searches for each hyperparameter in Lin et al. (2021).

In our experiments, we implemented DynSnap-ENS on the top of the base fine-tuning script. The ensemble size is set as 5 (equal to the ensemble size of bagging ensemble learners) and majority voting is used to generate ensemble predictions. We reuse base fine-tuning settings except that we set *cosine with restarts* as the learning rate scheduler and set the learning rate to restart every 3 epochs

	OVERLAP			CONTAINS-1			CONTAINS			BEFORE-1			BEFORE		
Method	P	R	F1	P	R	F1	P	R	F1	P	R	F1	P	R	F1
BASE	0.611	**0.482**	0.539	0.749	0.758	0.754	0.775	0.777	0.776	0.51	**0.428**	0.465	0.537	0.416	0.469
Seed-ENS	0.672	0.46	0.546	0.753	0.757	0.755	0.785	**0.79**	0.788	0.562	0.404	0.47	0.57	0.411	0.477
LRScheduler-ENS	0.652	0.48	0.553	0.741	0.758	0.749	0.789	0.781	0.785	0.535	0.406	0.462	0.568	0.396	0.467
Epoch-ENS	0.681	0.471	0.556	**0.774**	0.765	**0.769**	0.807	0.779	0.793	**0.599**	0.376	0.462	0.627	0.379	0.472
PretrainedModel-ENS	0.676	0.458	0.546	0.735	0.769	0.752	0.786	0.788	0.787	0.536	0.42	**0.471**	0.564	0.408	0.473
DataShuffle-ENS	**0.711**	0.458	**0.557**	0.737	**0.771**	0.754	0.806	0.788	**0.797**	0.586	0.384	0.464	0.617	**0.429**	**0.506**
DynSnap-ENS	0.695	0.464	**0.557**	0.769	0.762	0.766	**0.816**	0.778	0.796	0.579	0.381	0.459	**0.636**	0.404	0.494

	NOTED-ON-1			BEGINS-ON			NOTED-ON			ENDS-ON			OVERALL		
Method	P	R	F1	P	R	F1	P	R	F1	P	R	F1	P	R	F1
BASE	0.739	0.824	0.779	0.637	0.581	0.608	0.706	0.55	0.618	0.773	0.574	0.659	0.671	0.599	0.633
Seed-ENS	0.766	0.809	0.787	0.705	0.537	0.61	**0.794**	0.55	0.65	0.799	0.602	0.687	0.712	0.591	0.646
LRScheduler-ENS	0.765	0.81	0.787	0.669	0.569	0.615	0.792	0.543	0.644	0.763	0.582	0.66	0.697	0.592	0.640
Epoch-ENS	**0.771**	0.816	0.793	**0.771**	0.569	0.655	0.782	0.564	0.656	0.807	**0.635**	0.711	0.732	0.596	0.657
PretrainedModel-ENS	0.769	0.801	0.784	0.664	0.531	0.59	0.777	0.521	0.624	0.812	0.602	0.692	0.702	0.589	0.640
DataShuffle-ENS	0.758	**0.832**	0.793	0.682	0.562	0.616	0.758	0.536	0.628	**0.854**	0.553	0.672	0.723	0.590	0.650
DynSnap-ENS	0.768	0.822	**0.794**	0.726	**0.613**	**0.664**	0.777	**0.571**	**0.658**	0.831	0.623	**0.712**	**0.733**	**0.602**	**0.661**

Table 1: Ensemble model performance on THYME test colon data. NONE - no relation, CONTAINS-1 - arg 2 contains arg 1, CONTAINS - arg 1 contains arg2, BEFORE-1 - arg 2 before arg 1, BEFORE - arg 1 before arg 2, NOTED-ON-1 - arg 2 noted on arg 1, BEGINS-ON - arg 1 begins on arg 2, NOTED-ON - arg 1 noted on arg 2, ENDS-ON - arg 1 ends on arg 2. NONE scores are omitted from the table and the OVERALL is the macro average score excluding NONE.

which, based on the base setting, allows the model to converge to a reasonable state before each restart. The total number of epochs for each training run is 15 and we save the top 4 models for pruning based on validation accuracy. The random seeds and shuffling datasets for the sequential training runs are the same with the 5 options described in Section 3.2. The logic behind the above settings is to retain the benefits from the base fine-tuning settings as much as possible. Codes and settings to reproduce the results are available here[2].

4 Results and Discussion

We show model performance in Table 1. Compared with BASE, all ensemble methods boost the overall F1 score, with DynSnap-ENS achieving the highest improvement, 2.8% absolute. The improvement is mainly due to the increase in precision, 6.2% absolute. This complies with the theoretical findings in Wang et al. (2020) that ensemble can improve prediction accuracy (i.e. precision). However, there is no proof that ensembling can improve recall.

Among the bagging ensembles, diversity in epoch number (Epoch-ENS) leads to the largest improvement, 2.4% absolute. Diversity in data order (DataShuffle-ENS) and random seeds (Seed-ENS) achieve the next best improvement, 1.7% and 1.3% absolute, while diversity in learning rate schedulers (LRScheduler-ENS) and PubMedBERT variants (PretrainedModel-ENS) obtain the least improvement, 0.7% absolute. In general, we see that selecting a single model is a riskier choice than ensembling several models when trying to avoid overfitting or underfitting the training data.

However, all sources of diversity are not equal, with the diversity from different epochs of a training run being most helpful, and diversity of learning rate schedulers and diversity of PubMedBERT variants helping little. A possible reason is that both LRScheduler-ENS and PretrainedModel-ENS have only 3 components while the other ensemble learners have 5 components, as Wang et al. (2020) proved that a better precision can be achieved if more component learners are combined. However, that would not explain the superiority of Epoch-ENS to DataShuffle-ENS and Seed-ENS, and an improvement of the ensemble's performance is not guaranteed if many poor learners are combined. DynSnap-ENS outperforms all the other ensemble learners, likely because it takes advantage of all the individual types of diversity: data, model parameters, epochs, and learning rate. Figure 1 presents the training history on learning rate, training loss, and validation accuracy along epochs. We can observe that learning behavior changes a lot with respect to each source of diversity. DynSnap-ENS combines those sources in a computationally effi-

[2] `https://github.com/christa60/transformer-dynamic-snapshot-ensemble`

cient way and selects top single learners (marked in yellow squares) from a more diversified pool to guarantee an improvement in the final ensemble learner.

5 Conclusion

We investigated ensemble methods in fine-tuning transformer-based pretrained models for clinical NLP tasks, specifically temporal relation extraction from the clinical narrative. Our experimental results on the THYME++ data showed that ensembling can further boost performance, and that dynamic snapshot ensembling is especially effective. Future works include: 1) investigating the impact of ensemble size in model performance; 2) exploring hyperparameters regarding the snapshot strategy and pruning algorithm; 3) testing the trained ensemble learners on an expanded set of clinical domain tasks.

Acknowledgements

The study was funded by R01LM013486, R01LM10090 and U24CA248010 from the Unites States National Institutes of Health. The content is solely the responsibility of the authors and does not necessarily represent the official views of the National Institutes of Health.

References

Emily Alsentzer, John Murphy, William Boag, Wei-Hung Weng, Di Jindi, Tristan Naumann, and Matthew McDermott. 2019. Publicly available clinical BERT embeddings. In *Proceedings of the 2nd Clinical Natural Language Processing Workshop*, pages 72–78, Minneapolis, Minnesota, USA. Association for Computational Linguistics.

Iz Beltagy, Kyle Lo, and Arman Cohan. 2019. SciBERT: A pretrained language model for scientific text. In *Proceedings of the 2019 Conference on Empirical Methods in Natural Language Processing and the 9th International Joint Conference on Natural Language Processing (EMNLP-IJCNLP)*, pages 3615–3620, Hong Kong, China. Association for Computational Linguistics.

Steven Bethard, Guergana Savova, Martha Palmer, and James Pustejovsky. 2017. SemEval-2017 task 12: Clinical TempEval. In *Proceedings of the 11th International Workshop on Semantic Evaluation (SemEval-2017)*, pages 565–572, Vancouver, Canada. Association for Computational Linguistics.

Leo Breiman. 1996. Bagging predictors. *Machine learning*, 24(2):123–140.

Dan CireşAn, Ueli Meier, Jonathan Masci, and Jürgen Schmidhuber. 2012. Multi-column deep neural network for traffic sign classification. *Neural networks*, 32:333–338.

Jacob Devlin, Ming-Wei Chang, Kenton Lee, and Kristina Toutanova. 2019. BERT: Pre-training of deep bidirectional transformers for language understanding. In *Proceedings of the 2019 Conference of the North American Chapter of the Association for Computational Linguistics: Human Language Technologies, Volume 1 (Long and Short Papers)*, pages 4171–4186, Minneapolis, Minnesota. Association for Computational Linguistics.

Yu Gu, Robert Tinn, Hao Cheng, Michael Lucas, Naoto Usuyama, Xiaodong Liu, Tristan Naumann, Jianfeng Gao, and Hoifung Poon. 2021. Domain-specific language model pretraining for biomedical natural language processing. *ACM Trans. Comput. Healthcare*, 3(1).

Jinhyuk Lee, Wonjin Yoon, Sungdong Kim, Donghyeon Kim, Sunkyu Kim, Chan Ho So, and Jaewoo Kang. 2020. Biobert: a pre-trained biomedical language representation model for biomedical text mining. *Bioinformatics*, 36(4):1234–1240.

Chen Lin, Timothy Miller, Dmitriy Dligach, Steven Bethard, and Guergana Savova. 2021. EntityBERT: Entity-centric masking strategy for model pretraining for the clinical domain. In *Proceedings of the 20th Workshop on Biomedical Language Processing*, pages 191–201, Online. Association for Computational Linguistics.

Ilya Loshchilov and Frank Hutter. 2016. Sgdr: Stochastic gradient descent with warm restarts. *arXiv preprint arXiv:1608.03983*.

Leslie N Smith. 2017. Cyclical learning rates for training neural networks. In *2017 IEEE winter conference on applications of computer vision (WACV)*, pages 464–472. IEEE.

William F. Styler IV, Steven Bethard, Sean Finan, Martha Palmer, Sameer Pradhan, Piet C de Groen, Brad Erickson, Timothy Miller, Chen Lin, Guergana Savova, and James Pustejovsky. 2014. Temporal annotation in the clinical domain. *Transactions of the Association for Computational Linguistics*, 2:143–154.

Haixun Wang, Wei Fan, Philip S Yu, and Jiawei Han. 2003. Mining concept-drifting data streams using ensemble classifiers. In *Proceedings of the ninth ACM SIGKDD international conference on Knowledge discovery and data mining*, pages 226–235. AcM.

Lijing Wang, Dipanjan Ghosh, Maria Gonzalez Diaz, Ahmed Farahat, Mahbubul Alam, Chetan Gupta, Jiangzhuo Chen, and Madhav Marathe. 2020. Wisdom of the ensemble: Improving consistency of deep learning models. *Advances in Neural Information Processing Systems*, 33:19750–19761.

Thomas Wolf, Lysandre Debut, Victor Sanh, Julien Chaumond, Clement Delangue, Anthony Moi, Pierric Cistac, Tim Rault, Remi Louf, Morgan Funtowicz, Joe Davison, Sam Shleifer, Patrick von Platen, Clara Ma, Yacine Jernite, Julien Plu, Canwen Xu, Teven Le Scao, Sylvain Gugger, Mariama Drame, Quentin Lhoest, and Alexander Rush. 2020. Transformers: State-of-the-art natural language processing. In *Proceedings of the 2020 Conference on Empirical Methods in Natural Language Processing: System Demonstrations*, pages 38–45, Online. Association for Computational Linguistics.

Kristin Wright-Bettner, Chen Lin, Timothy Miller, Steven Bethard, Dmitriy Dligach, Martha Palmer, James H. Martin, and Guergana Savova. 2020. Defining and learning refined temporal relations in the clinical narrative. In *Proceedings of the 11th International Workshop on Health Text Mining and Information Analysis*, pages 104–114, Online. Association for Computational Linguistics.

Jingjing Xie, Bing Xu, and Zhang Chuang. 2013. Horizontal and vertical ensemble with deep representation for classification. *arXiv preprint arXiv:1306.2759*.

Exploring Text Representations for Generative Temporal Relation Extraction

Dmitriy Dligach[1], Timothy Miller[2], Steven Bethard[3], and Guergana Savova[2]

[1]Loyola University Chicago
[2]Boston Children's Hospital and Harvard Medical School
[3]University of Arizona
[1]dd@cs.luc.edu
[2]{first.last}@childrens.harvard.edu
[3]bethard@email.arizona.edu

Abstract

Sequence-to-sequence models are appealing because they allow both encoder and decoder to be shared across many tasks by formulating those tasks as text-to-text problems. Despite recently reported successes of such models, we find that engineering input/output representations for such text-to-text models is challenging. On the Clinical TempEval 2016 relation extraction task, the most natural choice of output representations, where relations are spelled out in simple predicate logic statements, did not lead to good performance. We explore a variety of input/output representations, with the most successful prompting one event at a time, and achieving results competitive with standard pairwise temporal relation extraction systems.

1 Introduction

Extracting temporal information from texts is critical in the medical domain for prognostication models, studying disease progression, and understanding longitudinal effects of medications and treatments. The standard route for extracting temporal information is by casting it as a relation task between time expressions and medical events. This relation extraction task is approached by forming relation candidates by pairing potential relation arguments and training a classifier to determine whether a relation exists between them. This pairwise approach is taken by a state-of-the-art temporal relation extraction system (Lin et al., 2019), which uses a pretrained language model such as BERT (Devlin et al., 2019) for representing the training examples.

The goal of this paper is to investigate a generative approach to relation extraction as an alternative to the traditional pairwise method. We investigate whether it is possible for a sequence-to-sequence (seq2seq) model such as T5 (Raffel et al., 2020), BART (Lewis et al., 2020), and SciFi (Phan et al., 2021) to ingest a chunk of clinical text, often containing multiple sentences, and generate human-readable output containing all relation instances in the input. This goal proved to be more ambitious than we anticipated, but ultimately we succeeded in designing input/output representations that were competitive with state-of-the-art.

Using generative models for relation extraction has received little attention and no work exists on using these models for temporal relation extraction. Paolini et al. (2021) use natural language to encode sentence-level relations but mapping the output text to the input arguments is not trivial and requires an alignment algorithm. Huang et al. (2021) formulate relation extraction as a template generation problem but their approach requires a complex cross-attention guided copy mechanism. We explore sentence- as well as cross-sentence relations and encode relations in a structured and human-readable form in which the relation arguments can be easily mapped to the reference entities in the input.

In our experiments, we use SemEval-2016 Task 12: Clinical TempEval data (Bethard et al., 2016), which annotated time expressions, events, and temporal relations, specifically the CONTAINS relation that links times and events to their narrative containers (Pustejovsky and Stubbs, 2011). For example, in Table 1 the time expression *postop* in the second sentence contains the event *chemotherapy*.

Proceedings of the 4th Clinical Natural Language Processing Workshop, pages 109 - 113
July 14, 2022 ©2022 Association for Computational Linguistics

2 Methods

2.1 Input and output representation variants

While a natural input/output representation would have been to keep everything fully in the realm of words (e.g., the NATURAL row in table 1), this would have made reconstructing the character offsets of these relations difficult. For example, if the system produced *1998 contains tumor* for an input where the surface form *tumor* appeared multiple times (a common occurrence in clinical data), we would not be able to determine which *tumor* event to link to the date.

Thus, we focused on representations where we could deterministically recover the character offsets of the events and times being related. We took as input chunks of text, typically spanning multiple sentences to capture cross-sentence relations. We appended a slash character and an integer index to each event and time expression to disambiguate surface forms that occured multiple times in the text. We also marked all reference events and time expressions with special tags to make the candidates for relation arguments transparent to the model. Examples of such input formatting can be found in the bottom three rows of table 1.

Given this setup, our original goal was a seq2seq model that would take as input the formatted text and generate all temporal relations as output. Our first input/output representation encoded the relations as predicate logic statements with *contains* as the predicate, event/time indices as the arguments, and predicates sorted by the position of the first argument (table 1, RELATIONS variant). The sorting is necessary to introduce a notion of order into an otherwise order-less relation extraction problem, i.e., to transform a set prediction problem into a sequence prediction problem.

Our second input/output representation encoded the temporal relations as classifications over each event or time, where the model must predict a temporal container for each event and each time, generating the underscore character if no container is found (table 1, CONTAINERS variant). Preliminary error analysis had indicated that models based on the RELATIONS variant struggled to decide when to produce or omit an argument, and the CONTAINERS variant removed that choice.

Our final input/output representation was similar to CONTAINERS, but rather than asking the model to predict all temporal containers, it prompted the model with a focus event or time and asked only for the temporal container for that. We achived this by attaching the index of the focus event or time at the end of the formatted input text after a vertical bar separator character, and using as output only the index of the container event or time or underscore to indicate no relation (table 1, 1-CONTAINER variant). Thus, for every chunk of text, the number of examples that we generate equals the total number of events and times in the chunk.

Note that traditional pairwise relation extraction models, require $O(n^2)$ examples to encode the relations, where n is the total number of events and times in the chunk. Our RELATIONS and CONTAINERS representations require m training examples, where m is the number of chunks ($m << n$) and our 1-CONTAINER representation requires n examples, thus potentially reducing training time and memory requirements.

2.2 Models

For seq2seq models, we compare BART, T5, and SciFive (a clinical version of T5). The models are trained to receive a chunk of text and generate output as described in section 2.1.

Chunk size plays an important role in input/output representations: short chunks have fewer relation instances and seq2seq models have less trouble predicting them correctly. But short chunks miss long-distance relations, which often span multiple sentences. Longer chunks are harder for seq2seq models, but they capture more long-distance relations. This tension plays a role in the performance of our models and we treat chunk size as a hyperparameter that we tune on the development set.

Additionally, we observe that our 1-CONTAINER variant does not require a full auto-regressive decoder since models only need to generate a single integer (the index of the container). We thus study two encoder-only models. In BERT-softmax, we follow the standard text classification approach with BERT: add a randomly-intitialized softmax layer on top of the last layer's contextualized represenatation of the `[cls]` token, where the sofmax is over all items in the vocabulary. In BERT-similarity, we instead compute similarity (the dot product) between the `[cls]` token and all word piece embeddings in the vocabulary, apply softmax to the similarity scores, and select the item with the largest score. Note that the classification layer of BERT-softmax must be trained from scratch, while

Variant	Input	Output
NATURAL	2001: Left breast lumpectomy followed by radiation therapy. She received no postop chemotherapy. She was given tamoxifen for five years and then Femara.	2001 contains lumpectomy. postop contains chemotherapy. five years contains tamoxifen.
RELATIONS	**task**: relext; **text**: <t> 2001/0 </t>: Left breast <e> lumpectomy/3 </e> followed by radiation <e> therapy/4 </e>. She received no <t> postop/1 </t> <e> chemotherapy/5 </e>. She was given <e> tamoxifen/6 </e> for <t> five years/2 </t> and then <e> Femara/7 </e>.	contains(0; 3) contains(1; 5) contains(2; 6)
CONTAINERS	**task**: relext; **text**: <t> 2001/0 </t>: Left breast <e> lumpectomy/3 </e> followed by radiation <e> therapy/4 </e>. She received no <t> postop/1 </t> <e> chemotherapy/5 </e>. She was given <e> tamoxifen/6 </e> for <t> five years/2 </t> and then <e> Femara/7 </e>.	contains(0; _) contains(3; 0) contains(4; _) contains(1; _) contains(5; 1) contains(6; 2) contains(2; _) contains(7; _)
1-CONTAINER	**task**: relext; **text**: <t> 2001/0 </t>: Left breast <e> lumpectomy/3 </e> followed by radiation <e> therapy/4 </e>. She received no <t> postop/1 </t> <e> chemotherapy/5 </e>. She was given <e> tamoxifen/6 </e> for <t> five years/2 </t> and then <e> Femara/7 </e>. | 3	0

Table 1: Sample input/output (I/O) representation variants. Bold text indicates task prompt conventions. Note that the 1-Container variant shows only one relation; seven more instances would be required to represent classifications for all eight input events and times.

BERT-similarity does not require any layer to be trained from scratch.

2.3 Experiments

We use BART (facebook/bart-base), T5 (t5-base), SciFive (razent/SciFive-base-Pubmed_PMC), and BERT (bert-base-uncased) from the HuggingFace model hub[1]. Our code is based on the HuggingFace Transformers library (Wolf et al., 2020) and will be released publically upon publication. We use AdamW optimizer and tune its learning rate and weight decay as well as other model hyperparameters such as chunk size, beam size, and the number of epochs on the official Clinical TempEval development set. After tuning the models, we retrained on the training and development sets combined. We report the results on the Clinical TempEval test set using the official evaluation script.

We compare to three baselines from Lin et al. (2019). BERT-T and BioBERT are standard pairwise relation extraction BERT-based ('bert-base' and 'biobert', respectively) models that generate relation candidates by pairing all events and times in a 60-token chunk of text and train a three-way classifier to predict whether a relation exists between them. The negative class represents the no-relation scenario. The positive class is split into two labels, CONTAINS, and CONTAINED-BY, depending on the order of the arguments. BERT-TS augments the aforementioned BERT system with high-confidence 'silver' instances obtained through self-training. The BioBERT-based system is currently the state-of-the-art on this dataset.

Chunks: We apply simple preprocessing to the TempEval data to generate the inputs and outputs for our models as follows: (1) we split the corpus into sections (e.g. medications, family history), which are marked with standardized section headers; (2) we split sections into sentences using a simple regular expression; (3) we form chunks by concatenating adacent sentences up to the *chunk_size* hyperparameter. A sample chunk is shown in table 1.

[1] https://huggingface.co/models

N	Model	I/O Representation	Chunk	P	R	F1
1	BERT-T (Lin et al., 2019)	Pairwise	n/a	0.735	0.613	0.669
2	BERT-TS (Lin et al., 2019)	Pairwise	n/a	0.670	0.697	0.683
3	BioBERT (Lin et al., 2019)	Pairwise	n/a	0.674	0.695	0.684
4	BERT-softmax	1-CONTAINER	50	0.714	0.530	0.608
5	BERT-similarity	1-CONTAINER	50	0.712	0.540	0.615
6	BART	RELATIONS	50	0.709	0.231	0.348
7	BART	CONTAINERS	75	0.480	0.266	0.342
8	BART	1-CONTAINER	175	0.651	0.671	0.661
9	T5	RELATIONS	50	0.675	0.570	0.618
10	T5	CONTAINERS	75	0.684	0.625	0.654
11	T5	1-CONTAINER	75	0.718	0.632	0.672
12	T5	1-CONTAINER	175	0.717	0.675	**0.696**
13	SciFive	RELATIONS	50	0.669	0.503	0.574
14	SciFive	CONTAINERS	75	0.657	0.609	0.632
15	SciFive	1-CONTAINER	175	0.691	0.683	0.687

Table 2: Generative relation extraction and baseline performance on Clinical TempEval test set using reference relation arguments (events and times). Top three systems include current SOTA (line 3) on this dataset.

3 Results and Discussion

Only one input/output variant was competitive with baseline systems: the 1-CONTAINER variant (table 2, lines 12 and 15) performed at least as well or better than all three baselines (lines 1-3). T5's good performance is notable since it is more comparable with BERT-T (line 1), which, unlike the other two baselines did not have acccess to additional training examples (BERT-TS) or in-domain data (BioBERT). On the other hand, suprisingly, SciFive did not have an advantage over T5 despite having been pretrained on in-domain data.

Our encoder-only systems (lines 4 and 5) performed much worse than the comparable 1-CONTAINER variant for the seq2seq models. This is likely due to the lack of a full pretrained decoder, although the similarity-based variant (line 5) mitigated that disadvantage a little.

BART performed worse than the other seq2seq models across all input/output variants although its performance could potentially be improved by a much more extensive hyperparameter search. We leave an exploration into why its "out-of-the-box" performance was inferior for future work.

Chunk size issues: The number of reference relations can grow quadratically with the size of the input as the number of potential relation arguments in the input grows (e.g. it is possible for a time expression to contain multiple events). Because of this, the CONTAINERS input/output variant had a problem on the output side: we observed that the seq2seq maximum length limit (512 word pieces) was not enough to accomodate all relation instances for chunk sizes above 75-100 word pieces. Our 1-CONTAINER input/output variant mitigates that problem by essentially trading the output size for a larger number of training examples, resulting in the best performance (line 12). However, the 1-CONTAINER variant (line 11) is still better when we set the chunk size to the same value as the best CONTAINERS variant (line 10). This hints at a fundamental advantage of this type of model over a full seq2seq model. We hypothesize that this is due to a difficulty on the part of seq2seq models to produce structured outputs such as predicate logic statements.

4 Conclusion

Engineering input/output representations for seq2seq models proved difficult as obvious choices of output representations, such as explicit relations encoded as predicate logic statements led to poor performance. By exploring alternative input/output representations, we were able to improve performance. Our 1-CONTAINER input/output variant with a T5 model was competitive with or better than the current state-of-the-art without requiring additional training data. This is likely due to several factors. First, predicting one relation at a time allowed the model to mitigate the limitation on the maximum length of the output and capture long-distance relations, which was more challenging for the other variants. Second, it required generating only a single word, which is more like the text generation tasks the seq2seq models were trained on than generating predicate logic expressions like the other variants required. Future research may want to explore different pretraining objectives for seq2seq models that would be more appropriate when downstream tasks require generating structured output.

Acknowledgements

Research reported in this publication was supported by the National Library Of Medicine of the National Institutes of Health under Award Numbers R01LM012973 and R01LM010090. The content is solely the responsibility of the authors and does not necessarily represent the official views of the National Institutes of Health.

References

Steven Bethard, Guergana Savova, Wei-Te Chen, Leon Derczynski, James Pustejovsky, and Marc Verhagen. 2016. SemEval-2016 task 12: Clinical TempEval. In *Proceedings of the 10th International Workshop on Semantic Evaluation (SemEval-2016)*, pages 1052–1062, San Diego, California. Association for Computational Linguistics.

Jacob Devlin, Ming-Wei Chang, Kenton Lee, and Kristina Toutanova. 2019. BERT: Pre-training of deep bidirectional transformers for language understanding. In *Proceedings of the 2019 Conference of the North American Chapter of the Association for Computational Linguistics: Human Language Technologies, Volume 1 (Long and Short Papers)*, pages 4171–4186, Minneapolis, Minnesota. Association for Computational Linguistics.

Kung-Hsiang Huang, Sam Tang, and Nanyun Peng. 2021. Document-level entity-based extraction as template generation. In *Proceedings of the 2021 Conference on Empirical Methods in Natural Language Processing*, pages 5257–5269.

Mike Lewis, Yinhan Liu, Naman Goyal, Marjan Ghazvininejad, Abdelrahman Mohamed, Omer Levy, Veselin Stoyanov, and Luke Zettlemoyer. 2020. BART: Denoising sequence-to-sequence pre-training for natural language generation, translation, and comprehension. In *Proceedings of the 58th Annual Meeting of the Association for Computational Linguistics*, pages 7871–7880, Online. Association for Computational Linguistics.

Chen Lin, Timothy Miller, Dmitriy Dligach, Steven Bethard, and Guergana Savova. 2019. A BERT-based universal model for both within- and cross-sentence clinical temporal relation extraction. In *Proceedings of the 2nd Clinical Natural Language Processing Workshop*, pages 65–71, Minneapolis, Minnesota, USA. Association for Computational Linguistics.

Giovanni Paolini, Ben Athiwaratkun, Jason Krone, Jie Ma, Alessandro Achille, RISHITA ANUBHAI, Cicero Nogueira dos Santos, Bing Xiang, and Stefano Soatto. 2021. Structured prediction as translation between augmented natural languages. In *International Conference on Learning Representations*.

Long N Phan, James T Anibal, Hieu Tran, Shaurya Chanana, Erol Bahadroglu, Alec Peltekian, and Grégoire Altan-Bonnet. 2021. Scifive: a text-to-text transformer model for biomedical literature. *arXiv preprint arXiv:2106.03598*.

James Pustejovsky and Amber Stubbs. 2011. Increasing informativeness in temporal annotation. In *Proceedings of the 5th Linguistic Annotation Workshop*, pages 152–160, Portland, Oregon, USA. Association for Computational Linguistics.

Colin Raffel, Noam Shazeer, Adam Roberts, Katherine Lee, Sharan Narang, Michael Matena, Yanqi Zhou, Wei Li, and Peter J Liu. 2020. Exploring the limits of transfer learning with a unified text-to-text transformer. *Journal of Machine Learning Research*, 21:1–67.

Thomas Wolf, Lysandre Debut, Victor Sanh, Julien Chaumond, Clement Delangue, Anthony Moi, Pierric Cistac, Tim Rault, Remi Louf, Morgan Funtowicz, Joe Davison, Sam Shleifer, Patrick von Platen, Clara Ma, Yacine Jernite, Julien Plu, Canwen Xu, Teven Le Scao, Sylvain Gugger, Mariama Drame, Quentin Lhoest, and Alexander Rush. 2020. Transformers: State-of-the-art natural language processing. In *Proceedings of the 2020 Conference on Empirical Methods in Natural Language Processing: System Demonstrations*, pages 38–45, Online. Association for Computational Linguistics.

Author Index

Association for Computational Linguistics
209 N. Eighth Street
Stroudsburg, Pennsylvania 18360

ISBN 978-1-7138-5625-2

9 781713 856252

CURRAN ASSOCIATES INC.
proceedings.com